Field Guide to the U.S. Economy

Field Guide
to the U.S. Economy

(Revised and Updated)

A Compact and Irreverent Guide to Economic Life in America

Jonathan Teller-Elsberg, Nancy Folbre, James Heintz
with the Center for Popular Economics

THE NEW PRESS

NEW YORK
LONDON

Requests for permission to reproduce selections from this book should be mailed to: Permissions Department,
The New Press, 38 Greene Street, New York, NY 10013

Published in the United States by The New Press, New York, 2006
Distributed by W. W. Norton & Company, Inc., New York

LIBRARY OF CONGRESS CATALOGING-IN-PUBLICATION DATA
Teller-Elsberg, Jonathan.
Field guide to the U.S. economy : a compact and irreverent guide to economic life in America / Jonathan Teller-Elsberg, Nancy Folbre,
James Heintz ; with the Center for Popular Economics.—Rev. and updated.
p. cm.
Rev. ed. of: The ultimate field guide to the U.S. economy. 2000.
Includes bibliographical references.
ISBN-13: 978-1-59558-048-1
ISBN-10: 1-59558-048-4 (pbk.)

The New Press was established in 1990 as a not-for-profit alternative to the large, commercial publishing houses currently
dominating the book publishing industry. The New Press operates in the public interest rather than for private gain, and is
committed to publishing, in innovative ways, works of educational, cultural, and community value that are often deemed
insufficiently profitable.

www.thenewpress.com

Book design by Lovedog Studio
This book was set in Adobe Garamond

Printed in Canada

2 4 6 8 10 9 7 5 3 1

Contents

Acknowledgments

Our first debt of gratitude is to the readers of previous editions of the *Field Guide* who have told us that it is a useful and entertaining book that deserves updating. One of our strongest supporters has been University of Wisconsin professor Erik Olin Wright, who not only encouraged us to write a new edition but also suggested new topics and commented on early drafts of this manuscript.

Many other individuals contributed in one way or another to make this revision possible, including fellow staff economists at the Center for Popular Economics. Jim Boyce, Mark Brenner, Jim Crotty, Jerry Epstein, Dean Robinson, and University of Massachusetts Labor Center professors Dale Melcher and Eve Weinbaum all gave us extensive comments on the previous edition. Emily Kawano, executive director of the Center for Popular Economics, provided necessary logistical support and lent a critical eye to the developing manuscript. Suresh Naidu helped us better focus several pages and was a general source of advice throughout, as was Arjun Jayadev.

Matt Clifford helped draft several pages in Chapter 2. Anita Dancs drafted most of Chapter 5, an effort well beyond the call of duty, and additional contributions came from Teresa Ghilarducci and Marty Wolfson. Cecilia Conrad and Lisa Saunders reviewed drafts of Chapter 4 and gave much helpful advice. Michael Ash, Kiaran Honderich, and Jim Westrich provided guidance in revising Chapter 7. Ash also pointed out a critical but easy-to-miss problem with data in Chapter 2, and Al Blostin, at the Bureau of Labor Statistics' National Compensation Survey, provided the solution's final missing link. Matt Riddle helped with sources and ideas for Chapter 8, and Hector Saez reviewed a draft of the chapter and suggested improvements. Wendy Teller-Elsberg supplied numerous suggestions throughout the writing process. She, Bob Dworak, and Caroline Carr provided copyediting and final comments as the manuscript approached completion.

McMaster University professor Martin Daly and Harvard University School of Public Health professor Ichiro Kawachi were very helpful in the development of page 1.8. Jeannette Wicks-Lim and Cornell University professor Robert Frank provided advice critical to the drafting of page 2.5.

Naturally, this book could never have reached your hands if not for the support and labor of everyone at The New Press, in particular our editor, Ellen Reeves, her assistant, Jessica Colter, and managing editor Maury Botton. Our copyeditor Sue Warga, proofreader Sarah Groff-Palermo, book designer Brian Mulligan, and cover designer Stewart Cauley all did a fantastic job. Our thanks go also to all those involved behind the scenes, from The New Press to the bookstores and libraries that connect our work to the wider world.

We want to express our sincerest thanks to the dozens of artists who contributed the cartoons that make this book special. All of them were willing to work within our meager budget. We encourage you to check out their Web sites and books:

- Kirk Anderson, www.kirktoons.com
- Khalil Bendib, www.bendib.com
- Clay Bennett, www.claybennett.com
- Steve Benson, www.azcentral.com/arizona republic/opinions/benson/
- Ruben Bolling, "Tom the Dancing Bug," www.ucomics.com/tomthedancingbug
- Barbara Brandon-Croft, "Where I'm Coming From," www.ucomics.com/barbarabrandon
- Clay Butler, "Sidewalk Bubblegum," www.sidewalkbubblegum.com
- Russell Christian, portfolios.com/russell christian
- M. e. Cohen, www.politicalcartoons.com
- Barry Deutsch, "Ampersand," www.amptoons.com
- Darrin Drda, "Channel X," www.darrindrda.org
- Arcadio Esquivel, www.politicalcartoons.com
- Brian Fairrington, www.politicalcartoons.com
- Peter Hannan, www.peterhannan.com
- Nicole Hollander, "Sylvia," www.nicole hollander.com
- The team of Gary Huck and Mike Konopacki, www.solidarity.com/hkcartoons
- Sandy Huffaker, www.politicalcartoons.com
- Marc Hughes, www.marchughes.com
- Jimmy Ilson
- Olle Johansson, www.politicalcartoons.com
- Sabrina Jones, www.sabrinaland.com
- Keith Knight, "(Th)ink," www.kchronicles.com
- Mike Lane, www.politicalcartoons.com
- Sergio Langer, www.politicalcartoons.com
- Michael Leunig, c/o Penguin Books Australia
- R. Jay Magill, www.creativehotlist.com/r-magill
- Barrie Maguire, www.newsart.com
- Stephanie McMillan, "Minimum Security," www.minimumsecurity.net
- Jim Meehan, www.newsart.com
- Stephen Notley, "Bob the Angry Flower," www.angryflower.com
- Jeff Parker, www.politicalcartoons.com
- Ted Rall, www.rall.com
- Mikhaela Reid, "The Boiling Point," www.mikhaela.net
- Joe Sayers, "Thingpart," www.jsayers.com
- Osmani Simanca, www.politicalcartoons.com
- Carol Simpson, "CartoonWork," www.cartoon work.com
- Andy Singer, "No Exit," www.andysinger.com
- Chris Slane, www.politicalcartoons.com
- Jen Sorensen, "Slowpoke," www.slowpoke comics.com

- Tom Tomorrow, "This Modern World," www.thismodernworld.com
- Dan Wasserman, www.boston.com/news/globe/editorial_opinion/oped/wasserman/
- Matt Wuerker, "Lint Trap," www.mwuerker.com

Finally, we are grateful to the following friends of CPE and the *Field Guide* for generously purchasing numerous copies of this new edition long in advance of publication. Their purchases established our artwork budget. Without them this book would be much less fun to read and would have been much less fun to write. They are: Randy Albelda and fellow UMass–Boston faculty, Michael Ash and Krista Harper, Alexandra Bernasek, Shannon Brockman and Andy Elsberg, Jim and Pamela Crotty, Mickey and Margie Elsberg, Paula England, Jerry Epstein, Marianne Ferber, John Fitzgerald, Gerald Friedman and Debra Jacobson, Sut Jhally, Emily Kawano, Karen and Jerry Levitis, Julie Nelson, Susan and Saul Nimowitz, Manuel Pastor, Frances Fox Piven, Katha Pollitt, Juliet Schor and Prasannan Parthasarathi, Peter Skott, Timothy Smeeding, Diana Strassmann, Wendy Teller-Elsberg, Marty Wolfson and fellow Notre Dame faculty, and Howard and Roslyn Zinn.

The Bottom Line

IF THERE WERE JUST ONE BOTTOM LINE, THE U.S. economy would be easier to understand. We could pretend that it was one big checking account, and we could look at our monthly statement to see how we were doing. We could see who made the deposits and who made the withdrawals, and we could figure out who got what and why.

It's not that simple because an economy is more than a set of accounts: it's a system of production and distribution. People put their labor, their talents, and a little bit of their souls into it and take their livelihoods out of it. Some people get rich, some get poor; sometimes the overall economy grows, sometimes it falters. Not even the best economists in the world understand exactly how it works.

But most people want to know more about it, if only because they're worried about the bottom line of their own checkbooks. News reports describe a growing economy, but the real wages of the typical U.S. worker are no higher now than they were in the early 1970s. New medical technologies abound, but many families can't afford health insurance. The unemployment rate is low, but even experienced professionals and managers remain susceptible to the downsizing, outsourcing, and offshoring of their jobs. People are also worried about the larger economic trends affecting their communities, their country, and their world: the movement of U.S. corporations abroad, growing income inequality, and the threat of major environmental problems.

Those who know a great deal about the U.S. economy are often exceedingly fond of it. Economic experts are far more likely to extol the virtues of the system than to criticize it. Prevailing orthodoxy holds that the economy does not need critics, watchdogs, or gadflies of any sort and, indeed, works much better without them. Typical economics courses confine much of their attention to the theory of competitive markets and treat the economy as a self-regulating system. Even when they address issues of public policy, economists often teach students that there is an inevitable trade-off between economic equality and efficiency. The message, in ordinary language, is that social justice is just too expensive.

Some economists (like us) disagree. We believe that economic power in the U.S. is unevenly distributed and easily abused and that current economic policies are inefficient as well as unfair. We also believe that good citizens should be good critics, and that controversy and debate over economic issues are central to the democratic process. This book compiles useful information for noneconomists (as well as students and teachers) who want to know more about the U.S. economy. The facts and figures we highlight reflect our personal values and our political concerns. But we stop short of developing any one interpretation of U.S. economic trends or advocating any particular social policies. We aspire to inform and provoke, enlighten and enliven economic debate.

This *Field Guide* is the fourth version we have published. It is designed to serve as an accessible, concise reference for answering specific questions as well as an informative overview of the U.S. economy. Each page stands alone as a description of an economic fact or trend but also fits into a chapter that systematically covers a particular topic. You might want to read the book from cover to cover. More likely, you'll want to scan the table of contents, pick a page title that interests you, and follow your nose. The ten chapters are followed by a Toolkit section, a Glossary, and bibliographic Sources and Notes. Each of the first four chapters explains the economic position of a group of people: "Owners," "Workers," "Women," and "People of Color." The next chapters cover a particular area of concern: "Government," "Welfare and Education," "Health," "Environment," "Macroeconomics," and "The Global Economy." The last two chapters, in particular, use some technical terms that make them more difficult than the earlier ones. If you are having trouble, be sure to consult the Glossary.

Each chapter opens with a brief overview that ties its pages together around a main theme. The pages of each chapter progress from the general to the specific, providing a variety of types of information—descriptions of widely discussed trends, explanations of basic economic concepts, and, occasionally, more speculative analysis of possibilities for change. We use the most recent information available to us at the time of our writing (the middle of 2005), but because collecting and analyzing economic data is a difficult, time-consuming process, many of our sources lag a couple of years behind.

The ten sections in the Toolkit provide quick tutorials to help readers who are unfamiliar with economic theory. These tutorials are designed to help readers interpret and use economic statistics. They include reminders about how to read graphs, as well as explanations of things like price indices and the poverty line. We have included explanatory notes for many pages in the Sources and Notes section. The Glossary provides clear, simple definitions of technical terms.

This book has been shaped by its most immediate audience. For the past 27 years, the Center for Popular Economics has organized and taught workshops on economic issues for community organizers and activists. Our students constantly demanded more information, more explanation, more documentation. Every year, we added to a pile of classroom handouts; every year we found it harder to keep our pile organized and up-to-date. In the summer of 1984, we took the initial step of transferring our handouts to computer files and began to experiment with computer-generated graphs. Our students loved the results. "Make it a book," they exclaimed, "but make it more fun." Their enthusiasm fanned our ambition to produce an illustrated guide to the U.S. economy.

The first edition was a big hit and was adopted for use in many classrooms across the country. Fans, friends, students, and colleagues soon began asking for updates. A second version, published in 1995, included a great deal of new material focusing on hot political issues. As 1998 rolled around we realized that the book needed to keep evolving, and the third edition came out in 2000—precisely the moment when so many changes to the economy and to economic policies kicked off. It wasn't long before we began thinking about writing this new edition. You can find additional articles in the spirit of the *Field Guide* at our Web site, www.fguide.org, where we will post any corrections that are necessary. If you notice an error in the book, please let us know by writing us at feedback@fguide.org or via The New Press.

What you have here represents our commitment to a kind of economics that is popular in the best sense of the word—it's aimed at ordinary people. Put these facts and figures to good use. "Never doubt," wrote anthropologist Margaret Mead, "that a small group of thoughtful, committed citizens can change the world. Indeed, it is the only thing that ever has."

Chapter 1: **Owners**

FROM EASY STREET TO SKID ROW, THE HAVES AND have-nots coexist in towns across America. But who actually owns what in the United States? This chapter looks at the distribution of family wealth and the structure of corporate power.

Them that's got usually get. Individuals compete against each other in a capitalist economy, their success partly determined by the wealth they bring with them to the market. When they leave, those who started out wealthy often take home even more.

Chart 1.1 shows that the richest 10% of all households own 80% of the financial wealth in America. The bottom 80% of households have only 9%. These inequalities are more extreme than in the past. As Chart 1.2 points out, the wealthiest 1% of households took home more than half of the new financial wealth created between 1983 and 2001.

While many families own a bit of wealth, most of it is invested in their own home. Chart 1.3 shows that the richest, on the other hand, own most of their wealth in the form of business equity, real estate, stocks, bonds, mutual funds, and trusts. Those who think that the playing field is level as we move into the new century should check out Chart 1.4. In 2001, the financial wealth of white households, on average, was 38 times that of African American households and a mind-boggling 210 times that of Hispanic households.

Chart 1.5 shows the difference between the average pay of corporate chief executive officers (CEOs) and those who work as retail clerks or medical doctors. The increasing difference between rich and poor is pictured in Chart 1.7, which shows how higher-income households have gained ground. The majority of Americans have enjoyed only modest gains over the past 20 years. Economic inequality has social side effects. Chart 1.8 shows that U.S. states and Canadian provinces with greater inequality also tend to have higher murder rates.

RUSSELL CHRISTIAN

Wealth bestows more than just a high standard of living. It also provides the means for influencing political outcomes. Chart 1.9 details the relative size of contributions that business, labor, and single-issue organizations made to political candidates and their support groups in 2004. Chart 1.10 shows the difference in spending between winners and losers of congressional campaigns. Concentration in control over the media, another form of political influence, is documented in Chart 1.11.

Concentrated economic power can lead to crimes that are enormously costly to society. Chart 1.12 shows that investors hoodwinked by Enron executives lost more than twice as much as victims of all property crimes in 2002.

As Chart 1.13 shows, global corporations are now so big that they make the economies of entire countries look puny. The biggest kid on the block is Wal-Mart, whose growth is illustrated in Chart 1.14. Many fear that Wal-Mart, like the proverbial 800-pound gorilla, can do whatever it wants, regardless of the consequences.

While the concentration of economic power in the United States might feel overwhelming, there are reasons to be optimistic. The socially responsible investing described in Chart 1.15 has been growing fast, suggesting that many ordinary people disagree with "business as usual." Chart 1.16 explains how more workers are becoming owners. In the long run, this may help increase their voice and influence over their own destinies.

1.1 Who Owns How Much?

"THE RICH ARE DIFFERENT FROM you and me," said F. Scott Fitzgerald. "Yes," replied Ernest Hemingway. "They have more money." More specifically, they have more wealth, an accumulation of money and other assets.

In 2001, the richest tenth of U.S. households owned 80% of the country's financial assets. The bottom four-fifths owned only 9%. Financial assets include cash, bank deposits, corporate stocks, and private or public bonds.

It's nice to be wealthy: you get income whether or not you work. A plush cushion protects you from the ups and downs of the business cycle.

Those who enjoy the advantages of wealth have benefited from Republican control of Congress and the presidency. The federal estate tax once took a big bite out of large inheritances. Although it never affected more than the wealthiest 2% of Americans, it has raised a substantial amount of revenue. This tax is now being phased out and is set to disappear completely in 2010. Less wealthy Americans will have to make up the difference, either by paying more in taxes or making do with fewer government services.

EVER SINCE THE MARKET TURMOIL LAST OCTOBER, THERE'S BEEN A LOT OF TALK IN THE MEDIA ABOUT THE IMPORTANCE OF THE *SMALL INVESTOR.*

WALL STREET'S NOT JUST FOR THE *RICH* ANYMORE! WHY, IT SEEMS LIKE *EVERY*-ONE OWNS A PIECE OF THE MARKET THESE DAYS!

AT LEAST, EVERYONE WE KNOW-- EH, BETTY?

TOM TOMORROW

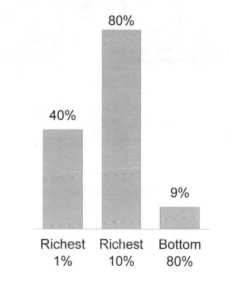

Distribution of financial wealth in 2001 (by groups of households)

Richest 1%	Richest 10%	Bottom 80%
40%	80%	9%

1.2 **Very Rich, Getting Richer**

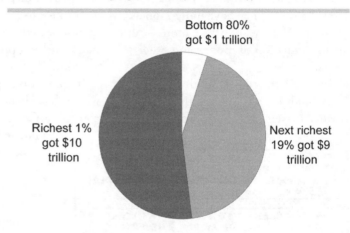

Distribution of new financial wealth, 1983–2001 (in $2004)

Bottom 80% got $1 trillion

Richest 1% got $10 trillion

Next richest 19% got $9 trillion

IF THOU HAST, THOU SHALT receive. That seems to be the rule in the U.S. Between 1983 and 2001, the value of all financial wealth in the U.S. grew by over $20 trillion (in 2004 dollars). But not all groups of Americans benefited equally from that growth. The richest 1% of households took in over half of all that increase in wealth, and the next richest 19% got almost all the leftovers.

In the 1970s, the distribution of wealth was similar in most of the industrialized countries. But by the 1980s, wealth inequality in America had become extreme by international standards.

Business assets, financial securities, and mutual funds account for about 78% of the wealth of the top 1%. Less wealthy households haven't shared in the boom to the same extent. Nearly 18% of households have as much debt as assets, or more, so their net wealth is zero or negative.

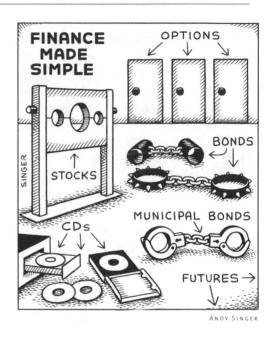

1.3 What's Wealth Made Of?

WHAT YOU OWN CAN BE just as important as how much you own. Most people's wealth, if they have any, is in the form of a home. That's not only a way to hold wealth; it also puts a roof over their heads. But in a financial emergency a home can be hard to sell quickly. And the burden of mortgage debt can be heavy, particularly when interest rates rise.

Rich households own much more wealth that is "liquid," meaning that it can be converted into cash easily. Some common liquid assets are savings accounts, stocks, bonds, and mutual funds. In 2001, the richest 10% of households controlled nearly 85% of all individually owned stocks and mutual funds and 90% of all business equity.

Just over half of all households own corporate stock. However, most own it indirectly through mutual funds and, more commonly, pensions. Only direct owners can hope to influence corporate policies through election of boards of directors and approval of shareholder resolutions.

Major components of wealth, by household groups in 2001

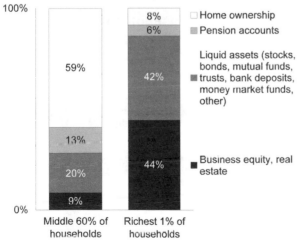

- □ Home ownership
- ▨ Pension accounts
- ▦ Liquid assets (stocks, bonds, mutual funds, trusts, bank deposits, money market funds, other)
- ■ Business equity, real estate

Middle 60% of households: 59%, 13%, 20%, 9%

Richest 1% of households: 8%, 6%, 42%, 44%

ANDY SINGER

5

The Color of Wealth

I N TIMES OF STRESS, WEALTH makes a crucial difference. A sudden income drop due to job loss or illness can mean poverty. When hard times hit, the typical white household is more likely to have reserves to fall back on, with 38 times the average financial wealth of black households and 210 times that of Hispanic households. The Gulf Coast disaster in 2005 made this clear, when thousands of poor, predominantly black residents of New Orleans lacked the means to evacuate the city before Hurricane Katrina struck.

Wealth passed down the generations explains much of this disparity. In 2001, some 21% of white households reported having received an inheritance at some time, with an average value of $274,000. Only 8% of African American and 3% of Hispanic households had received inheritances, averaging $78,000 and $22,000, respectively.

Of course, the high average value for whites masks a lot of real financial struggling: 13% of white households had no wealth at all in 2001. But that's true for a much larger proportion of blacks and Hispanics. That year, about one-third of black and Hispanic households had no wealth.

R. JAY MAGILL

Median financial wealth of households in 2001

Hispanics	$200
Blacks	$1,100
Whites	$42,100

1.5 CEO Pay

THE AVERAGE RETAIL CLERK IN the U.S. would have to work for 419 years to earn what the average corporate chief executive officer (CEO) makes in a single year. That's a boost for CEOs, whose average pay is growing again after dipping in 2001 and 2002. Between 2003 and 2004, workers saw their earnings increase by an average of 2.2%, while CEOs received an average raise of 15%.

The best-paid employees are also company owners. Much of the compensation CEOs get includes stock options—the ability to purchase company stock at better-than-market prices.

The benefits are enormous. When Oracle CEO Lawrence Ellison exercised his stock options in 2001, he made over $700 million.

Are CEOs worth it? Higher pay does not guarantee superior performance; companies with the highest-paid CEOs often do worse than other firms. While Oracle was making Ellison a very, very rich man, the market value of the company fell 57% and nearly 1,300 workers were laid off.

R. JAY MAGILL

Average pay of CEOs compared to retail clerks and medical doctors in 2004

Retail clerk	$22,930
Medical doctor	$138,490
CEO	$9,600,000

They Didn't Do It Alone

FINALLY! I'VE MADE IT TO THE TOP OF MY PROFESSION!

SINGER

ANDY SINGER

HOW DID THE RICHEST PEOPLE in America get their money? Stories in the media tout the saga of the "self-made man" (and occasional woman) who picked himself up by his bootstraps and made good.

Luck favors the prepared, and working hard certainly helps people achieve success, but social and family connections play a significant role in acquiring wealth.

The easiest way to get wealth is to inherit it. Each year *Forbes* magazine profiles the 400 wealthiest individuals in the U.S. In 2004, ten of the new people on the list were all from the same family. Each inherited enough to make the list without making any money on their own. *Responsible Wealth*'s 2004 report "I Didn't Do It Alone" highlights the way rich individuals have gotten a social boost. People they interviewed identified several key factors that helped them become rich. Some emphasized the advantages of privilege, like inheritance and race. Others emphasized government-provided services, like subsidized college tuition and investments in technological research. And others noted old-fashioned luck.

> "Most wealth comes out of the commons and individuals add a little bit on top of that. But because of the way capitalism is set up, for adding that little bit, you get to grab an enormous share of what comes out of the commons."
>
> —*Peter Barnes, co-founder of Working Assets*

> "To turn $100 into $110 is work. To turn $100 million into $110 million is inevitable."
>
> —*Seagram's heir Edgar Bronfman*

> "It's very difficult to go to a bank and borrow money to start a business or to expand a business if you are black in this country. You can borrow money to buy a car or a boat or a house, but when you go to talk about borrowing $10 million dollars or $20 million dollars, big time money to expand a business, you get a very chilly reception."
>
> —*Maceo Sloan, founder and chair of Sloan Financial Group*

1.7 Scraping By

MANY PEOPLE LIVE FROM paycheck to paycheck, year after year, without much to show for it. When income just covers the basic costs of living, building up even small amounts of wealth becomes impossible.

The inequality between households has grown over the last generation. Between 1983 and 2003, average income for households in the top 5% grew by $108,987. The gains were far smaller for every other income group. In 2003, the 20% of households with the least earnings scraped by with an average income of just $9,996, only $839 more in real terms than what they had 20 years earlier.

Income and wealth are related in two ways. People with high incomes can accumulate wealth, and this wealth can generate additional income. But for most people, income is just a means of surviving.

Increase in mean household income, 1983–2003, by income group (in $2004)

Top 5%	$108,987
Highest fifth	$47,919
Fourth fifth	$13,869
Third fifth	$6,785
Second fifth	$3,345
Lowest fifth	$839

KIRK ANDERSON

9

1.8 Inequality Hurts

WHY SHOULD WE CARE about economic inequality? Many poor people in the U.S. today own cars and cell phones, luxuries that even millionaires lacked a hundred years ago. But the last century's luxuries are this year's necessities. It's hard to find and keep a job without a car and a phone. And human beings tend to define their standards of living in relative, rather than absolute, terms.

Extreme inequality reduces people's sense of inclusion in the larger community. It reduces the likelihood that they will be able to work together to solve problems. It also contributes to overt forms of social conflict.

Studies of U.S. states and Canadian provinces show that higher income inequality is associated with higher rates of homicide. In 1990,

for instance, the homicide rate in the U.S. was highest in Louisiana. That state also had the highest level of income inequality (as measured by a Gini coefficient—see the Glossary for details).

Homicide rates and income inequality in the U.S. (1990) and Canada (average 1988–1992)

WE'LL DO ANYTHING TO STOP CRIME!

BILLIONS FOR NEW PRISONS!

ROLLING BACK CIVIL LIBERTIES!

POLICE CRACKDOWNS! RANDOM BAG CHECKS! RACIAL PROFILING!

WHATEVER IT TAKES!

OKAY, THEN, HOW ABOUT REDUCING THE ECONOMIC INEQUALITY THAT LEADS TO CRIME?

DON'T BE RIDICULOUS—THAT'S CRAZY TALK!

AMPERSAND BY B. DEUTSCH

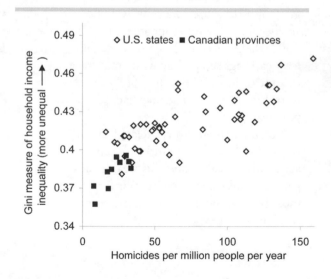

◇ U.S. states   ■ Canadian provinces

Gini measure of household income inequality (more unequal →)

Homicides per million people per year

1.9 The Price of Influence

EVERYONE KNOWS THAT MONEY talks, but in American politics it positively screams. Many individuals, corporations, and political action committees (PACs) influenced the 2004 elections by giving money to political parties and candidates.

Business outspent other interest groups by a large margin, with a combined investment of over $1.4 billion in its favored candidates. Unions raised one-tenth of that amount.

A new twist was the introduction of so-called 527 groups, like America Coming Together and the Club for Growth, which offered another avenue for spending political money. Created in 2002 after changes in election finance laws, 527s are legally required to be managed independently of political parties and candidates, but they do use their money to promote their preferred candidates.

In 2003–2004, the top contributors were retirement organizations, lawyers, real estate businesses, and investors. Oil, gas, and coal companies contributed over 15 times the amount environmentalists did, and the defense industry contributed more than four times as much as human rights advocates.

R. Jay Magill

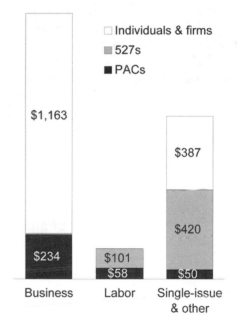

Contributions to political candidates, parties, and 527s, 2004 election (in $ millions)

- □ Individuals & firms
- ▨ 527s
- ■ PACs

Business: $1,163 / $234
Labor: $101 / $58
Single-issue & other: $387 / $420 / $50

1.10 **Dollar Democracy**

A MERICAN DEMOCRACY IS THE best money can buy: in 2004, winners of seats in the House of Representatives spent 3.7 times as much as losers did. Winners in the Senate spent an average of over $7.6 million, more than double what losers spent. Expensive elections are also a barrier to political choice: 115 representatives had no opponent or one who spent nothing. With money playing such a decisive role, it's no wonder many potential voters don't turn out on election day.

Once in office, members of Congress can more easily attract private contribu-

IF THE POOR DON'T LIKE IT, LET 'EM BUY THEIR *OWN* SENATORS!

TOM TOMORROW

tions, particularly if they sit on a powerful committee. In the House in 2004, 393 incumbents were reelected and only five were defeated. In the Senate, 25 incumbents were reelected, while only one was defeated.

The system of private financing makes it difficult for candidates to win without backing from special interest groups. Elected officials will remain beholden to those who put up the money until serious campaign reform is implemented and strictly enforced.

Average spending of winners and losers in congressional campaigns in 2004

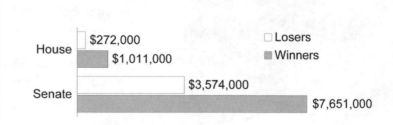

	Losers	Winners
House	$272,000	$1,011,000
Senate	$3,574,000	$7,651,000

12

1.11 Controlling Media

FROM BOOKS TO TV TO MOVIES to magazines to Internet portals, you could go for weeks getting all your news and entertainment through one giant corporation: Time Warner.

Ownership of the media industry has become increasingly concentrated. One company, Clear Channel, owns more than 1,000 radio stations in the U.S., some of which operate by remote control, playing prerecorded material.

Twenty years ago there were 50 corporations controlling the majority of media available to Americans. Mergers and buyouts have enlarged the companies and reduced the number of owners. In 2004, a majority of American newspapers, magazines, TV and radio stations, book publishers, and movie studios were controlled by just five corporations: Time Warner, Disney, News Corp., Bertelsmann, and Viacom.

This concentration allows a very few individuals to have enormous influence over news, information, and entertainment available to the public. And while the big media companies compete against each other in some ways, they also help each other out. In 2004, the five corporations engaged in 141 joint ventures and conducted hundred of millions of dollars of business among themselves.

FCC approves new ownership rules.

ÓSMANI SIMANCA (BEST OF LATIN AMERICA, CAGLE CARTOONS, BRAZIL)

Number of corporations controlling the majority of U.S. media, 1983–2004

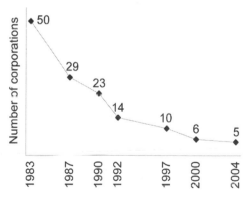

Number of corporations

50
29
23
14
10
6
5

1983 1987 1990 1992 1997 2000 2004

13

Corporate Crime

WHEN PEOPLE HEAR THE word "crime" they usually think of burglaries or carjackings reported on the local news. White-collar crime may be less dramatic, but it is no less significant. The corporate accounting scandals of the last few years have revealed the number of ways in which top management can distort financial records to exaggerate its success, inflate its stock, or avoid paying its taxes.

The first victims are the thousands of employees who lose their jobs—and often their pensions—when a company puffed up on fake profits goes bankrupt. Other victims are ordinary investors whose savings for college or retirement go down the tubes along with the company's stock.

The costs of these corporate crimes can be huge. Investors in Enron, just one of the corporations recently caught red-handed, lost approximately $32 billion (in 2004 dollars) when the company fell apart after its illegal accounting practices were discovered. Compare that to the gross loss to victims of property crimes in the U.S. in 2002: $15 billion.

Cost of Enron scandal vs. property crimes in 2002 (in billions of $2004)

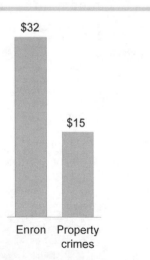

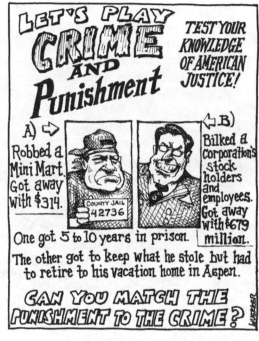

MATT WUERKER

1.13 Multinational Goliaths

THE SIZE OF TODAY'S GIANT corporations often dwarfs the economies of entire countries. In 2003, total sales of Wal-Mart, BP (formerly British Petroleum), and ExxonMobil each exceeded the gross domestic product of Indonesia. Together, the three are larger than the combined economies of the world's poorest 118 countries, with a total population of over 800 million people. While U.S. foreign policy places great emphasis on democracy and human rights when dealing with small countries, the same principles aren't applied to private businesses.

Multinationals have enormous global reach. Because they operate across national boundaries, regulation proves difficult. Their ability to move from one country to another gives them an edge when striking deals with local communities and governments. If a multinational feels that labor laws or environmental codes are too restrictive, it can always threaten to leave.

ANDY SINGER

World sales of selected multinationals and gross national product of selected countries in 2003 ($ billions)

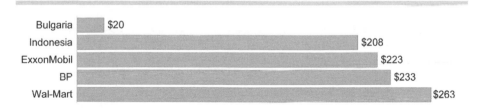

Bulgaria	$20
Indonesia	$208
ExxonMobil	$223
BP	$233
Wal-Mart	$263

The 800-Pound Gorilla

MEASURED IN TERMS OF ITS own growth, Wal-Mart is a great success story. By 2004, its sales were 285 times higher than in 1975. But much of this growth came at the expense of smaller local businesses. One Iowa study, for instance, found that small towns lost up to 47% of their retail trade when a Wal-Mart opened nearby.

Wal-Mart offers low prices for consumers in large part because it pays low wages to its workers. Many who work full time for the company are eligible for food stamps and other government assistance. The company has been sued for forcing employees to work unpaid overtime and also for discriminating against its women workers.

Wal-Mart throws its weight around in other ways as well. It forces suppliers to cut wholesale prices to the bone, reducing their profit margins and pressuring them to reduce wages for their workers. Indeed, many suppliers have been forced to relocate their production to China or other low-wage countries. In 2002, nearly 10% of all U.S. imports from China came to Wal-Mart.

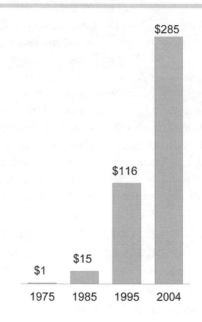

**Wal-Mart annual sales
(in billions of $2004)**

$285 — 2004
$116 — 1995
$15 — 1985
$1 — 1975

FINALLY, WE ENCOMPASS THE EARTH ENTIRELY WITH **ONE MASSIVE STORE.**

WELCOME, SHOPPERS!

ALL★MART

SOON THE WHOLE WORLD WILL BE ONE BIG, LOW-WAGE, NON-UNIONIZED, BENEFIT-LACKING, HAPPY ALL-MART FAMILY... WHO CAN ONLY AFFORD TO SHOP AT ALL-MART!

JEN SORENSEN, SLOWPOKECOMICS.COM

1.15 Owner Activism

R. JAY MAGILL

OWNERSHIP IS POWER. That's a problem when ownership is concentrated. But ownership can also be an avenue for positive change. Many people and institutions are using the power of ownership through what they call "socially responsible" investing.

Definitions of social responsibility vary. Some draw the line at tobacco companies, whose products are bad for people's health. Many avoid investing in companies that have broken environmental laws or tried to bust unions. Others screen out companies profiting from militarism and war. In the 1970s and '80s, investors who disapproved of South Africa's racist apartheid regime pulled their money out of companies doing business in that country, adding to the political pressures that eventually ushered in democratic rule.

The amount of money held in mutual funds and other accounts that specialize in socially responsible investing has grown substantially in the past 20 years.

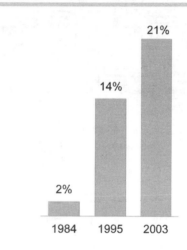

Socially responsible assets as a percentage of value of Standard & Poor's 500 Index

- 1984: 2%
- 1995: 14%
- 2003: 21%

In 1984, they were equivalent to only 2% of the value of the Standard & Poor's 500 (a stock index of 500 corporations); by 2003, the value of socially responsible investments was equivalent to 21% of the S&P 500.

17

magillós

R. JAY MAGILL

WORKERS CAN BE OWNERS, too, and many roads lead to greater worker ownership. Profit-sharing arrangements give workers a piece of the owners' income without actually transferring property. Employee stock ownership plans (ESOPs) establish a trust fund through which workers acquire new and existing company stock. In 2005, 10 million workers participated in ESOPs, with combined assets valued at over $500 billion. The National Center for Employee Ownership reports that, overall, approximately 25 million workers at for-profit companies owned stock in their employer in 2002.

Ownership is one thing; control is another. In most cases, worker ownership remains too small to provide much influence over corporate strategies. Worker-owners often don't have full voting rights. Employees can end up sharing the risks of ownership without having any voice in governing the firm—as many former Enron workers might emphasize.

One form of worker ownership that gives workers democratic control of the business is the worker cooperative, a company controlled by a one-person, one-vote system. Cooperatives have been successful in many industries, from manufacturing and construction to nursing and software design. This structure is especially well suited to smaller companies.

Chapter 2: **Workers**

RUSSELL CHRISTIAN

WHAT KIND OF JOBS DO AMERICANS HAVE? Who gets the big bucks and who works for peanuts? And why can't some people find any employment at all? This chapter looks at work in the United States, making connections between wages, unemployment, and income.

Average wages have not been working so well for the people who earn them. Chart 2.1 illustrates that recent years have seen a slight improvement, but not enough to make up for the lost ground of the 1970s and '80s. It also makes clear the stark economic differences among broad racial/ethnic groups in the U.S.

Those at the bottom of the pay scale have made even less progress. Low wages have resulted in poverty for millions of people, as seen in Chart 2.2. Chart 2.3 shows the long, miserable decline in the federal minimum wage. But some workers have been fighting back, and in hundreds of cities and counties they've won the right to higher local minimums, or "living wages," examples of which are listed in Table 2.4.

The problem of inequality is highlighted in Chart 2.5, which demonstrates that wage differences between the best- and worst-paid college graduates have grown sharply in recent decades. Chart 2.6 emphasizes the disparities in income for those with different levels of education and from different racial/ethnic backgrounds.

Of course, paychecks don't tell the whole story. Benefits are important as well. Chart 2.7 shows that fewer and fewer full-time workers are receiving health insurance through their jobs. Chart 2.8 tells a similar tale for retirement benefits. Without these benefits, working families are forced to stretch their stagnant wages even further.

The worst thing that can happen on the job is injury or death. Chart 2.9 shows the relative risk of these events by gender and race/ethnicity.

In the past, many workers could at least expect stable employment throughout much of their lives. But that expectation is breaking down and workers have good reason to be worried about the security of their jobs. Chart 2.10 shows that mass layoffs hit millions of workers each year. Many people get stuck without any work, but the risks of unemployment differ for various groups of Americans, as seen in Chart 2.11. Over time, unemployment looks a bit like a roller coaster, with ups and downs over the business cycle, as portrayed in Chart 2.12. Workers can also suffer from underemployment; some work part time because they can't find a full-time job, or give up looking for a job and drop out of the labor force. Chart 2.13 presents a total count of underemployment in the U.S. in 2004. Chart 2.14 illustrates that instead of steady, reliable work, millions have contingent jobs, work through temp agencies, or are scheduled only "on call."

Trade unions, hard hit by the loss of manufacturing jobs in the U.S., are struggling to develop new organizing strategies. Chart 2.15 provides an overview of current union membership by demographic group and economic sector. Despite being on the defensive, unions still help protect their members' standard of living. As Chart 2.16 shows, union members are much more likely than other workers to enjoy retirement, medical, and other benefits on the job.

2.1 The Wage Treadmill

R. Jay Magill

MANY AMERICAN WORKERS are on a treadmill, running faster and faster without getting ahead. In the 1950s and '60s, when the U.S. economy grew, workers shared in the prosperity. From the 1970s into the 1990s, workers' median weekly earnings, adjusted for inflation, took a tumble even when the overall economy was growing. This trend began to reverse itself in 1997, but real weekly earnings remain well below their 1973 peak.

Lower real hourly wages mean that people must work harder just to maintain their standard of living. Much of this burden falls on the shoulders of women. Over the 1990s, married couples with children added 151 hours to their average work year, equivalent to almost a month of full-time labor spent away from home. Overall, the average working American in 2004 spent the equivalent of six weeks more on the job than the average Western European.

Stagnant wages are particularly discouraging for those at the bottom. Many full-time workers don't earn enough to keep their families out of poverty. Also, racial and ethnic differences in earnings have become more extreme in recent years.

Median weekly earnings of full-time workers, 1970–2004 (in $2004)

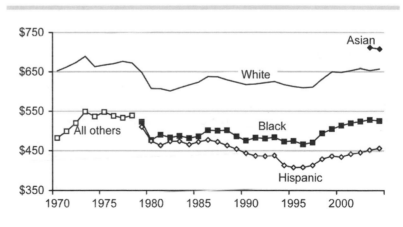

2.2 The Working Poor

HAVING A JOB DOESN'T ALWAYS MEAN YOU CAN PAY THE bills. A significant number of adults are classified as working poor— employed but with family incomes below the poverty line.

* In 2003, the working poor numbered 7.4 million, more than 20% of all poor people.

* Most of the working poor, 60%, worked full time.

* Of all workers who usually had a part-time schedule, about 11% fell below the poverty line, compared to about 5% for the labor force as a whole.

* Women who maintained families were twice as likely to be among the working poor as men who maintained families.

* Half of all poor full-time workers had no health insurance for the entire year.

The number of working poor tends to change along with the business cycle: as the economy grows, some escape to better paying jobs. Still, many people, particularly women, people of color, and those with less education, end up trapped in low-wage jobs for years on end. Even though they sometimes get small raises or slightly higher-paying jobs, these improvements are not sufficient to lift them over the poverty line.

Millions of working poor in the U.S.

Year		Value
1995		7.5
1999		6.8
2003		7.4

CAROL SIMPSON

2.3 The Minimal Minimum Wage

MINIMUM WAGES ARE SUP-posed to set a basic standard of decent living, but that standard has been slipping. Adjusted for inflation, the minimum wage was higher in 1950 than in 2004. In the 1950s and '60s, Congress boosted the minimum wage several times, more than enough to compensate for inflation. But since 1968, when it peaked in real value, its purchasing power has sunk. The federal minimum wage was last raised in 1997. The result was still low by historical standards, and inflation has pushed its value down ever since.

The low minimum wage means poverty for many families. At $5.15 an hour in 2005, a full-time worker brought home less than $11,000 a year. In 2004, over 2 million people were being paid the legal minimum wage or less. Two-thirds of them were women.

GARY HUCK. USED WITH PERMISSION, HUCK/KONOPACKI LABOR CARTOONS, SOLIDARITY.COM/HKCARTOONS/.

Federal minimum wage, 1950–2004 (in $2004)

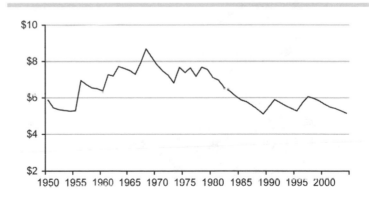

Raising the Floor

"ALL POLITICS IS LOCAL," quipped former congressman Tip O'Neill. Many community activists are trying to make economics local, too. The District of Columbia and 13 states have minimum wages above the federal level that are applicable to almost all workers in those states. Poor workers and their allies have convinced some cities and counties to go further. The idea is simple: raise wages so that someone working full time earns enough to support his or her family above the poverty line. By the end of 2004, there were 123 of these "living wage" ordinances in effect, often automatically adjusted for inflation. However, in most cases, the ordinance applies only to city employees and companies with city contracts.

Opponents argue that higher wages mean fewer jobs. While the ordinances do increase labor costs, the positive effect of higher worker morale can often increase productivity. Studies in several cities have found that job losses and costs to city budgets have been minimal.

HUCK/KONOPACKI LABOR CARTOONS
WWW.SOLIDARITY.COM/HKCARTOONS · FEB
KONOPACKI
©2005

LOCAL MINIMUM WAGE HIKES

LEAD, FOLLOW, OR GET OUT OF THE WAY!

MIKE KONOPACKI. USED WITH PERMISSION, HUCK/KONOPACKI LABOR CARTOONS, SOLIDARITY.COM/HKCARTOONS/.

Examples of hourly living wages set by municipal ordinances (as of March 2005)

DES MOINES, IA ($9.00)
BALTIMORE, MD ($8.85)
MILWAUKEE, WI ($7.53)
PORTLAND, OR ($8.54)
NEW YORK, NY ($10.10)
ST. PAUL, MN ($9.07)
LOS ANGELES, CA ($8.78)
NEW HAVEN, CT ($11.10)
BOSTON, MA ($11.29)
DURHAM, NC ($9.51)
OAKLAND, CA ($9.66)
SAN ANTONIO, TX ($8.85)
CHICAGO, IL ($9.43)
DETROIT, MI ($9.43)
LINCOLN, NE ($8.85)
TUCSON, AZ ($8.77)
MIAMI-DADE COUNTY, FL ($9.44)
DENVER, CO ($9.06)
ALEXANDRIA, VA ($11.36)
PITTSBURGH, PA ($9.12)
RICHMOND, CA ($12.47)
LOUISVILLE, KY ($9.50)

2.5 Unequal Pay

SOME WORKERS HAVE ALWAYS gotten paid more than others because of differences in education and training. But in recent years, pay inequality has increased even among people with similar levels of education.

For instance, the wage difference between the best-paid college-educated women (those with earnings higher than 90% of others) and the worst-paid (with earnings lower than 90% of others) rose dramatically between 1979 and 2003. While about $15 per hour separated the low-paid from the high-paid in 1979, by 2003 the gap was $25, as expressed in 2004 dollars. The trend for college-educated men was similar.

Earnings inequality has increased in a startling variety of jobs—among astronomers, barbers, hoist and winch operators, and biomedical engineers. At least half of all employees in 2004 were in occupations that saw increased inequality over the previous five years.

Some might argue that the labor market is simply offering greater rewards for effort and skill. But a number of institutional changes have contributed to "winner-take-all" dynamics. Cutbacks in public employment have been accompanied by cuts in the relative pay of government employees. Declining unionization and increased immigration have weakened the bargaining power of workers in many low-wage occupations.

Hourly wages of low-paid and high-paid college graduates (in $2004)

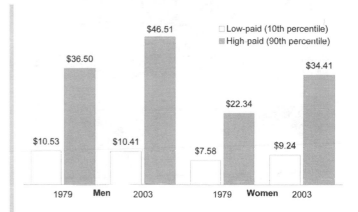

2.6 The College Premium

GO TO COLLEGE AND GET that degree. Otherwise, you'll have a hard time earning a decent living. Between 1979 and 2003, real wages for high school graduates fell, while those for college graduates rose. Average real wages for college graduates are now about twice as high as those of high school dropouts.

A college degree is valuable in part because it is still relatively rare. In 2003, only 27% of adults age 25 and older had completed a bachelor's degree.

The advantages of education are not shared equally. At every level, whites have higher average incomes, an advantage that grows with more education. The good news is that the wage gap between women and men has narrowed.

High school dropouts don't find many job opportunities. In 2001, fewer than 60% of dropouts between ages 16 and 24 were employed.

SPUD AND BARRY DEUTSCH

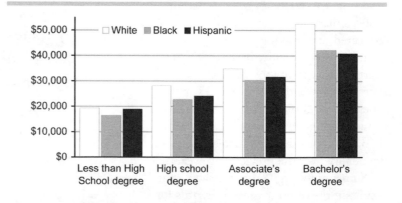

Average annual income in 2002 by race, Hispanic origin, and highest educational degree (age 18 and older)

2.7 Shrinking Health Benefits

WORKERS DON'T LIVE ON take-home pay alone. During World War II, employers began providing relatively generous benefit packages. But as these benefits became more expensive, employers started shifting costs to their workers. This trend has accelerated over the last 25 years. Between 1989 and 2004, the percentage of full-time workers with employer-provided medical insurance fell from 80% to 66%.

Large firms are more likely than small firms to offer benefits. Still, the cost to employees of participating in the health plan prevents many from buying in. In 1984, full-time employees at medium and large firms paid an average of $22 per week for single-person coverage and $65 for family coverage. By 2004, the cost to the worker, after adjusting for inflation, had almost doubled for single-person coverage and more than doubled for a family plan.

The situation is even tougher for employees at smaller firms, where over half of private industry workers find jobs. In 2004, only 60% of smaller businesses offered medical benefits, at an average cost of $74 per week for individual coverage and $307 for family coverage.

PETER HANNAN

Percentage of full-time workers in private industry covered by employer-provided medical insurance

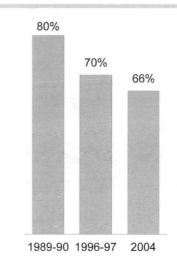

80%   1989-90
70%   1996-97
66%   2004

2.8 Rising Retirement Risk

FOR DECADES, MILLIONS OF American workers relied on pensions to see them through their golden years. While workers produced goods or services for the company to sell, the company put money aside to cover their retirement.

Now, many companies have either eliminated pension plans or shifted the financial risks of retirement onto employees. Traditional pensions offered "defined benefits" that guaranteed a certain level of retirement income. But employers prefer "defined contribution" plans in which they promise only a specific contribution. If the pension fund loses value—as a result, for instance, of a tumbling stock market—the retirees suffer the consequences.

As recently as 1995, more than half of employees at medium and large firms could look forward to defined benefits in retirement. By 2004 only a little more than a third could.

To make matters worse, many pension funds are dangerously underfunded. When companies can't meet their financial obligations, they can file for bankruptcy. Pension funds are only partially insured by the federal government, so employees can end up getting far less than they were promised.

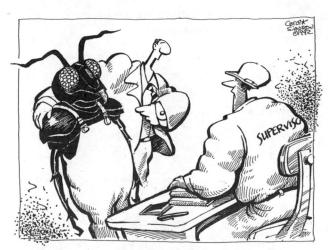

"His entire adult lifespan is exactly eight hours. He won't be around long enough to need benefits."

CAROL SIMPSON

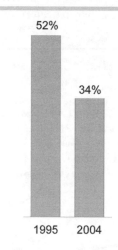

Percentage of employees at medium and large firms with defined benefit retirement plan

52% — 1995

34% — 2004

2.9 Dangerous and Deadly Jobs

MAKING A LIVING CAN sometimes be fatal. More than 5,500 workers died from injuries on the job in 2003. Men are the most common victims, and the risks are higher for Hispanics than other groups. An additional 2.3 million nongovernment workers suffered nonfatal work-related injuries or illnesses severe enough to require days off from work, a job transfer, or some other work restriction to help in recovery.

Not all workplace injuries are reported. Even when an employee is killed due to an employer's willful violation of workplace safety laws, the employer is almost never prosecuted for the crime.

There is some evidence that American workplaces are becoming less deadly. Since the government started keeping records in 1992, the rate of job-related deaths has been steadily dropping, from 5.2 to 4.0 deaths per 100,000 workers in 2003.

However, these statistics do not count the illnesses and deaths occurring off the job-site that result from long-term job exposure to toxic substances. Approximately 20,000 cancer deaths and 40,000 new cases of cancer each year in the U.S. are linked to people's occupations.

CAROL SIMPSON

Rate of workplace fatalities per 100,000 workers in 2003

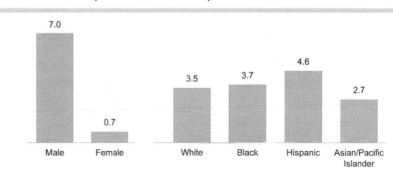

29

2.10 **Job Insecurity**

PEOPLE DEPEND ON THEIR JOBS FOR MORE than money. A job helps shape a person's identity and can provide a sense of personal accomplishment. Jobs also anchor people's lives, affecting where and how they raise their families.

Unfortunately, many people have good reason to fear job loss. Downsizing and outsourcing take a heavy toll. Even in a growth year like 2004, more than 1.5 million workers were affected by mass layoffs in which 50 or more workers lost their jobs at once. Most of those laid off usually find new jobs, but there's no guarantee that the new job will be as good as the old one.

Worries about job security can be as stressful as unemployment for workers and their families. In an era of downsizing, even keeping your job has drawbacks: when a business downsizes, the remaining workers are at higher risk for job-related injuries.

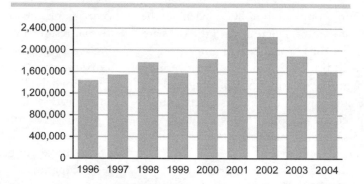

Annual unemployment insurance claims from mass layoffs, 1996–2004

JEN SORENSEN, SLOWPOKECOMICS.COM

2.11 Jobless

IF YOU HAVE BEEN ACTIVELY searching for a job in the last month but haven't found one, you are officially unemployed.

In 2004, the percentage of those unable to find work averaged 5.5%. But some groups had a tougher time than others. While whites had an unemployment rate of 4.8%, African Americans were more than twice as likely to be unemployed, at a rate of 10.4%. Teenagers were particularly vulnerable, with an unemployment rate of 17%. Even those ages 20 to 24 had a particularly hard time finding jobs.

Length of time unemployed also matters. The average duration of unemployment in 2004 was 19.6 weeks, well above the 15.4-week average for the past 20 years. Being out of work is hard on people. Studies show that it contributes to problems like child abuse and mental illness.

MIKHAELA REID

Unemployment rates in 2004

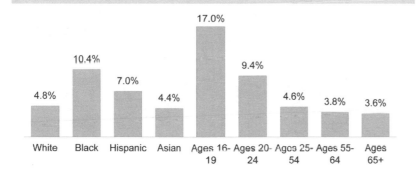

2.12 The Ups and Downs of Unemployment

THE UNEMPLOYMENT RATE reflects the roller coaster of the business cycle, but no one really understands its long-run trends. Between 1950 and 1974, a period of relatively steady economic growth, it generally remained under 6%. In the 1970s and '80s, it careened upward, almost reaching 10%. Since then it has settled down.

The official unemployment rate isn't a totally satisfactory measure. For example, people in prison and other institutions are not counted as part of the labor force and therefore are left out of unemployment statistics. The U.S. jail and prison population has been growing rapidly in the past decade and now includes over 2 million people.

A low unemployment rate still represents a large number of unemployed people. In August 2005, the rate of 4.9% represented 7.4 million people with bills to pay who were out looking for jobs.

Unemployment rate, 1950–2004
(noninstitutionalized civilians in
the labor force, age 16+)

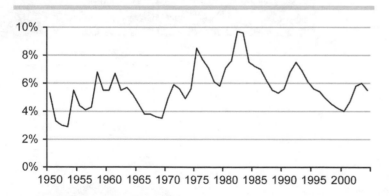

2.13 **Underemployment**

A LITTLE BIT OF WORK IS BETTER than none, but many people can't find enough. In 2004 about 4.6 million people worked part time only because they couldn't find full-time jobs. Another 1.6 million had given up looking, entering the category of "marginally attached and discouraged workers."

Adding these involuntary part-time and discouraged workers to the 2004 unemployment rate of 5.5% results in an *under*employment rate of approximately 9.7%. In other words, almost one in every 10 workers had insufficient employment.

Part-time workers are less likely than those working full time to receive medical or pension benefits from their employer. Underemployment in general is associated with depression, decreased self-esteem, and higher rates of alcohol abuse, especially among younger workers.

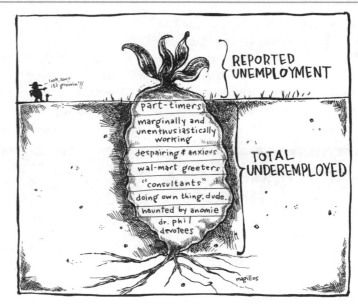

R. JAY MAGILL

Millions of underemployed workers by situation in 2004

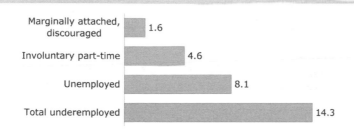

Marginally attached, discouraged	1.6
Involuntary part-time	4.6
Unemployed	8.1
Total underemployed	14.3

ONCE UPON A TIME, MANY people worked for the same company most of their lives. Employees were loyal to their company, and the employers were expected to return the favor. Nowadays, long-term relationships are rare.

"Contingent" workers are those who don't expect their job to last more than a year. In 2005, 5.7 million workers fell into this category. Workers are also categorized according to whether their job arrangement is traditional or not. Some nontraditional workers are those who work "on call" or through a temp agency. There were 2.5 million on-call and 1.2 million temp workers in 2001. These workers may or may not also be counted as contingent.

Some workers feel that these arrangements give them flexibility, and that opinion is becoming more common. Still, this flexibility comes at a price. The average pay for a full-time contingent, on-call, or temp worker is less than in a regular job arrangement. These workers are also less likely to enjoy retirement or health care benefits.

Millions of contingent and nontraditional employees in February 2005

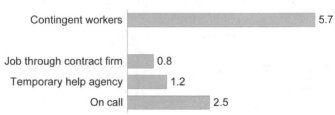

Contingent workers	5.7
Job through contract firm	0.8
Temporary help agency	1.2
On call	2.5

Who Belongs to Unions?

LABOR UNIONS REPRESENT THEIR members' interests, fighting for higher wages and better benefits, and working to settle grievances with employers. However, representation by unions is declining. Despite a brief resurgence in the 1990s, unions represented only 12.5% of American workers in 2004, the lowest level in decades.

Companies go to great lengths to stay free of unions, regularly violating employees' legal rights with little fear of real punishment. Employers fire pro-union workers and use intimidation and the threat of plant closure and layoffs to defeat unionization efforts.

A survey for the AFL-CIO, conducted by Peter D. Hart Research Associates in 2005, found that 53% of nonunion workers would vote for union representation if given the opportunity (38% said they'd vote no). If that hap-pened, organized labor would represent millions more workers.

Historically, union members have been disproportionately white and male. Today they are more diverse. While 12% of white workers are members, they are joined by 15% of African Americans, 11% of Asian Americans, and 10% of Hispanics. Women make up 43% of all unionized workers.

CAROL SIMPSON

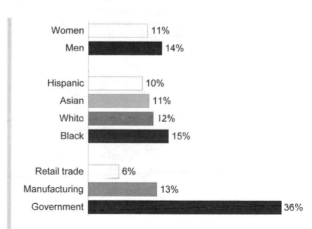

Percentage of employees belonging to unions in 2004

Women	11%
Men	14%
Hispanic	10%
Asian	11%
White	12%
Black	15%
Retail trade	6%
Manufacturing	13%
Government	36%

Unions at Work

COLLECTIVE BARGAINING PAYS off. Labor unions deliver important benefits to their members. In 2004, full-time workers in unions had median weekly earnings of $781, some 28% more than nonunion workers. In most occupations, the more heavily unionized the workers were, the higher their wages were compared to nonunionized workers in the same occupation.

Unionized workers in private industry tend to enjoy more benefits on the job as well. In 2004, 81% had retirement benefits, compared to 47% of nonunion workers. The situation was similar for health benefits. Of all workers with health benefits, nonunion workers had to pay a much larger share of the insurance premium than those in unions.

Union members are more likely to receive paid holidays, military leave, and vacations, and their average vacation time is longer than for their nonunion neighbors. They also receive benefits that are less tangible. Unions can give workers a voice on the job, making it harder for managers to treat employees unfairly or to violate labor laws.

CAROL SIMPSON

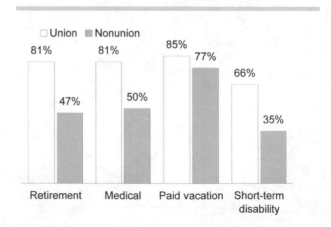

Percentage of workers with various benefits in 2004, by union affiliation

□ Union ■ Nonunion

	Retirement	Medical	Paid vacation	Short-term disability
Union	81%	81%	85%	66%
Nonunion	47%	50%	77%	35%

CHAPTER 3: Women

RUSSELL CHRISTIAN

You've come a long way—maybe. Imagine flipping on the television and watching a commercial about a tireless man who whisks the kids off to school, then does a load of laundry before driving to work. You probably won't see it anytime soon—a good reminder that gender inequalities remain a central feature of our economic life.

How has women's place in the economy changed? Chart 3.1 shows that after many decades of rapid increase, female participation in paid employment has leveled off. There are,

after all, only 24 hours in a day, and most women continue to take primary responsibility for family care. As Chart 3.2 points out, many women resort to part-time employment, the better to juggle competing demands on their time. Unfortunately, many part-time jobs don't offer much by way of pay or benefits.

The good news is that women have narrowed the wage gap. Chart 3.3 points to substantial improvements in the relative average earnings of full-time women wage earners across all racial and ethnic groups. But equally qualified women should earn exactly what men earn. They don't. And as Chart 3.4 indicates, even small differences in pay in a year add up to thousands of dollars over the course of a lifetime.

Women's traditional role in the household has always influenced their place in paid work. Chart 3.5 shows that many women workers remain in gender-typed, low-paid pink-collar jobs. Child care workers earn about the same per hour as parking lot attendants. According to Chart 3.6, even preschool teachers are poorly paid.

Women have moved into many well-paying professional jobs once monopolized by men. But substantial barriers still prevent promotions to top positions. Chart 3.7 reveals some dimensions of the "glass ceiling." In discrimination cases, the burden of proof lies with those who feel they have been unfairly treated. Yet women have won some notable victories in recent years, described in Chart 3.8. A case against the country's single largest private employer, Wal-Mart, recently got under way.

The workplace is not the only place where women experience disadvantage. Motherhood is economically risky. As Chart 3.9 shows, almost half of families living in poverty are maintained by women alone, more than double the percentage in 1959. Low levels of paternal child support provide a partial explanation. Unmarried mothers are now more likely to collect support than in the past. But Chart 3.10 documents how few receive the full amount they are owed.

Women devote more time than men to housework and care activities, even when they also work for pay. Chart 3.11 shows differences in the way men and women use time, while Chart 3.12 shows why many families with children report a "time crunch." The average number of hours of wage employment per household has gone up substantially over time.

Many young children are now cared for outside the home. Chart 3.13 describes the different arrangements parents rely on, emphasizing problems with the costs and quality of care. Many states are moving toward provision of early childhood education, but the U.S. government offers less generous support for child rearing than most other countries. As Chart 3.14 details, parents elsewhere typically enjoy paid leaves from work.

As of 2005, women have legal rights to contraception and abortion. But Chart 3.15 explains political and economic tactics used to restrict their access. Despite their many differences, women share some common interests, but it's not easy for them to influence government policies. Chart 3.16 documents the gender gap in political office holders. Women's reactions to the economic differences documented in this chapter might lead to a narrowing of that gap in the future.

3.1 To Market, to Market . . . but Not So Fast

AFTER FOUR DECADES OF dramatic increase, women's participation in paid employment seems to be leveling off. The percentage of all women between ages 25 and 54 who were in the labor force remained constant at about 74% between 1990 and 2000. Single mothers, struggling hard to make ends meet, were the only group of women whose employment increased.

Men may be taking on more care responsibilities, and those whose wives bring home a paycheck may feel less pressure to work for pay. The labor force participation rate of working-age men declined more sharply between 1990 and 2000 than in any other decade. As a result, the participation rates of men and women continued to converge.

In high-income families, a spouse can choose to opt out of paid employment.

But many families must rely on two earners, and they face difficult trade-offs. Market income can be used to buy many goods and services once produced in the home, but it is not a perfect substitute for time, especially when care of family members is concerned.

Labor force participation rates (men and women ages 25–54)

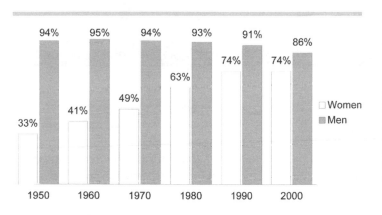

Year	Women	Men
1950	33%	94%
1960	41%	95%
1970	49%	94%
1980	63%	93%
1990	74%	91%
2000	74%	86%

CHRIS SLANE, NEW ZEALAND

39

3.2 **Part-Time Patterns**

WOMEN ORGANIZE THEIR work life differently from men. Largely as a result of family responsibilities, they are much more likely to end up in part-time jobs, those that require fewer than 35 hours per week. In 2004, almost 70% of the part-time labor force was female. Mothers of young children are particularly likely to work only part time in a given week. They also tend to work fewer weeks of the year.

Full-time work in the U.S. often demands more than 40 hours per week with little flexibility. Part-time jobs typically pay far less per hour than full-time ones, and they seldom offer benefits such as health insurance, vacations, or pensions. Career ladders or other opportunities for advancement are rare, and employers often require nonstandard and irregular work hours.

In some countries, such as France, employers are required to prorate benefits for part-time workers (allowing them benefits proportional to their work hours, rather than denying them coverage altogether). Such policies go a long way toward improving the quality of part-time jobs relative to full-time ones.

Percentage of all part-time workers in 2004 by gender (workers age 20+)

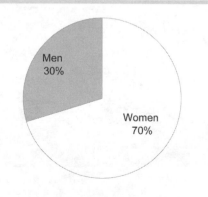

Men 30%

Women 70%

AMPERSAND BY B. DEUTSCH

3.3 Women Still Earn Less than Men

OVER THE PAST DECADES, women have substantially improved their economic position. But among full-time workers in 2002, women still earned only about 80 cents for every dollar that men earned.

For a long time, women's relative earnings were stuck at about 60%. Antidiscrimination laws that increased their access to professional training and higher-paying jobs contributed to a big push forward in the 1980s. Men's earnings increased very little after 1979, so a modest increase in women's earnings had a big statistical impact. Because relatively few women worked in manufacturing, they were less affected than men by the loss of jobs in that sector.

The difference between women's and men's wages is greatest among whites. Racial-ethnic inequality seems to mute the effect of gender.

TOM TOMORROW

Women's earnings as a percentage of men's earnings (year-round, full-time workers)

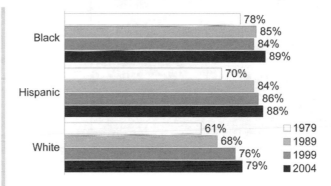

	1979	1989	1999	2004
Black	78%	85%	84%	89%
Hispanic	70%	84%	86%	88%
White	61%	68%	76%	79%

3.4 The Lifetime Earnings Gap

INEQUALITY ADDS UP. WOMEN earn less than men year after year, and they also take more time out of paid employment to care for family members. As a result, the earnings gap over many years is larger than the gap in any single year.

Between 1983 and 1998, women in the U.S. who worked full time for at least 12 years earned, on average, 64% of what men earned. But few women worked full time over this period. Among those who worked every year, but not necessarily full time, the earnings ratio was 56%. Among those who worked at least one year, excluding years when they did not work, the ratio was 44%. Overall, women who worked at least one year over the period earned only 38% of what men in the same age group earned. Such large differences in earnings reduce women's income security in the event of divorce, their pensions in old age, and their bargaining power in the home. While many women choose this sacrifice, they are constrained by social policies and cultural norms that make it hard to balance paid work with family work.

'Three-fourths of a penny for your thoughts...'

Women's long-term earnings relative to men's (workers ages 26–59 over the period 1983–1998)

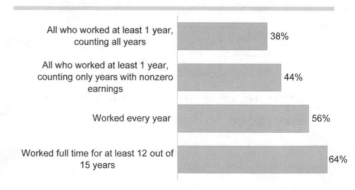

All who worked at least 1 year, counting all years	38%
All who worked at least 1 year, counting only years with nonzero earnings	44%
Worked every year	56%
Worked full time for at least 12 out of 15 years	64%

3.5 Pink-Collar Jobs

MANY WOMEN WORK IN jobs that don't fit the traditional blue-collar/white-collar distinction. They wear a metaphorical pink collar, doing work that often involves caring for others. Women represent the overwhelming majority of nurses, teachers, secretaries, and personal/home care aides.

Most occupations dominated by women are relatively poorly paid. Why don't more women choose to enter traditionally male occupations? They may face discrimination from employers or harassment from fellow workers. They may enjoy working with other women. They may value kinds of work that help others. They may also worry that "unfeminine" choices will lower their chances of success in dating and marriage.

Whatever their reasons for taking pink-collar jobs, most women working in them would like more room for career advancement and higher pay.

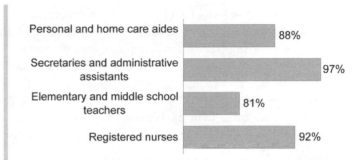

Women as a percentage of all employees in selected occupations in 2004

Personal and home care aides 88%

Secretaries and administrative assistants 97%

Elementary and middle school teachers 81%

Registered nurses 92%

CAROL SIMPSON

3.6 The Care Penalty

THE LABOR MARKET OFFERS little reward for the work of care. Jobs involving face-to-face interaction with young children are poorly paid compared to jobs that require far less skill and responsibility. Child-care workers are better educated than the general population, but in 2004 they earned about the same hourly wage as parking lot attendants. Preschool teachers earned less, on average, than tree trimmers.

Children, as well as grown-ups, are affected by the low level of pay. Turnover rates are high among child-care workers—about one-third leave their jobs every year, a discontinuity that makes it hard to maintain high-quality care.

Higher community standards and pay-equity policies could address this problem. In many countries, including Australia and France, child-care workers earn higher wages relative to other workers.

SPUD AND R. JAY MAGILL

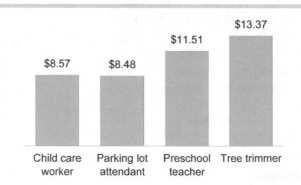

Mean hourly wages by occupation in 2004

Child care worker	Parking lot attendant	Preschool teacher	Tree trimmer
$8.57	$8.48	$11.51	$13.37

3.7 Glass Ceilings

A GLASS CEILING MAY BE hard to see, but it hurts when you bump your head against a barrier to upward mobility built on hidden bias and unspoken assumptions. Despite growing diversity in the workforce, women are seriously underrepresented in top-level management positions.

A census of the Fortune 500 corporations in 2003 conducted by the consulting firm Catalyst found that only 16% of corporate officers—and only 5% of the highest-paid officers—were women. The definition of "officer" was taken from the companies' own public filings.

Some companies do better than others. At Ikon Office Solutions, SLM Holding, Pacificare Health Systems, and Nordstrom, women hold over 40% of officer slots. Still, 90 Fortune 500 companies reported no women officers at all in 2000.

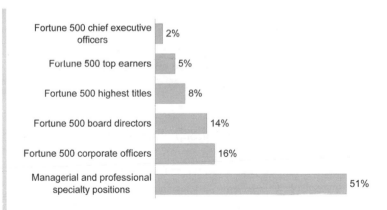

Women as a percentage of corporate management positions in 2003

Fortune 500 chief executive officers	2%
Fortune 500 top earners	5%
Fortune 500 highest titles	8%
Fortune 500 board directors	14%
Fortune 500 corporate officers	16%
Managerial and professional specialty positions	51%

3.8 Call a Lawyer

DISCRIMINATION AGAINST WOMEN IS NOT JUST wrong, it's against the law. More than 40 years after the passage of the Civil Rights Act of 1964, women are still fighting for their rights—and often winning. Some notable recent cases:

MERRILL LYNCH: An arbitration panel ruled that the company had systematically discriminated against a female broker, and the panel ordered the company to pay her $2.2 million. The complaint was part of a class action suit filed against the company in 1997.

FEDERAL EXPRESS: A female tractor-trailer driver claimed she was subjected to a hostile work environment based on her sex, and experienced retaliation when she complained. She was awarded $3.2 million.

UNITED AIRLINES: A group of female flight attendants filed suit claiming that the weight restrictions imposed on women were stricter than those imposed on men. In December 2002 a U.S. district court found in their favor, with a preliminary award of $36.5 million.

M. E. COHEN, M.E.COHEN@HUMORINK.COM

WAL-MART: Plaintiffs argue that both hourly and salaried women employees earn less than men with the same job title and that women are significantly underrepresented in management. Women who do become managers at the company take longer to reach that position.

3.9 Mothers, Children, and Poverty

MOTHERS ON THEIR OWN have become increasingly vulnerable to poverty. Their families represented almost half of all those living below the poverty line in 2003, a much larger share than in 1959.

This feminization of poverty reflects, in part, the pauperization of motherhood. Support from both fathers and the state remains relatively low, increasing the economic burden on mothers. Raising the next generation of workers and taxpayers is apparently not considered productive work.

Policy changes implemented in 1996 pushed many mothers into paid employment. But few earn wages sufficient to keep them and their children out of poverty. Child support enforcement remains a serious problem.

It's not just single mothers who suffer. When married women are just a husband away from poverty, they don't have much bargaining power in the home.

Percentage of all poor families maintained by women alone

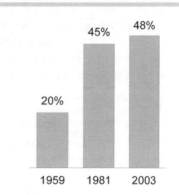

1959	1981	2003
20%	45%	48%

DID YOU KNOW THAT THE AVERAGE WOMAN'S STANDARD OF LIVING DROPS 73% DURING THE FIRST YEAR AFTER A DIVORCE?

DID YOU KNOW THAT THE AVERAGE MAN'S STANDARD OF LIVING IMPROVES 42% DURING THAT SAME YEAR?

I WILL ALWAYS LOVE YOU.

3.10 **Deadbeat Dads**

SOMETIMES YOU SEE THEIR faces on "Wanted" posters or hear about their wages being garnished. But deadbeat dads are still not paying up. Despite a significant boost in enforcement efforts, fewer than half of all custodial parents received the full amount of child support they were due in 2002. More than 40% of all custodial parents, who are mostly women, lacked any formal child support agreement.

Divorced mothers fare better than never-married mothers: almost half receive the full amount awarded. Compliance problems have created an entirely new industry—private detectives who track down delinquent spouses in return for a share of the settlement.

States have a big incentive to bear down on the fathers of children receiving public assistance, since the state can claim this money for itself. Many states also threaten to deny public assistance to unmarried mothers who fail to disclose paternity. Many low-income fathers are simply unable to pay what they owe. Sending them to jail doesn't help them earn money to support their children.

Percentage of custodial parents due child support who received the full amount

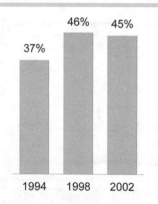

37% — 1994
46% — 1998
45% — 2002

3.11 Unpaid Work

WHILE MEN PUT MORE TIME into paid work, women put more time into unpaid services such as housework and the care of family and friends. These services may not carry a price tag, but they certainly have economic value. If they weren't provided outside the market, someone would probably have to pay for them.

Men and women over the age of 18 worked, on average, between 53 and 54 hours a week in 2003. Men devoted about 32 hours per week to paid work, compared to 20 for women. Overall, unpaid work amounted to about half of all work performed.

Housework, including activities such as cooking, cleaning, and shopping, accounted for 14 hours a week for men and 23 for women. Care for family, friends, and others included activities such as child care, tending to family members in separate households, and civic and religious activities. Men spent about 7 hours per week in such activities; women, about 12.

When women live in a household with children under the age of 6, the amount of time they devote to both care and housework increases dramatically, to almost 27 hours per week. Mothers of young children who also work for pay don't enjoy much leisure time. Fathers' time seems to be less affected by household composition.

Hours per week of paid and unpaid work in the U.S. in 2003

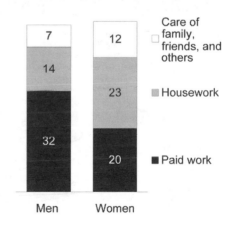

	Men	Women	
Care of family, friends, and others	7	12	☐
Housework	14	23	▨
Paid work	32	20	■

COPYRIGHT BY NICOLE HOLLANDER

49

3.12 Time Crunch

OFTEN THE ONLY WAY TO EARN more money is to give up more time. The increase in married women's participation in paid employment in recent decades has reduced the time available for family care. Increases in the average weekly work hours of married couples have contributed to higher income but created a time crunch. In 1968, husbands and wives together put in less than 55 hours of paid work per week. By 2002 they were putting in almost 65 hours per week.

Many parents trying to balance work and family responsibilities find it difficult to do so. Nearly three-quarters of working adults say they have little or no control over their work schedules. Part-time jobs don't pay well and often lack benefits. Some employees are pressured into working overtime.

Many employees lack the flexibility they need to care for sick children without losing pay, forfeiting vacation time, or having to invent some excuse for leaving work.

Elder care is also a big responsibility. Changes in health care practices, including shorter hospital stays, have increased the burden of informal care.

ALL I CAN FIGURE OUT, LINDA, IS THAT YOU MUST BE SUFFERING FROM SOME SORT OF REPETITIVE MOTION ILLNESS.

I COULD HAVE TOLD YOU THAT, DOC. IT'S CALLED TWO JOBS AND A FAMILY!

HUCK/KONOPACKI LABOR CARTOONS - FEB

MIKE KONOPACKI. USED WITH PERMISSION, HUCK/KONOPACKI LABOR CARTOONS, SOLIDARITY.COM/HKCARTOONS.

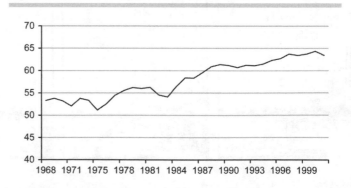

Weekly hours in paid work of husbands and wives combined (families with children)

3.13 The Demand for Child Care

MOTHERS IN OUR SOCIETY are expected to work for pay. They are not eligible for public assistance unless they do. But good child care is expensive and hard to find—especially for families without grandparents and other relatives available to help out.

In 2002, about 30% of children younger than five with employed mothers were in center-based care (child-care center, Head Start, or preschool). Almost as many were cared for primarily by a parent juggling work schedules, arranging shift work, or working at home. Care by relatives such as grandmothers also played a large role. About 13% of families relied on care by a nonrelative in the provider's home (sometimes called family day care).

Recent evidence suggests that center-based care helps enhance school readiness. High-income children are likely to enjoy such high-quality, educational care. Low-income children are more likely to be plunked down in front of a television set. While low-income families enjoy greater eligibility for government assistance, they often end up on a waiting list.

Some states, including Georgia, Florida, and California, are moving toward publicly funded universal preschool for four- and five-year-olds.

child-care subsidy, no child-care subsidy, no child-care subsidy, child-care subsidy...

R. JAY MAGILL

Primary child care arrangements for children under age 5 with employed mothers in 2002

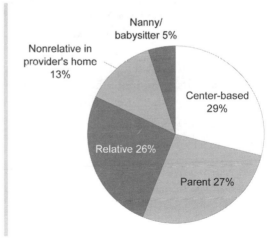

Nanny/babysitter 5%

Nonrelative in provider's home 13%

Center-based 29%

Relative 26%

Parent 27%

3.14 Family Policies Around the World

THE PARENTAL LEAVE AND CHILD CARE BENEFITS offered in northwest Europe, Canada, and Australia are far more generous than those in the United States.

∗ The U.S. is one of only five affluent countries worldwide that do not offer paid parental leave. Denmark, Finland, Norway, and Sweden offer particularly generous maternity leave: 30–42 weeks at close to full wage replacement. In the U.S. the Family and Medical Leave Act of 1993 provides only 12 weeks of unpaid leave for those employed by firms with 50 or more employees.

∗ Many countries also offer paternal leave, which encourages fathers to play a more active role. In Sweden, parental leaves can be shared or used by one parent, but one nontransferable month is reserved for the father and one for the mother, to encourage sharing. During their child's first year, more than one-half of fathers use some leave. Swedish fathers use nearly one-third of all paid temporary leave to stay home and care for sick children under 12.

∗ Many northwest European countries make it easier for families to balance paid work and family work. They set shorter workweeks, provide a minimum of twenty days paid vacation, and promote high-quality part-time

R. JAY MAGILL

employment. In Sweden, parents have the right to work six hours a day (at prorated pay) until their children turn eight.

∗ Most northwest European countries provide high-quality early childhood education and care programs either free or for a very low cost.

3.15 Reproductive Rights and Wrongs

THE TOP FIVE PROBLEMS FOR SEXUAL AND reproductive health in 2004:

1. HEALTH PROFESSIONALS ARE ALLOWED TO DENY WOMEN THEIR CONTRACEPTIVE PRESCRIPTIONS

Recent federal and state legislation makes it easier for health care providers and insurers to refuse to offer or cover sexual and reproductive health services, including prescriptions for emergency contraceptives and birth control pills. Pills to treat male erectile dysfunction, by contrast, are heavily advertised and widely available.

2. GOVERNMENT-SPONSORED IGNORANCE PUTS YOUNG PEOPLE AT RISK

Since 1996, nearly $1 billion in state and federal funds has been spent on abstinence-only education that forbids any discussion of contraceptives except to describe how they can fail.

3. ACCESS TO ABORTION IS RESTRICTED

Although the law of the land guarantees women the right to an abortion within the first few months of pregnancy, political pressures and terrorist attacks on family planning clinics have made it difficult for women to obtain the procedure. More than half of all metropolitan counties in the U.S. lack an abortion provider.

JEN SORENSEN, SLOWPOKECOMICS.COM.

4. MEDICAID SUPPORT FOR FAMILY PLANNING IS IN JEOPARDY

More than one in three low-income women of reproductive age depend on Medicaid for health care, and the program pays for nearly one in four births in the U.S. Yet the Bush administration advises sharp reductions in benefit guarantees.

5. A GAG RULE IS IMPOSED ON HEALTH CARE PROVIDERS OVERSEAS

President George W. Bush reinstated a rule requiring nongovernmental organizations outside the United States to forgo use of their own funds to provide abortions or abortion counseling, or to engage in any advocacy related to their country's abortion laws in order to be eligible for U.S. family planning assistance.

The Political Gender Gap

WOMEN WOULD GET MORE help from public policy if they held more political power. While they make up 51% of the adult population in the U.S., they hold only a small fraction of elective offices at almost every level of government.

Combined work/family responsibilities may increase women's reluctance to run for office. Many voters may hold the traditional view that men should be in charge. Lower levels of individually controlled wealth and income may discourage women from participation in what has become an increasingly costly electoral process.

Women don't invest as heavily in political campaigns as men do. In 2000, they made only one-quarter of all contributions greater than $200 to political candidates. Historically, women have been more likely to donate to issue-oriented causes than to election campaigns. New organizing efforts that speak more directly to their interests might change their priorities.

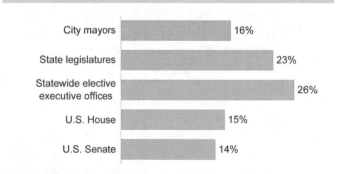

Percentage of elective positions held by women in 2005

- City mayors — 16%
- State legislatures — 23%
- Statewide elective executive offices — 26%
- U.S. House — 15%
- U.S. Senate — 14%

Who do you *really* want to see in the White House?

Mikhaela B. Reid for Women's eNews ★ 2004

MIKHAELA REID/WOMEN'S ENEWS, WOMENSENEWS.ORG

CHAPTER 4: **People of Color**

ECONOMIC OPPORTUNITIES IN AMERICA ARE determined both by the color of people's skin and by the contents of their wallets. While it's hard to find data describing the fate of every ethnic group, statistics show that blacks and Hispanics are more likely than whites to die in infancy, to grow up in poverty, to experience unemployment, and to spend time in prison.

Table 4.1 describes the composition of the U.S. population in 2003, while Chart 4.2 explores the ethnic diversity of Hispanics, Asians, and Pacific Islanders in more detail. Immigration dynamics have a big impact on current demographics. Chart 4.3 documents recent trends in legal immigration, while Chart 4.4 describes the composition of the undocumented workers whose annual flow into the U.S. now rivals that of legal immigrants.

Blacks and Hispanics are particularly susceptible to joblessness. As Chart 4.5 indicates, their unemployment rates vary over the business cycle but remain consistently higher than those of whites. Chart 4.6 shows that educational attainment

RUSSELL CHRISTIAN

can't fully explain these differences. In 2004, black college graduates fared only slightly better than white high school graduates.

Educational attainment is going up overall. Still, as Chart 4.7 illustrates, race and ethnicity can impinge on attainment of college diplomas. Partly as a result, blacks and Hispanics are more likely than whites to end up in dead-end jobs. Chart 4.8 shows that they are overrepresented in less-skilled service occupations and underrepresented in managerial and professional positions. Inequalities in earnings are one obvious result.

Chart 4.9 compares the median weekly earnings of black and Hispanic men and women to those of whites. In recent years, these inequalities have gotten worse. High unemployment, unequal educational opportunities, and low-paying jobs have a cumulative effect. As Chart 4.10 shows, blacks and Hispanics are far more susceptible to poverty than whites.

Unemployment figures for people of color would look much worse if the prison population were included in the statistics. Incarceration rates in the United States are much higher than in other developed countries, and as Chart 4.11 shows, a much higher percentage of African American than white men are in prison. Families and communities are disrupted. The special problems that children of prisoners experience are described in Chart 4.12.

Single-mother households face enormous economic challenges and a high risk of poverty. Chart 4.13 shows how likely black, Hispanic, and white households are to be maintained by women alone. Chart 4.14 points out that white households are less likely than others to be raising children at all, a factor that may help explain relatively low levels of support for public policies to reduce child poverty.

Discrimination based on race and ethnicity grows less acceptable every year. Yet it continues to leave a visible trail. Chart 4.15 describes the backlash against affirmative action programs at colleges and universities. A variety of experiments and comparisons, documented in Chart 4.16, prove that we remain a long way away from color-blind ideals.

4.1 **Who We Are**

THE U.S., TRADITIONALLY DESCRIBED AS A melting pot, is more like a salad bowl. In 2003, more than a quarter of the population had ethnic backgrounds that set them apart from the politically dominant white population.

Many people can lay claim to more than one ethnic identity, and the Census Bureau now takes this into account. But in 2000, fewer than 3% of people described themselves as belonging to more than one racial/ethnic category.

In 2003, blacks and Hispanics accounted for 13% and 14% of the population, respectively. Asian/Pacific Islanders made up about 4% and Native Americans about 1%. Because these groups are concentrated in certain geographic areas, they often represent a much larger percentage of the population in their own communities.

All these groups are growing faster than non-Hispanic whites, who are projected to represent only slightly more than 50% of the population in 2050.

Racial and ethnic composition of the U.S. population (actual and projected)

	2003	2050
White non-Hispanic	67%	52%
Black	13%	13%
Hispanic	14%	25%
Asian/Pacific Islander	4%	10%
Native American	1%	1%

JIM MEEHAN

4.2 Asian and Hispanic Diversity

MANY PEOPLE STRONGLY identify with their nation of origin. The broad ethnic categories used by the Census Bureau conceal enormous diversity, particularly among Hispanics and Asian/Pacific Islanders.

Individuals with a Mexican heritage represented about 58% of the Hispanic population in 2000, concentrated largely in the Southwest, where many have lived for generations. Puerto Ricans were the second-largest category, followed by Cubans and those from other countries of Central and South America.

Among Asians or Pacific Islanders, Chinese and Filipinos are the most numerous. Most Chinese have long been citizens. Other groups include many recent immigrants.

JEFF PARKER, FLORIDA TODAY

Components of Hispanic and Asian/Pacific Islander population in 2000

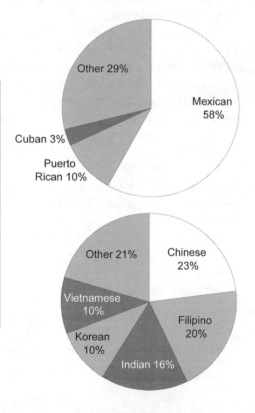

4.3 Potential Citizens

T HE UNITED STATES IS FAMOUS for being a nation of immigrants, and employers are often happy to have new sources of workers. Not all legal immigrants become citizens right away, but they do become eligible to apply.

Current immigration rates have increased substantially since the 1960s, although they remain lower than they were in the early twentieth century. The annual average of legal immigrants per 1,000 residents reached 3.4 between 1991 and 2000. As a result, the foreign-born population in the U.S. almost doubled over that decade, reaching about 12% of our population by 2002. The composition of immigrants has also shifted. Today, many more come from Latin America and Asia than from Europe.

Some immigrants are highly educated, and studies show that most

CLAY BUTLER, SIDEWALK BUBBLEGUM

Average annual number of legal immigrants per 1,000 U.S. population

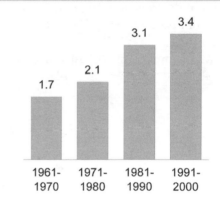

1961-1970	1971-1980	1981-1990	1991-2000
1.7	2.1	3.1	3.4

immigrants, whatever their education, contribute more in taxes than they use in benefits. But increases in the supply of labor tend to lower wages. As a result, employers benefit more from immigration than workers do.

4.4 Illegal Immigrants

THE ANNUAL FLOW OF undocumented workers now roughly matches that of legal immigrants. They represent almost a third of the foreign-born population in this country, and about 5% of the U.S. labor force.

Many immigrants risk their lives to sneak across the Mexican border in search of a better life for themselves and their children. Not all come from Latin America. Undocumented Asian and Filipino workers also enter the U.S. in substantial numbers (often through Mexico). While still largely concentrated in the Southwest, undocumented workers are now a highly visible presence in states such as Colorado and Georgia.

The government has stepped up efforts to police the border, but done little to punish employers who hire illegal workers. The *Wall Street Journal* has famously called for "open borders" in order to increase the supply of labor. Some Republicans, including President George W. Bush, have called for amnesty programs like those implemented in the 1990s. But both liberal and conservative groups remain divided on this issue.

M. E. COHEN, M.E. COHEN/HUMORINK.COM

Legal status of the foreign-born population in 2004

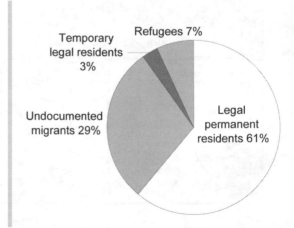

Refugees 7%

Temporary legal residents 3%

Undocumented migrants 29%

Legal permanent residents 61%

4.5 Last Hired

UNEMPLOYMENT IS A GAME of musical chairs. When the music stops, not everyone has a seat, and it's mostly blacks and Hispanics left standing. These racial/ethnic differences have persisted through many business cycles over the years.

In 2004, 10% of blacks and 7% of Hispanics could not find jobs, while only 5% of whites were in the same predicament. Black and Hispanic workers are often the first fired as well as the last hired, suffering disproportionately from job cuts.

Persistently high unemployment rates discourage people from looking for work or drive them into the underground economy. Black male labor force participation rates have dropped considerably in recent years.

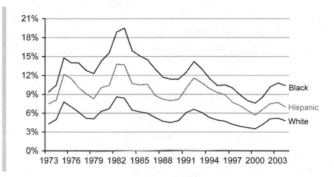

Unemployment rate by race and Hispanic origin, 1973–2004

4.6 Unemployment by Degrees

A COLLEGE DIPLOMA CONFERS real advantages, including higher probability of employment, better wages, and good health. Unemployment rates are highest among those without a high school diploma. But racial/ethnic differences remain significant even when education is taken into account. College-educated blacks and Hispanics had higher unemployment rates than their white counterparts in 2004. If affirmative action leads to reverse discrimination, as some critics argue, one would expect to see exactly the opposite pattern.

Among individuals without a college degree, Hispanics have lower unemployment rates than blacks, probably because of immigration dynamics. Uncertainties and insecurities often force recent immigrants to seek out labor-intensive, low-wage jobs wherever they are. And many illegal immigrants don't show up in unemployment statistics.

SPUD AND BARRY DEUTSCH

Unemployment by educational attainment in 2004

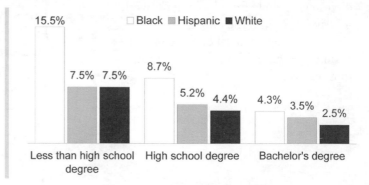

4.7 The Education Gap

THE GOOD NEWS IS THAT, over time, all Americans are improving their access to education. Since 1960, the percentage of people over age 25 with high school degrees has increased dramatically for whites and blacks in particular. Hispanics have enjoyed more modest gains.

College completion rates have also improved. But they remain relatively low, and racial/ethnic disparities loom large. More than 25% of whites over age 25 now have a college degree, compared to only about 17% of blacks and 11% of Hispanics.

Cuts in aid for college students have reinforced a decline in the percentage of low-income high school graduates going on to college. Budget cuts also shrank tutorial and counseling programs for disadvantaged students. Challenges to affirmative action programs at many state universities have also reduced opportunities for black and Hispanic students.

Percentage of persons age 25+ with high school or college degrees

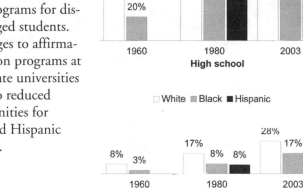

High school

1960 — White 43%, Black 20%
1980 — White 69%, Black 51%, Hispanic 44%
2003 — White 85%, Black 80%, Hispanic 57%

□ White ■ Black ■ Hispanic

College

1960 — White 8%, Black 3%
1980 — White 17%, Black 8%, Hispanic 8%
2003 — White 28%, Black 17%, Hispanic 11%

More Menial Work

HISTORICALLY, BLACKS AND Hispanics have been confined to jobs whites wanted to avoid, like domestic service. Today, they are disproportionately represented in jobs that involve housekeeping for the economy as a whole, such as cleaning offices, growing and preparing food, waiting tables, and caring for children and the elderly. About a quarter of blacks and Hispanics work in service jobs.

Not surprisingly, they are underrepresented at the top of the occupational ladder, in managerial and professional occupations. Only 26% of blacks and 17% of Hispanics held such jobs in 2004, compared with 36% of all white workers.

Despite the visibility of a few highly paid athletes and media stars, few families of color enjoy an affluent lifestyle. About 8% of black and Hispanic families had incomes over $100,000 in 2002, compared with 19% of white households.

(th)ink

BY KEITH KNIGHT

My goodness. You barely even notice it's there..

How do you keep it so clean?

I invite one of 'em up to wash it every once in a while..

CEO

CEO

©K.KNIGHT 2001

keefflix@hotmail.com

WRITE!! P.O. Box 591794 San Francisco CA 94159-1794

ONE MAN'S CEILING IS ANOTHER MAN'S FLOOR

(TH)INK BY KEITH KNIGHT

Employed civilians, by occupation, race, and Hispanic origin in 2004

□ Service ■ Managerial and professional

White: Service 15%, Managerial and professional 36%
Black: Service 24%, Managerial and professional 26%
Hispanic: Service 24%, Managerial and professional 17%

4.9 **Wage Inequalities**

OR A BRIEF PERIOD IN THE U.S., RACIAL/ETHNIC inequality appeared to be declining. In the 1960s and early 1970s, black and Hispanic workers narrowed the gap between their median earnings and those of their white counterparts.

But increasing inequality in wages as a whole—including a widening gap between more-educated and less-educated workers—reversed that trend. Between 1979 and 2004, most men and women of color lost ground relative to whites of the same gender.

A weakened public commitment to challenging racial and ethnic segregation, along with an influx of immigrants willing to work in low-wage jobs, had a particularly visible impact on the relative earnings of Hispanics.

Median weekly earnings of blacks and Hispanics as a percentage of those of whites of the same sex (full-time workers)

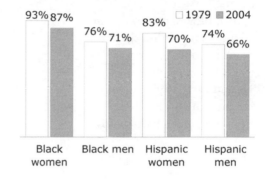

☐ 1979 ■ 2004

	Black women	Black men	Hispanic women	Hispanic men
1979	93%	76%	83%	74%
2004	87%	71%	70%	66%

4.10 The Color of Poverty

MANY PEOPLE THINK POVERTY is somebody else's problem, and racism makes it easier to blame the victim. But history shows that poverty is systemic. Persistent inequalities, as well as unemployment and rips in the social safety net, have left blacks and Hispanics more vulnerable to poverty than whites.

In the 1980s and early 1990s, increasing unemployment and cuts in federal social spending had a particularly sharp impact on people of color. Public support for families with dependent children declined, leaving many kids vulnerable.

Poverty rates fell during the economic expansion of the late 1990s. But even in 2001, after 10 years of uninterrupted economic growth, close to a quarter of all blacks and Hispanics lived below the poverty line.

Percentage of people with incomes below the poverty line in 2003, by race and Hispanic origin

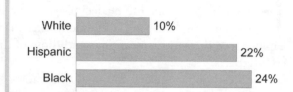

White 10%
Hispanic 22%
Black 24%

SPUD AND MARC HUGHES

4.11 **Doing Time**

INCARCERATION RATES IN THE United States are higher than in any other democracy in the world, and a disproportionate share of those in prison is black. In 2003, there were 3,590 black men and women serving prison sentences for every 100,000 black residents in the country. Only 503 whites per 100,000 were in the same situation.

A majority of inmates—over 50% in the federal system—are drug offenders. Americans don't use more drugs than people in other rich countries do. But if they are caught, they are far more likely to go to jail. Mandatory sentencing rules leave judges with little discretion, even for individuals arrested for possession of a small quantity of an illegal drug. While many drug treatment programs have proven effective, they remain underfunded, with long waiting lists in most states.

The social costs of incarceration are high. A year of prison costs more per person than a year of college. Jail time does little to

CLAY BUTLER, SIDEWALK BUBBLEGUM

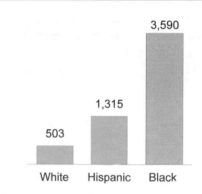

Number of sentenced prisoners per 100,000 residents in 2003, by race and Hispanic origin

White	Hispanic	Black
503	1,315	3,590

develop employable skills, and it disrupts families and communities. As a result, it reproduces conditions that contribute to high crime rates.

Almost 60% of all black male high school dropouts born between 1965 and 1969 had spent some time in prison by 1999.

4.12 Children and Prison

MORE THAN 10 MILLION CHILDREN HAVE HAD A parent spend some time behind bars in the U.S., an experience that has often left them traumatized or neglected. The public money spent on foster care and welfare services for these children adds to the social costs of incarceration.

Mothers are the fastest-growing segment of the prison population. Black women are seven times more likely than white women to be incarcerated, a disparity related more to prosecution for petty crimes than for serious ones. The war on drugs has played a significant role as well. According to a report from the Bureau of Justice Statistics, 67% of the parents in federal prison are drug offenders whose sentences average more than 10 years.

A journalist who has spent time studying families affected by incarceration observes, "For children of nonviolent drug offenders in particular, the experience can be morally as well as emotionally corrosive: They may lose respect for a legal system that, in their eyes, has shown their parents so little in the way of justice."

Children who lack adequate family and community support are likely to face incarceration themselves. Rates of arrest, detention, and incarceration are higher for blacks than for whites. Black juvenile offenders are more likely to be placed in lockup facilities, regardless of the offense, than white juveniles.

SABRINA JONES, THE REAL COST OF PRISONS PROJECT, REALCOSTOFPRISONS.ORG

MOTHERS ON THEIR OWN cope with the triple burden of paying the bills, doing the housework, and looking after the kids. The proportion of families maintained by women alone is especially high among blacks and Hispanics.

These families are vulnerable to poverty because they typically rely on the earnings of a single adult. Few receive much financial help from absent parents. Many live in poverty even if they receive public assistance.

Widowed and divorced mothers tend to fare better than those who never marry. But that doesn't mean that simply urging mothers to marry will solve the problem. Low-income individuals are less likely to marry whether they have children or not.

Greater education and better job opportunities tend to increase the probability of marriage as well as boosting earnings.

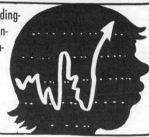

Personal Economic Indicators

The I'll-Be-Feeding-My-Kids-Ramen-Noodles-Again-Tonight Consumption Composite

The No-Insurance-and--Medical-Bills-So-High-I'm-Getting-Sicker-Just-Worrying-About-Trying-to-Pay-Them Weighted Average

MIKHAELA REID

Percentage of families with children under 18 maintained by women alone in 2003

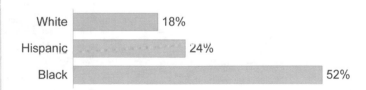

White — 18%
Hispanic — 24%
Black — 52%

4.14 Who's Raising the Kids?

WE DEPEND ON A FUTURE generation of workers and citizens to take care of us in our old age and help repay our public debt. But participation in the task of raising this generation varies substantially across racial/ethnic groups.

In 2003, fewer than half of all white families included individuals under age 18, compared with 56% of black families and 63% of Hispanic families. White families include a higher proportion of elderly members.

Taxpayers don't like to pay for "other people's children." In communities with a high level of racial/ethnic diversity, elderly voters are less supportive of spending on schools. Public programs in the U.S. provide better income security and benefits for the elderly than for children.

Parents who are not citizens, as well as many of those who have been convicted of a felony, are not allowed to vote.

SPUD AND BARRY DEUTSCH

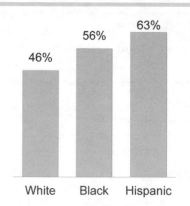

Families with children under 18 as a percentage of all families in 2003, by race and Hispanic origin

46% White
56% Black
63% Hispanic

4.15 Affirmative Action in Higher Education

MOST AMERICANS EMBRACE THE values of diversity and a level playing field. When asked if they favor efforts to improve the position of blacks and other minorities, they answer with a resounding yes. On the other hand, forms of affirmative action that can be interpreted as preferential treatment are under attack.

Affirmative action policies remain in effect at many elite colleges, where they have helped strengthen the backbone of the black middle class. The University of Michigan recently withstood a Supreme Court challenge to its affirmative action policies. However, the University of California has suspended programs explicitly aimed at increasing black and Hispanic enrollment. Declines in both application and acceptance rates among these groups have occurred.

Some state university systems, including California, Florida, and Texas, now guarantee admission to in-state high school graduates ranked at the top of their class. Such "color-blind" policies have the effect of increasing the percentage of black and Hispanic students admitted. On the other hand, they may penalize students who attend competitive high schools and enroll some who are less well prepared for college.

MATT WUERKER

4.16 **Evidence of Discrimination**

* Researchers who sent fictitious resumes to help-wanted ads in Boston and Chicago newspapers found that those with white-sounding names, such as Emily and Greg, received 50% more callbacks for interviews than those with African American–sounding names, such as Lakisha and Jamal. A higher-quality resume elicited a much greater increase in callbacks for whites than for blacks.

* Experimenters in New York City who sent teams of black, white, and Hispanic men with equivalent resumes to apply for entry-level jobs found that whites fared significantly better. Indeed, whites with felony convictions listed fared about as well as blacks or Hispanics with no criminal history. The effect of a criminal conviction was much more negative for black and Hispanic than for white men.

* African Americans and Hispanics who buy or refinance homes are more likely to have "subprime mortgages" that are substantially more costly. In 2004 about 29% of African Americans and 15% of Hispanics paid extra, compared to about 10% of white Americans. Bankers argue that these differences merely reflect differences in credit risk.

* African Americans were almost three times as likely as whites to be charged markups on car loans financed by General Motors Acceptance Corporation.

CHAPTER 5: **Government**

SOME PEOPLE DENOUNCE BIG GOVERNMENT AS the source of all our economic woes. Even those who favor public spending worry about current priorities. Citizens who want their voices to be heard need a clear understanding of government spending and taxation in the U.S. This chapter provides such an overview.

Chart 5.1 reveals the size of federal, state, and local government spending relative to gross domestic product. Chart 5.2 offers an international perspective. Compared to other high-income countries, our public sector represents a relatively small percentage of overall economic activity.

Chart 5.3 analyzes the composition of federal spending, offering a detailed breakdown of expenditures targeted to low-income households and the unemployed. These constitute less than a fifth of total spending, and as Chart 5.4 shows, many of the programs most vital for meeting poor people's basic needs have been scaled back in recent years.

Despite growing concerns about terrorism within our borders, the traditional armed forces account for the bulk of national security spending described in Chart 5.5. Our military spending dwarfs that of other countries. Chart 5.6 reveals that it composes almost half of all global military expenditures.

Chart 5.7 puts federal bookkeeping in perspective, describing a roller coaster ride from the budget surpluses of the late

RUSSELL CHRISTIAN

1990s to the looming deficits that followed. The government must borrow money to finance these deficits, adding to public debt. Chart 5.8 documents recent increases in the burden of debt that will fall heavily on future generations.

The government levies a variety of taxes to raise revenue. Between 1960 and 2005, both corporate income and excise taxes declined in relative importance, while taxes on wages increased, as seen in Chart 5.9. In recent years, budget-busting cuts in personal income tax rates have been implemented. Chart 5.10 documents the uneven impact. Benefits have gone primarily to those at the top of the income pyramid.

Chart 5.11 focuses on state and local taxes, explaining their regressive impact: low-income families pay a larger share of their income than high-income families do. Corporations get off easy because of the many loopholes in the tax code, some of which are described in Table 5.12.

Corporations wield significant political as well as economic power. Table 5.13 traces the effects of their lobbying "investments" on public policy. Individual citizens, by contrast, seem discouraged about the prospects of having a significant impact. A large percentage of Americans do not vote. As Chart 5.14 reveals, political participation tends to decrease with household income.

The Social Security system that Republicans would like to privatize continues to enjoy the allegiance of most Americans. As Chart 5.15 documents, this program has contributed to significant reductions in poverty among the elderly. As our population ages, the costs of this program will grow. But Chart 5.16 shows why economic growth is likely to generate additional revenues. If economic growth slows, the simplest way to raise additional revenues would be to lift the cap that currently limits the Social Security taxes paid by high earners.

5.1 How Big Is Government?

MANY PEOPLE COMPLAIN about Big Government. In 2004, direct federal outlays were $2.3 trillion; state and local governments spent about $1.3 trillion. Together they were equivalent to 31% of U.S. GDP.

But while the public sector consumes a lot of resources, it also provides important services. Public schools educate most Americans. Social Security and food stamps supply a safety net. Roads enable people to get to school, work, and the grocery store. Emergency services and disaster relief help people cope with unexpected crises. When the economy takes a turn for the worse, government policy can give it a boost. Without government spending, too few of the public goods and services that we rely on would be produced. Some would not be available at all.

The public sector also generates a lot of jobs. In 2004, national, state, and local governments employed more than 23 million people, or about 16% of the workforce. Public employment often provides women and people of color with better job opportunities than the private sector does.

WHAT CONSERVATIVES MEAN BY "SMALLER GOVERNMENT"

I'M SORRY YOUR BOSS STOLE YOUR PENSION BUT THE S.E.C. LACKS STAFF TO INVESTIGATE YOUR CLAIM

DUE TO BUDGET CUTS AND UNDERSTAFFING, WE INCREASED YOUR CLASS SIZE TO 86 KIDS

I'M SORRY, YOU DON'T QUALIFY FOR MEDICAL ASSISTANCE. HAVE YOU EVER TRIED PRAYER?

LIBRARY CLOSED
HOURS:
1PM-7PM
(MONDAY)

SINGER

ANDY SINGER

Government spending and GDP in 2004 (in $ trillions)

State & local government spending	1.3
Federal government spending	2.3
Gross domestic product	11.6

5.2 **Government Spending Elsewhere**

GOVERNMENTS COME IN ALL shapes and sizes, some bigger than others. In relative terms, the U.S. has one of the smallest public sectors of any industrialized country. In 2005, government spending amounted to 36% of U.S. GDP, compared to 39% in Canada, 54% in France, and 57% in Sweden.

The size of the public sector is less important than its ability to deliver. While the U.S. government spends a smaller proportion of its GDP than Canada, more than 15% of Americans lack health insurance. In Canada, everyone is covered, with much lower per capita medical care costs.

Priorities vary widely from country to country. In the U.S., the military chews up a much larger portion of federal dollars than in other developed countries, which spend more on social services and economic security. Government spending on education, infrastructure, research, and family welfare can improve a country's competitive position in the global marketplace.

R. Jay Magill

Government spending as a percentage of GDP in selected countries in 2005

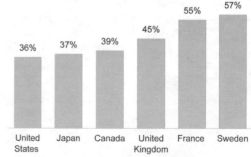

5.3 **Where Federal Dollars Go**

PICTURE YOUR TAX DOLLAR snipped into different-sized pieces that show how the federal government spends it. In 2005, one-quarter paid for Social Security and other retirement programs, and 12% paid for Medicare. These programs benefit almost all Americans during their lifetimes. Almost one-fifth went to the military and another 7% to interest payments on the national debt. While most Americans think that welfare programs are huge, only 17% was spent on programs specifically targeted to help low-income families and the unemployed.

In the last few decades, both Social Security and Medicare have grown significantly, partly because of increases in the number of elderly persons. Military spending goes up when the nation goes to war. Between 2001 and 2005, spending in this category shot up by more than 50%.

Components of the federal budget in 2005

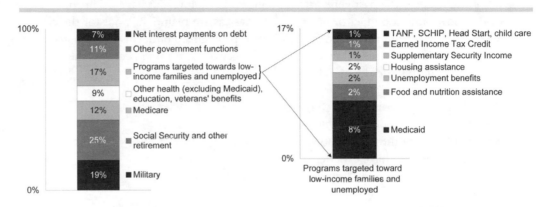

SPUD AND MARC HUGHES

77

5.4 Expanding Holes in the Social Safety Net

OUR SOCIAL SAFETY NET HAS frayed over the past generation. Government budget priorities have shifted away from many programs that help people in or near poverty who are struggling with basics like food and housing bills.

Spending on food assistance fell from 7.6% of the federal budget in 1980 to 5.3% in 2005, even though millions of American households have experienced hunger in recent years. Spending on housing assistance fell from 5.4% to 4.1% in those years, despite a growing shortage of affordable housing. Many Americans have lost their jobs in recent years due to downsizing and outsourc-ing. Yet public commitments to training and employment have declined.

It's easy to blame the poor for their own problems. Politicians seem to get a bigger boost from tax cuts for the rich.

SERGIO LANGER
(BEST OF LATIN
AMERICA, CAGLE
CARTOONS,
EL CLARIN,
ARGENTINA)

Spending on selected social programs as a percentage of the federal budget

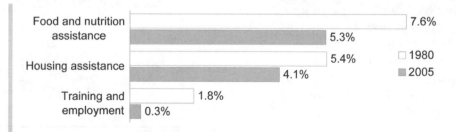

	1980	2005
Food and nutrition assistance	7.6%	5.3%
Housing assistance	5.4%	4.1%
Training and employment	1.8%	0.3%

5.5 **National Security Priorities**

MAINTAINING NATIONAL security requires more than military might. Preventive measures such as diplomacy and peace-keeping can reduce armed conflict. Domestic efforts to improve port security and protect chemical and nuclear plants could help protect against terrorist attacks. Such efforts receive relatively little support from the federal government, which spent almost $9 on the military for every $1 it spent on nonmilitary security spending in 2005.

National security spending in 2005

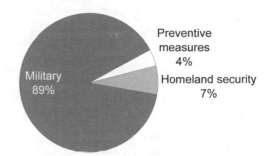

Military 89%

Preventive measures 4%

Homeland security 7%

The cost of military operations is high, in both human and dollar terms. After two years of the war in Iraq, Congress had already committed over $200 billion, with much more to follow. Meanwhile, the government spends less than $1 billion a year securing loose nuclear materials that could fall into dangerous hands.

Security experts argue that if we eliminated unnecessary, redundant, and outdated weapons, not only could we redirect some of that money to more useful nonmilitary security measures, but we could actually decrease overall security spending, freeing up money for other national priorities.

5.6 Policing the World

THE UNITED STATES is responsible for nearly half of all military spending in the world. Our NATO allies account for almost another quarter. Other close allies, such as Japan and Australia, together provide at least 8% of additional military spending. Taken together, this military clout far outweighs that of the countries typically identified as potential threats.

REPRODUCED FROM *THE TRAVELLING LEUNIG* BY MICHAEL LEUNIG, PUBLISHED BY PENGUIN AUSTRALIA

The U.S. military is not only big, but spread out around the world. More than 250 Army, Navy, Marine, or Air Force personnel were located in each of 24 different countries in 2005, with thousands more at sea.

Of course, the largest concentration has been in Iraq. In May 2003, President Bush declared, "Major combat operations in Iraq have ended." Between then and October 2005, nearly 2,000 U.S. troops were killed and over 14,000 wounded. A minimum of about 10,000 Iraqi civilians were also killed in that period. In 2005, the U.S. spent approximately $5 billion each month on military efforts in Iraq.

World military spending in 2004

Rest of the world
20%

Cuba, Iran, Libya, North Korea, Sudan, Syria
2%

Other close allies
8%

U.S.
47%

NATO allies
23%

5.7 **Back in the Red**

IN 1998, FOR THE FIRST TIME IN nearly 30 years, the U.S. government brought in more money than it spent. But this new era of surpluses didn't last. By 2002, the combination of a recession, large tax cuts, and increases in military spending had taken their toll, resulting in more than $150 billion in red ink.

Deficits are not necessarily bad. When growth slows down and unemployment creeps up, deficit spending can give the economy a boost. But some forms of deficit spending are better than others. Government investments in infrastructure and education can increase future economic growth. Tax cuts for the affluent that simply lead to more consumption don't have such a positive effect.

Whatever their short-term impact, very large deficits are unsustainable. Deficit spending adds to the total debt. As debt climbs, more public resources go to pay bondholders, instead of to programs that benefit the population.

Federal government deficits and surpluses as a percentage of GDP, 1950-2005

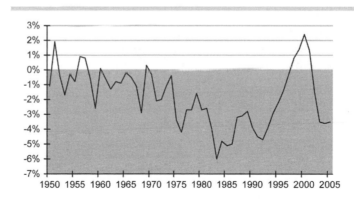

5.8 Borrowed Money

IMAGINE THAT AMERICA HAS one big credit card. Whenever spending plans go over budget and the government is running a deficit, it just charges the difference, adding the new shortfall to the outstanding debt.

Economic growth from 1950 to 1980 helped reduce the debt significantly, from about 95% of gross domestic product (GDP) to little more than one-third. The 1980s witnessed a resurgence of borrowing, and the size of the debt in relation to the economy quickly grew. During the late 1990s, cuts in spending and stronger economic growth again reduced the overall debt, but recent deficits drove it back up again. By August 2005, the debt had reached $7.9 trillion, equivalent to two-thirds of GDP.

Public borrowing can help fund productive investments. But debt reduces economic flexibility, and its burden grows if interest rates go up.

R. JAY MAGILL

Gross federal debt as a percentage of GDP, 1950–2005

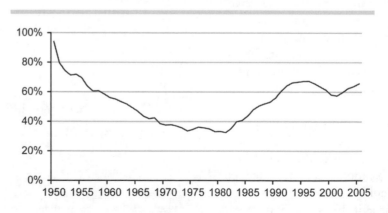

5.9 Shifting the Burden

HEARING THE WORDS "APRIL 15" can make many people break out in a cold sweat, fearing an attack of incomprehensible fine print. But the income tax is only the most visible of personal taxes. Payroll taxes for Social Security and Medicare now contribute a much larger share of total federal tax revenues than in the past. Meanwhile, the portion coming from corporations and excise or sales taxes has plummeted.

Social Security taxes became more prominent for several reasons. Many women entered paid employment over this period and began paying into the system. The Social Security tax rate was increased during the 1980s. Also, the retirement age was increased, so workers began staying on the job longer, increasing the number of years they paid Social Security taxes.

These longer-term trends have recently been accompanied by steep reductions in taxes on income derived from wealth, like the capital gains tax. As a result, the tax burden has shifted away from the wealthy and toward ordinary working people. Social Security taxes are paid only on earnings under $90,000.

CLEARLY, IT WOULD BE **UNAMERICAN** TO EXPECT LARGE CORPORATIONS TO SHOULDER AN EQUITABLE SHARE OF THE TAX BURDEN...SO IT'S UP TO ALL OF **US** TO PITCH IN AND DO OUR PART-- TO TURN THIS ECONOMY **AROUND!**

I COULD SELL MY **CLOCK RADIO**-- TO HELP PAY OFF THE **DEFICIT!**

I COULD DONATE MY **PENNY JAR** TO G.E.-- TO SPUR **INVESTMENT!**

THAT'S THE SPIRIT!

TOM TOMORROW

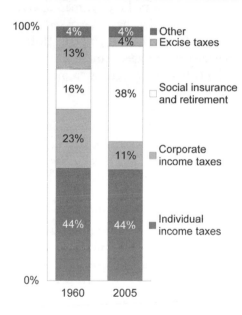

Sources of federal receipts, 1960 and 2005

	1960	2005
Other	4%	4%
Excise taxes	13%	4%
Social insurance and retirement	16%	38%
Corporate income taxes	23%	11%
Individual income taxes	44%	44%

Taking Home the Bacon, More and Less

D URING A TIME OF COLOSSAL new government projects—fighting wars, expanding Medicare drug benefits, and rebuilding Gulf Coast communities wiped off the map by hurricanes—our leaders have not asked Americans to tighten their belts. Instead, they have encouraged Americans to go out and buy fancy new belts with money from new tax cuts.

Not everyone gets the same party favor. The tax cuts instituted between 2001 and 2005 heavily favor higher-income families. The total value of these tax reductions from 2001 to 2010 is projected to reach nearly $2 trillion. The top 5% of all taxpayers will get 44% of that reduction, substantially more than the amount going to the bottom 80%. The disparity is starker in light of the average reduction for individual taxpayers. While the poorest 20% will receive an average annual tax break of $81, the richest 1% will keep an extra $42,618 each year. Their average tax break alone is worth more than the average total annual income of more than half the people in the country.

REPRODUCED FROM *GOATPERSON AND OTHER TALES* BY MICHAEL LEUNIG, PUBLISHED BY PENGUIN AUSTRALIA

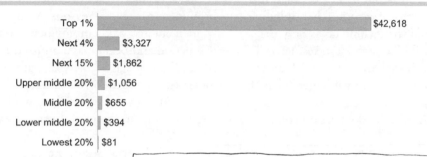

Average annual federal tax reduction between 2001 and 2010, by income group of taxpayer

Income group	Tax reduction
Top 1%	$42,618
Next 4%	$3,327
Next 15%	$1,862
Upper middle 20%	$1,056
Middle 20%	$655
Lower middle 20%	$394
Lowest 20%	$81

Robin Hood, Robin Hood,
You'd be napalmed in the wood,
I am very sad to say,
If you were alive today

Leunig

5.11 **Unfair Shares**

FEDERAL TAXES MAY GET MOST of the attention, but state and local taxes are nothing to sneeze at. In the U.S., poor families pay a larger share of their income in state and local taxes than rich families. In 2002, the bottom fifth of nonelderly married couples paid 11% of their incomes in sales, income, and property taxes. Not only did the richest 1% pay a smaller share, but they could also more easily deduct a portion of their state taxes from federal taxes. Including this federal offset, the richest families' state and local tax burden was only 5%.

When taxes take a bigger bite out of low incomes, they're called regressive. Both sales and property taxes fall into this category. They are the main sources of revenue for state and local governments. Most income tax plans work in the opposite direction. Their progressive structure takes a larger share from the affluent.

During the 1990s, many states cut income taxes, which had the effect of making overall taxes more regressive.

Average state and local taxes as a share of family income in 2002 (nonelderly married couples)

Income group	Lowest 20%	Top 1%
Sales & excise taxes	8%	1%
Property taxes	3%	1%
State/local income taxes	1%	5%
Total	11%	7%
Total after federal offset	**11%**	**5%**

5.12 Corporate Tax Loopholes

WHILE THE FEDERAL AND STATE GOVERNMENTS STRUGGLED with economic recession and jobless recovery between 2001 and 2003, corporate tax avoidance sapped public budgets even further. For example, the federal Treasury lost $50 billion a year or more to the "Bermuda tax avoidance" scheme, which enabled U.S. corporations to reincorporate in a country with no corporate taxes.

Two studies of more than 250 profitable companies by the Institute on Taxation and Economic Policy found that avoidance of federal and state taxes from 2001 to 2003 padded corporate pockets with an extra $217 billion. More than one-quarter of these corporations avoided state income taxes entirely in at least one of those years, and almost one-third escaped federal taxes, even while they reported billions of dollars in profits to their stockholders. Some of them went even further, hustling up federal and state tax refunds totaling over $13 billion.

LADIES AND GENTLEMEN! IN THE CENTER RING...

...THE AMAZING! THE STUPENDOUS!...

...CORPORATE TAX LOOPHOLE...

...FOR YOUR ENTERTAINMENT AND ,OF COURSE, AT YOUR EXPENSE!

GARY HUCK. USED WITH PERMISSION, HUCK/KONOPACKI LABOR CARTOONS, SOLIDARITY.COM/HKCARTOONS/.

Some methods used to avoid state corporate income taxes

Extorting states into providing tax "incentives"

Dell Computer extracted a $230 million tax break from North Carolina in return for establishing a new assembly plant there.

Profit shifting

Toys "R" Us set up a subsidiary in no-tax Delaware that charged royalties to all Toys "R" Us stores around the country. These royalties are tax-deductible in the states where the stores are located, and the profits of the subsidiary are never taxed in Delaware.

Asset-transfer shelters

The majority of banks in Wisconsin have set up subsidiaries in tax-haven Nevada. They arrange their books so that much of their income appears in Nevada, while many business expenses are listed in Wisconsin. The income in Nevada escapes taxation. Meanwhile, they get tax deductions for their expenses in Wisconsin.

5.13 Buying Favors

HAVING MONEY OPENS DOORS on Capitol Hill. Each year, special interest groups spend wads of cash to influence national legislation and spending priorities. Millions of dollars go directly to politicians in the form of campaign contributions, and billions are spent on lobbyists who cruise the halls of Congress promoting their clients' interests.

Industries that gave large campaign contributions in recent election cycles enjoyed favorable legal changes.

Many corporations have also benefited from no-bid and cost-plus contracts with the federal government. A no-bid contract is one that is awarded without any competition to find the lowest-cost option. With cost-plus contracts, the company can spend as much as it wants and the government promises to pay those costs, plus a certain percentage extra for profit.

Examples of recent lobbying and policy changes

ENERGY SECTOR

POLITICAL SPENDING: $50.6 MILLION (2004)

The energy bill signed into law August 2005 contained more than $10 billion in tax breaks and subsidies for oil, coal, and gas industries, while doing little to reduce U.S. dependence on fossil fuel.

CORPORATE MEDIA

POLITICAL SPENDING: $26.7 MILLION (1999–2002)

The Federal Communications Commission (FCC) issued new rules in June 2003 that increase the power of the biggest media conglomerates. A federal appeals court overturned the new rules in 2004. The struggle continues as the FCC works on rewriting the rules.

TOM TOMORROW

FINANCE AND CREDIT COMPANIES

POLITICAL SPENDING: $10.4 MILLION (2004)

Though about half of all personal bankruptcies are caused in part by medical problems, and large banks are extremely aggressive in promoting the use of credit cards, Congress passed legislation in 2005 making it much tougher for those in over their heads to recover from unmanageable debt.

EMOCRACY IS JEOPARDIZED WHEN POLITICIANS ignore the people. It's also a problem when people ignore politicians. A large fraction of Americans keep silent on election day for a variety of reasons: apathy, disgust with the options, disenfranchisement of convicted felons, and election rules that make it difficult for some to participate. In the 2004 presidential elections, 64% of citizens 18 years and older went to the polls. In most of Europe, 75% or more of the voting-age population participates in elections.

Who makes it to the polls? One of the strongest determining factors is income. The turnout rate for those with annual family income below $15,000 was 45% in 2004, compared to 81% for those making $100,000 or more.

Those with higher levels of education are also more likely to vote. In the 2004 elections, the voting rate for people with a bachelor's degree was 80%. For those without a high school diploma it was less than 40%.

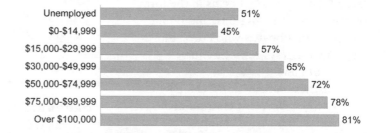

Percentage of citizens age 18 and older who voted in the 2004 elections, by family income and unemployment status

Unemployed	51%
$0-$14,999	45%
$15,000-$29,999	57%
$30,000-$49,999	65%
$50,000-$74,999	72%
$75,000-$99,999	78%
Over $100,000	81%

TOM TOMORROW

5.15 **Old Faithful**

THE SOCIAL SECURITY SYSTEM, established in 1935, has been gradually expanded to provide better income security for retirees, lifting millions out of poverty. In 1966, those 65 and older had a poverty rate of 29%, almost triple that of adults under 65. By 2003, their poverty rate had fallen to 10%.

Social Security taxes workers' paychecks to finance benefits for the retired and disabled. Currently, the system brings in more money than it pays out, creating a surplus that is kept in a trust fund. Some argue that this surplus will be insufficient to meet future needs, and they also worry about the effects of the larger federal deficit. Those who advocate "privatization"— allowing individuals to invest their Social Security funds themselves—understate the increased risk of that type of reform. If the investment gamble didn't pay off, low-income workers would have little to fall back on.

Percentage of people in poverty, by age group, 1966–2003

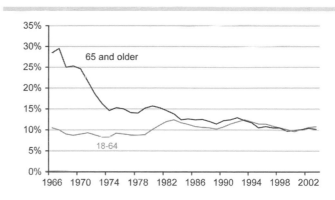

89

5.16 Real Solutions for Social Security

THE SOCIAL SECURITY TRUST FUND IS OVERSEEN by a board of trustees whose job is to make sure that sufficient money is being set aside from current taxes to meet future obligations. Their estimates are necessarily based on predictions of future economic growth. In their "optimistic" scenario (GDP growth of 2.7% per year), the money currently set aside is sufficient. In their "intermediate" scenario (GDP growth of 2% per year), the surplus will be used up by 2042, and Social Security would not be able to pay the full benefits that retirees expect. Actual growth in GDP over the past 25 years has averaged about 3%.

No one can accurately predict the future. But if growth does slow in ways that put pressure on Social Security, one simple change could solve the problem. Currently, wages above $90,000 are exempt from Social Security taxes. Eliminating this cap—so that the existing tax would be applied equally to these top wages, not just lower earnings—would provide a significant boost to revenues and prevent a shortfall.

Social Security trustees' optimistic and intermediate predictions of trust fund balance, 2005–2080 (in trillions of $2005)

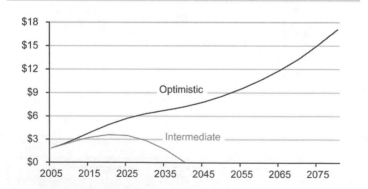

CHAPTER 6: Welfare and Education

A DECENT ECONOMIC SYSTEM SHOULD OFFER everyone a chance to achieve prosperity. Unfortunately, the U.S. is not as decent as it used to be. Income inequality has increased and more children live in poverty. Young people know they need a college education to get ahead, but many can't afford one. Many families barely earn enough to meet their basic needs, and they remain vulnerable to disasters such as hurricanes.

Family incomes increased steadily between 1950 and the mid-1970s. Since then, only married couples with a wife in the paid labor force have managed to boost their incomes enough to raise the median. Chart 6.1 shows that neither single mothers nor families with a wife at home enjoyed much improvement. Chart 6.2 examines the relative prosperity of rich and poor. The top 5% is doing just fine. But the bottom 40% of households have seen their share of total income decline.

What does poverty really mean? Nobody likes the official definition, which, as Chart 6.3 points out, overestimates economic privation in some ways and underestimates it in others. But politicians are reluctant to tamper with such a controversial issue. Chart 6.4 shows that individuals living with children, as well as those who are foreign-born (especially noncitizens), are particularly vulnerable to poverty. Chart 6.5 traces poverty trends by age. While the expansion of Social

Security has significantly reduced poverty among the elderly, a high percentage of children continue to live in families with incomes below the poverty line.

Poverty hurts kids. Chart 6.6 summarizes the reasons why it also hurts the country as a whole. We should be asking how public policy could address this problem. Changes in the rules governing public assistance have reduced the number of welfare recipients, but they haven't done much to reduce poverty. Chart 6.7 provides evidence of growing holes in the social safety net.

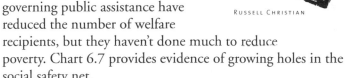

RUSSELL CHRISTIAN

One way to help low-income parents become self-sufficient is to offer subsidized child care. Many states expanded child-care services in the late 1990s, but in recent years, budget pressures have squeezed hard. Chart 6.8 explains why child-care remains in short supply.

Poverty is not inevitable. The United Kingdom, a country with a political history similar to our own, has recently launched a campaign to completely abolish poverty among children. Chart 6.9 explains the progress the British have made toward achieving this goal. The United States, on the other hand, continues to squander money on what can only be called corporate welfare. Chart 6.10 describes some of the programs that pro-business conservatives themselves have singled out as a waste of taxpayers' money.

We live in the richest country in the world, yet many people stand in line at food pantries, soup kitchens, and shelters. Chart 6.11 describes the kinds of households that most frequently suffer from food insecurity. Chart 6.12 shows that, after accounting for general inflation, rents and mortgage payments have both increased over time. Declines in the supply of affordable housing lead to homelessness. Families with children often find themselves out on the street; they represent 40% of the homeless population described in Chart 6.13. Access to emergency shelters remains inadequate, and more than 20% of families seeking assistance are turned away.

All parents want their children to succeed in school, but the quality of education varies according to where families live. Differences in per capita spending across states are pictured in Chart 6.14. Differences across school districts within a given state are often equally extreme. Education doesn't stop at age 18, but free public education does. The price tag on a college education is going up. Chart 6.15 tracks the increases for both private and public colleges and points out that financial aid hasn't grown enough to compensate. As Chart 6.16 shows, family income continues to exert a significant impact on probabilities of success.

6.1 Family Income

JOE SAYERS

MANY FAMILIES ARE working harder and harder, yet barely maintaining their standard of living. Median familiy incomes have increased only slightly since the 1970s except for married couples with a wife in the paid labor force.

The benefits of sending a second earner into the labor force are clear. The accompanying costs—such as increased spending on child care, elder care, and meals purchased outside the home—are less visible. When more hours are devoted to paid employment, fewer hours are available for nonmarket work, leisure time, and sleep.

Like married women, single mothers increased their hours of paid employment after the implementation of new work rules under the Temporary Assistance to Needy Families (TANF) program established in 1996. This shift nudged their family income up a bit.

Growing differences in family structure have contributed to increases in income inequality. Two-earner families without children have more money to spend on luxuries than do single mothers who are struggling to combine paid work with family responsibilities.

Median family income, 1950–2001 (in $2004)

6.2 Low-Income Households Get a Smaller Share

THE RICH KEEP ON GETTING richer. The recession and decline of stock prices in 2000 reduced the share of the top 5% of households by a small blip but did little to close the distance between top and bottom.

Differences in buying power have always been immense, with the top 5% claiming a bigger chunk of all household income than the bottom 40%. But today's disparities are extreme. We seem to be moving toward a form of economic apartheid in which the rich hardly even see the poor unless they are televised in the aftermath of a hurricane or other natural disaster.

Inequality increases social stresses, contributing to higher crime rates and a sense of insecurity at work. Inequality among children violates basic principles of equal opportunity. Of course, inequality does offer some benefits for those at the top—it lowers the relative cost of hiring gardeners, maids, and nannies.

COPYRIGHT BY NICOLE HOLLANDER

Shares of total household income received by groups of households

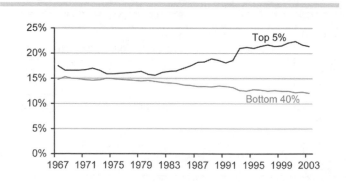

6.3 Defining Poverty

THE POVERTY LINE, DESIGNATED BY THE U.S. Census Bureau, varies according to family size and composition. In 2003, it was $18,660 for a four-person family with two children. In the same year, the median income for all family households was $53,991.

* Defined in the 1960s as the amount of money required for a subsistence diet multiplied by 3, the poverty line is updated yearly to account for inflation.

* Many experts argue that the poverty line is outmoded because food costs are a smaller share of family budgets today—rent and transportation costs have increased substantially. Another problem is that the focus on income ignores the value of noncash benefits such as food stamps and Medicaid.

* The poverty line also fails to take into account the costs of child care for working parents. Families in which parents work for pay need more income in order to maintain the same standard of living as families in which a mother has more time available to devote to household tasks.

* Most European countries define poverty in relative terms. In the United Kingdom, for instance, all households with income below 60% of the median income are deemed poor.

LUXURY ITEMS (shampoo etc.)
telephone
oils & sweets
holiday gifts
HEALTH CARE
CHILD CARE
transportation
electricity
RENT
DIAPERS/SHOES
clothing
SOLIDS
LIQUIDS
the poverty-level food pyramid

R. Jay Magill

6.4 The Likelihood of Being Poor

POVERTY THREATENS SOME people more than others. Family composition matters. In 2003, married-couple families had a poverty rate of 5%. Female-headed families with no husband present had a rate of 28%. Nearly 18% of all children under 18 lived below the poverty line.

Immigration status also matters. The poverty rate for foreign-born noncitizens in 2003 was almost twice as high as for individuals born in the U.S.

Many families are poor despite the fact that they have members who work full time. The current federal minimum wage of $5.15 adds up to an annual income of less than $11,000. Even when the value of the Earned Income Tax Credit for two children is added in, a single wage earner doesn't come close to keeping a family of four out of poverty. Whether a married couple can succeed with both partners working for pay depends on the cost and availability of child care.

KIRK ANDERSON

Percentage of families and persons in poverty in 2003

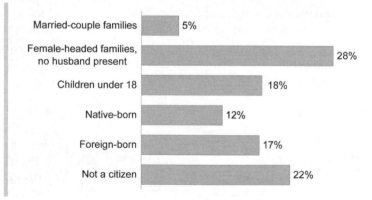

Married-couple families	5%
Female-headed families, no husband present	28%
Children under 18	18%
Native-born	12%
Foreign-born	17%
Not a citizen	22%

6.5 Poverty Among Children and the Elderly

MANY OF THE ELDERLY ARE POOR, BUT AS A group they are better off than children, whose overall poverty rate was 18% in 2003 compared to 10% for those 65 or over. Social Security has done a relatively good job of improving the standard of living of the elderly. Without the income it provides, more older Americans would live in poverty today.

Many children are poor because they live in families that receive little or no financial support from an adult male.

Government assistance is stingy. Even those families eligible for the primary cash welfare program, Temporary Assistance for Needy Families (TANF), receive only small, time-limited benefits.

Why can't we do better? Most other advanced industrial countries provide a better social safety net for their citizens. Their poverty rates for children, the elderly, and families maintained by women alone are all lower as a result.

Percentage of children and elderly in poverty

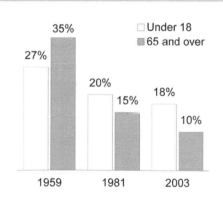

□ Under 18
■ 65 and over

1959: 27%, 35%
1981: 20%, 15%
2003: 18%, 10%

97

6.6 **Poverty Hurts Kids**

Poverty among children presents even more serious problems than poverty among adults. It violates principles of equal opportunity and reduces the productivity of our future labor force.

* Children in poverty perform less well on standardized tests than other children and are more likely to have behavioral problems.

Tom Tomorrow

* Children in poverty are more likely than other children to be overweight and suffer from other chronic health problems such as asthma.

* Children in poverty are far more vulnerable to neglect and abuse than children in other families.

* Children in poverty are more likely to be separated from their parents than other children. About seven out of every thousand children lived in foster care in 2003. Most came from low-income families.

* Poverty rates among children vary dramatically across states. In 2002, 27% of all children in Mississippi lived in families with incomes under the poverty line, compared to 11% in Wisconsin.

6.7 Welfare Farewell

IN 1996, CONGRESS REPLACED THE WELFARE program known as Aid to Families with Dependent Children (AFDC) with Temporary Assistance for Needy Families (TANF). The long-run consequences remain unclear.

TANF requires recipients to find employment or be placed in unpaid jobs for 20 hours a week as quickly as possible, and it sets a maximum lifetime limit of 60 months of public assistance. Unlike AFDC, it offers no guarantee that families with young children under the poverty line will receive public assistance.

Between 1996 and 2000, the economy was booming. Employment among single mothers increased and the child poverty rate decreased. Welfare rolls declined dramatically. Since 2001, however, employment has fallen among both single and married mothers and the child poverty rate has headed back up. TANF caseloads declined or remained flat, raising concerns that the program is not meeting current needs. Only 33% of poor children were receiving TANF in 2002.

No one knows exactly what happens to families kicked off public assistance. Between 1999 and 2002, the share of all families who had left welfare but were not employed, did not have an employed partner, and were not receiving income from Supplemental Security Income rose from 10% to 14%.

Struggling single mom, two kids, in poverty, little hope, on welfare.

Struggling single mom, two kids, in poverty, little hope, on welfare. with low paying job

WELFARE REFORM'S SUCCESS

KIRK ANDERSON

6.8 **Kid Care**

MANY PARENTS HAVE TO WORK LONGER AND harder to pay their bills. This means they have to find someone to look after their kids when they are not in school. This can cost a lot of money.

* Low-income families are particularly burdened. Not all are able to find a family member or friend to babysit for free. Poor families who were forced to pay for child care in 2003 spent, on average, one-third of their income on it.

* Welfare reforms adopted in 1996 increased political pressure to subsidize child care. Federal and state child-care assistance to low-income working families grew substantially between 1996 and 2001 and the number of children served more than doubled.

* Since then, however, support has declined. Despite the high cost of child care, 23 states have decreased the availability of subsidies for it since 2001, and only 18% of all eligible children actually receive subsidies.

SPUD AND JIMMY ILSON

* The quality of care varies widely. Low compensation for child-care workers leads to high turnover rates and unpredictable social environments for toddlers.

* Many low-wage earners work irregular hours or at night, a factor that makes it especially difficult for them to find reliable, high-quality child care.

6.9 Ending Child Poverty in the U.K.

> "Poverty is a scar on our nation's soul."
> —*Gordon Brown,*
> *chancellor of the exchequer, United Kingdom*

THE UNITED KINGDOM HAS TRADITIONALLY HAD one of the highest child poverty rates in Europe. But in 1999, the new Labour government made a public commitment to end child poverty by 2020. The intermediate target was to halve child poverty by 2010.

By 2005, the United Kingdom could show significant progress toward this goal. The number of children living in households with income below 60% of the median had been reduced by 25%.

The strategies adopted included tax and benefit policies that increased financial support for all families with children, but particularly those with low income. The level of benefits aimed specifically at poor families was raised. Increases in subsidized child care enabled parents to seek paid employment.

The extra spending amounted to less than 1% of the United Kingdom's gross domestic product per year. Many policy experts argue that a similar commitment on the part of the United States could substantially reduce child poverty and promote economic growth.

SPUD AND BARRY DEUTSCH

6.10 Corporate Welfare

GOVERNMENT PROGRAMS THAT PROVIDE unique benefits to specific industries or companies represent corporate welfare. Many of the biggest companies in America have been on the dole, including Wal-Mart, General Motors, Boeing, Archer Daniels Midland, and Enron. Why should companies like these receive direct grants, subsidized loans, or insurance financed by taxpayers?

✳ The conservative Cato Institute estimates that the federal government spent a total of $92.6 billion on corporate welfare in fiscal year 2002. They singled out the Market Access Program of the Agriculture Department, which helps exporters of agricultural products pay for overseas development campaigns; the Advanced Technology Program of the Commerce Department, which gives research grants to high-tech companies; and the Foreign Military Financing program, which funds purchases of U.S.-made weapons by foreign governments.

✳ State and local governments also hand out money to businesses. Subsidies for sports stadiums are popular, even though studies show they do little to promote local economic development. The primary beneficiaries are wealthy team owners who often sell their team franchises at a huge profit.

✳ Large businesses often bargain with communities, demanding major tax breaks, free or reduced-price land, or infrastructure assistance in return for the promise of creating jobs. One recent study reports that Wal-Mart has received more than $1 billion in subsidies over several decades. Yet Wal-Mart often destroys almost as many jobs as it creates, driving smaller, more community-based retailers out of business.

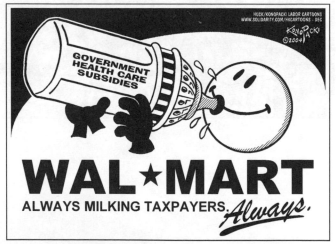

Mike Konopacki. Used with permission, Huck/Konopacki Labor Cartoons, solidarity.com/hkcartoons/.

6.11 **Bare Cupboards**

THE DEPARTMENT OF Agriculture defines "food insecurity" as lack of consistent access to enough food to ensure active, healthy living. It estimates that about 11% of all households—and about 18% of all children—experienced food insecurity in 2003.

The number of families in major cities seeking assistance at food pantries, soup kitchens, and shelters is going up. In one of the few efforts to monitor such trends, the U.S. Conference of Mayors surveyed 27 cities in December 2004. They found that requests for food assistance by families with children had increased by 13% over the previous year. They also found that, on average, 20% of all requests for emergency food assistance went unmet.

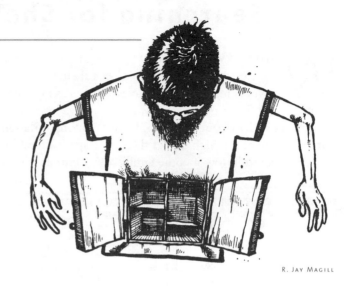

R. Jay Magill

Proportions of different household types experiencing food insecurity in 2003

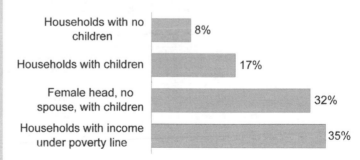

Households with no children — 8%

Households with children — 17%

Female head, no spouse, with children — 32%

Households with income under poverty line — 35%

6.12 Searching for Shelter

WHILE SKYROCKETING housing prices make homeowners feel rich, they increase the burden on first-time buyers. Most new houses and apartments available for rent are aimed at the high end of the market. As a result, low-income families are finding it increasingly hard to find shelter.

Average rents and mortgage payments have increased since 1975, even after taking inflation into account. The averages conceal huge regional differences. Central cities suffer more from affordability problems than suburban or rural areas. The ratio of housing costs to income is particularly high in Los Angeles, Miami, and New York.

Real earnings have declined for many low-income workers, while the cost of shelter has gone up. As a result, almost one-third of American households now spend more than 30% of their income on housing, often leaving them without enough to spend on food and health care. Many other Americans are forced to live a long distance from their place of work, devoting substantial amounts of both time and money to their daily commute.

Average monthly rents and mortgage payments, in 1975 and 2004 (in $2004—contract rents and before-tax mortgage payments)

□ 1975 ■ 2004

Rents: $588, $630
Mortgage payments: $862, $960

6.13 **Mean Streets**

I F PEOPLE CANNOT AFFORD A PLACE TO LIVE, THEY ARE
at risk of becoming homeless. In 27 cities surveyed by the U.S.
Conference of Mayors in 2004:

* Requests for emergency shelter increased by an average of 6%
  over 2003.

* An average of 23% of requests for emergency shelter by
  homeless people went unmet.

* Approximately 40% of the homeless population consisted of
  families with children; about 49% were African American,
  35% white, and 13% Hispanic.

* City officials identified a lack of affordable housing as the
  main cause of homelessness.

The National Low Income Housing Coalition reports that "the
cost of rental housing in the U.S. is out of reach of the vast majority
of low wage earners and people who are elderly or disabled with
public income benefits."

RALL © 1997 TED RALL. REPRINTED WITH PERMISSION OF
UNIVERSAL PRESS SYNDICATE. ALL RIGHTS RESERVED.

6.14 Poor Schools for Poor Kids

MOST PUBLIC SCHOOLS IN THE U.S. RELY HEAVILY on property taxes for their funding. Since wealthy school districts generate higher tax revenues, they generally spend more money on their students. Inequalities in per-pupil expenditure are pronounced.

While the U.S. Constitution makes few references to education, many state constitutions promise educational opportunity for all citizens. Reformers have successfully won lawsuits forcing at least some equalization of school spending in more than 16 states. In most cases, court-ordered mandates have significantly increased per-student funding in poor districts.

But school financing changes have not been entirely successful and have sometimes encouraged overall cuts in spending. And even if further initiatives within states succeed, differences across states will likely remain significant. In 2003–2004, for example, students in New York enjoyed per-pupil expenditures more than twice as high as those in Utah.

MIKHAELA REID

Average per-pupil expenditures across states in 2003–2004

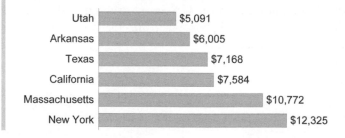

Utah	$5,091
Arkansas	$6,005
Texas	$7,168
California	$7,584
Massachusetts	$10,772
New York	$12,325

6.15 The Price of College

COLLEGE GRADUATES ENJOY A big premium in both wages and benefits, making a diploma worth more than its weight in gold. But it takes a lot of gold to get one. In 2002–2003, the average price of attending a public university was more than $10,000 per year. At a private university the average price was three times as high.

Students able to take advantage of financial aid pay substantially less than the "sticker price" charged by their universities. Increases in tuition and fees, however, have outpaced increases in financial aid.

Public universities have kept a tighter lid on prices than private universities, partly by hiring more part-time and temporary faculty and packing more students into large lectures. As prices for public and private higher education diverge, differences in quality are becoming increasingly apparent.

Yet the level of government support for students at both types of institutions is about the same. In 2000, public subsidies, including financial aid, averaged about $10,000 per student at both private and public universities.

"I sure hope Social Security is around when I'm 65. I'll need it to finish paying off my college loans."

CAROL SIMPSON

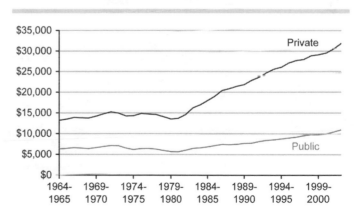

Average real price of attendance at public and private universities, 1964–1965 to 2002–2003 (in $2004)

6.16 Who Graduates from College?

IF EVERYONE HAD EQUAL ACCESS TO A COLLEGE education, family income would have less impact on chances for economic success. But affluent kids have an important advantage: they are substantially more likely to enroll in college and more likely to graduate than their low-income counterparts. In 1999–2000, only 7% of individuals from low-income families had completed a bachelor's degree by age 24, compared to 52% of those from high-income families.

Affluent families can help out more with college costs and tend to contribute a much higher share of total tuition and fees. A majority of families with incomes over $50,000 report that they are saving for their children's college education. Below that level of income, however, only a minority of families do so. The most common explanation offered is simply insufficient funds.

Financial aid significantly increases the likelihood that poor students will graduate from college. But direct grants for low-income families have declined substantially relative to tuition rates. "Need-blind" financial aid, once provided by many elite private schools to those who met their strict admissions criteria, is now harder to find.

MIKE KONOPACKI. USED WITH PERMISSION, HUCK/KONOPACKI LABOR CARTOONS, SOLIDARITY.COM/HKCARTOONS/.

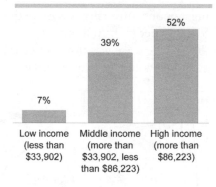

Percentage of individuals achieving a bachelor's degree by age 24 in 1999–2000, by family income

Low income (less than $33,902)	Middle income (more than $33,902, less than $86,223)	High income (more than $86,223)
7%	39%	52%

CHAPTER 7: **Health**

THE U.S. HEALTH CARE SYSTEM has been sick for years, but political bickering and special interests continue to block an effective cure. The problems are chronic: many Americans lack health insurance, prices for care keep climbing at a rapid pace, and the quality of care too often depends on a person's ability to pay.

RUSSELL CHRISTIAN

Chart 7.1 compares health spending in the United States and other high-income countries. Other countries are able to provide their residents with health care for a smaller fraction of gross domestic product. They also get more bang for their health care buck: Chart 7.2 reveals that despite higher spending in the U.S., life expectancy is longer in these other countries. Chart 7.3 demonstrates that leaving most health care provision to the marketplace has contributed to America's high costs. While government-provided insurance costs more per person in the U.S. than elsewhere, it covers relatively few people; many Americans must also make large out-of-pocket payments and purchase expensive private insurance to cover the gap.

Prices for medical goods and services have been rising fast, as seen in Chart 7.4. Since 1980, health care prices have grown more than twice as fast as prices in the overall economy. The combination of financial stress and more limited access to health care means that those with lower income don't feel as healthy as those with higher income, as indicated in Chart 7.5. Finding affordable health insurance is not easy, and Chart 7.6 shows that nearly one-third of low-income Americans have no coverage at all. Disparities in coverage among Americans from different racial and ethnic groups are striking. Chart 7.7 points out that Asian Americans and African Americans are almost twice as likely, and Native Americans and Hispanic Americans are roughly three times as likely, to be without health insurance as whites are. One result, pictured in Chart 7.8, is that black and Native American infants are much more likely than white infants to die before their first birthday.

High prices and limited public support can drain household resources. Chart 7.9 shows that the lowest 20% of earners in America spend 18% of their pretax income on health care, while the top 20% of earners spend only 3%. Chart 7.10 indicates that a large proportion of women undergo abortions because they feel they cannot afford a child. This is especially true for those below the official poverty line. Struggling with finances takes a toll on mental health. Chart 7.11 shows that people who are lower down the income ladder have higher odds of suffering from an anxiety or depressive disorder than those higher up. Stresses are compounded when the high costs of health care and the complexities of health insurance contribute to financial collapse. Chart 7.12 documents the large fraction of all personal bankruptcies that result, in part, from medical expenses that get out of control.

We could avoid many of the fatal diseases that strike down Americans each year. Chart 7.13 points out that many deaths are preventable. But it's difficult to change unhealthy behaviors, especially when industries promote them through advertising. Drug companies set a terrible example. Chart 7.14 shows that they spend more on marketing and administration—and take home more in profits—than they spend developing new and better drugs.

These problems are even more pressing in the international arena. Chart 7.15 describes the terrible impact that HIV/AIDS is having around the world, emphasizing the huge global effort necessary to rein in the epidemic. Chart 7.16 makes the impacts of poverty on health clear, showing that large portions of the world's people live without the clean water and sanitation needed for a healthy life.

7.1 Hey, Big Spender

THROWING MONEY AT A PROBLEM DOESN'T necessarily make it go away. The U.S. spends a far greater share of its gross domestic product (GDP) on health care than other industrialized countries. Even though health care expenditures equaled more than 14% of total U.S. GDP in 2001, nearly 40 million people lacked medical insurance.

Americans rely on a hodgepodge of private insurance, public assistance, and out-of-pocket payments that finances luxury treatment for some but begrudges basic care to others. In most other wealthy countries, the government either provides care directly or insures everyone. This can reduce multiple layers of bureaucracy, resulting in more efficient and egalitarian provision of health care.

Doctors and hospitals in the U.S. are increasingly torn between the pressure to protect profits and the desire to provide decent health care. Many feel trapped in a system that often pits these objectives against each other.

SPUD AND MARC HUGHES

Health care expenditures as a percentage of GDP in 2001

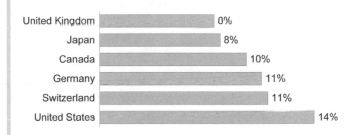

United Kingdom	0%
Japan	8%
Canada	10%
Germany	11%
Switzerland	11%
United States	14%

7.2 Spend More, Live Less

AMERICANS GET LESS BANG FOR THEIR HEALTH care buck than citizens of other industrialized countries. Despite high levels of average health spending per person, people in the U.S. don't live as long. Per capita health spending in Italy, Spain, and France is only half that in the U.S., yet citizens of those countries live an average of almost 3 years longer than Americans.

Why can't the U.S. buy its way to the top of the health charts? Many other countries guarantee basic health care for all their citizens, but the U.S. allocates services principally to those who can pay for them. Unequal access and the high cost of care add up to a less healthy population.

Income inequality itself is stressful. Numerous studies between countries, U.S. states, and U.S. cities show that, all else being equal, greater inequality is associated with lower life expectancy for rich as well as poor. Even if you have money, your neighbor's poverty can be bad for your health.

Life expectancy and health spending per capita in 1999

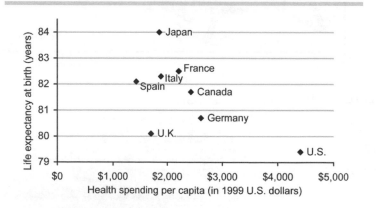

BARRIE MAGUIRE

7.3 You Get What You Pay Double For

I N MOST HIGH-INCOME COUNTRIES, THE government provides all citizens with public health insurance. In Canada, Japan, and most of Europe, public spending covered at least 70% of health care costs in 2003. In the U.S., public spending covered only 44% of costs.

By centralizing health care payments, these countries avoid redundant bureaucracies and can bargain with corporations for lower prices. This keeps overall costs down while providing quality health care for everyone. Governments in these countries spent an average of $2,343 or less per person in 2003 to provide universal health care.

In 2003, U.S. public health care spending averaged $2,502 per person—including everyone in the country—even though the government insured only about 30% of the population. Residents of the U.S. spent an average additional $3,133 per person to get the care they needed, while private spending in other high-income countries averaged only $718 per person.

AMPERSAND BY B. DEUTSCH

Average spending per person for health care in 2003 ($U.S., adjusted for purchasing power)

	▓ Public spending	☐ Private spending
United States	$2,502	$3,133
Switzerland	$2,212	$1,569
Germany	$2,343	$653
Canada	$2,099	$904
United Kingdom	$1,861	$370
Japan	$1,743	$396

7.4 The Unhealthy Cost of Care

INFLATION HAS LONG AILED THE U.S. economy, but in recent years price increases for medical care have become pathological. While overall consumer prices rose by 129% between 1980 and 2004, the costs of medical care grew more than twice as much. The fastest growth has been in hospital services, with prescription drug and medical supply costs in second place.

Technological change contributes to rapidly rising costs. But the fact that other countries have had more success controlling expenses without sacrificing quality suggests that our health care system itself is ailing. This problem can't be solved by the Band-Aid reforms offered by politicians dependent on campaign cash from the insurance and drug industries.

BARBARA BRANDON-CROFT

Average price increases for all consumer items and categories of medical care, 1980–2004

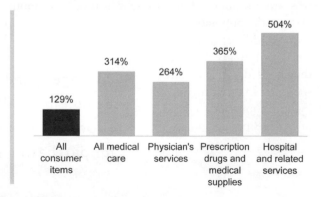

Earn More, Feel Better

MONEY CAN'T BUY GOOD HEALTH, BUT IT SURE helps. In 2003, people in poverty were almost four times as likely to describe their health as "fair or poor" than those in families with income above 200% of the poverty line. Within the more affluent group, 74% reported "excellent or very good" health, compared to only 51% of those below the poverty line. Health also differs by race/eth-nicity. Among both the poor and the middle class, blacks and Hispanics report feeling worse on average than whites.

Because many lower-income households lack affordable insurance, they often delay care until medical problems turn critical. In 2002, 69% of adults and 51% of children who had no insurance for the entire year postponed medical care because they couldn't afford to pay for it.

Some people get caught in a health-poverty trap. Poor health makes it difficult to find and keep a well-paying job. But without a job, people can't get the health insurance they need. In 2002, close to one-third of adults in poverty had a health condition that limited their ability to work.

Percent of people reporting different levels of health in 2003, by race, Hispanic origin, and poverty status

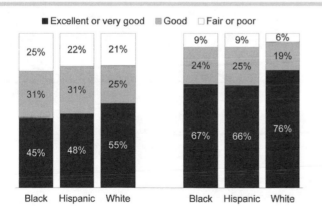

- ■ Excellent or very good
- ▨ Good
- ☐ Fair or poor

Below poverty line

	Black	Hispanic	White
Fair or poor	25%	22%	21%
Good	31%	31%	25%
Excellent or very good	45%	48%	55%

200% of poverty line or higher

	Black	Hispanic	White
Fair or poor	9%	9%	6%
Good	24%	25%	19%
Excellent or very good	67%	66%	76%

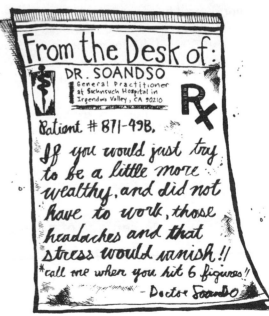

From the Desk of:
DR. SOANDSO
General Practitioner
at Suchnsuch Hospital in
Irgendwo Valley, CA 90210

Rx

Patient # 871-49B,

If you would just try to be a little more wealthy, and did not have to work, those headaches and that stress would vanish !!
*call me when you hit 6 figures !!
- Doctor Soandso

R. JAY MAGILL

7.6 Too Poor for Care

WHEN POOR PEOPLE GET SICK, THEIR OPTIONS FOR HELP are limited. Many end up in the emergency room, taking whatever services they can get. Medicare provides assistance to those 65 years or older and Medicaid and the State Children's Health Insurance Program (SCHIP) target poor families, but eligibility is limited and access notoriously difficult. In 2002, over 6 million children met the eligibility requirements to receive Medicaid or SCHIP but were not covered by the programs and were left without any insurance.

In 2002, close to one-third of all people in households with incomes below 150% of the poverty line had no medical coverage. The cost of insurance affects higher-income households as well. Among those with income over twice the poverty threshold, 11% lacked insurance, nearly double the rate in 1984.

Many of the uninsured have jobs: in 2003, half of all poor full-time workers lacked medical coverage for the entire year.

CLAY BUTLER, SIDEWALK BUBBLEGUM

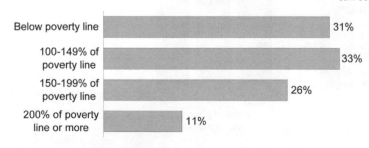

Percentage of people under age 65 lacking health insurance in 2002, by household poverty status

Below poverty line	31%
100-149% of poverty line	33%
150-199% of poverty line	26%
200% of poverty line or more	11%

People of Color Lack Insurance

SINCE HEALTH INSURANCE costs a lot, it's hardly surprising that groups with low average incomes don't have as much. In 2002–2003, about a fifth of African Americans and Asian Americans and a third of Hispanics lacked insurance, compared to 11% of whites. The racial/ethnic insurance gap was narrower for people living in poverty: across all groups, roughly a third of the poor had no coverage.

Unequal access to medical care contributes to poor health for people of color. In 2002, life expectancy for African Americans was five years less than the overall U.S. average. The percent of Native Americans dying from diabetes was more than double that of whites.

Both regional and historical factors help explain why Hispanics are particularly likely to be uninsured.

Often they have jobs with low pay and few benefits. Also, many are immigrants who lack information about the U.S. health system and may not realize that programs exist that can help them. In 2003, almost half of all noncitizens lacked insurance.

KHALIL BENDIB, WWW.BENDIB.COM

Percentage of people without health insurance (average 2002–2003)

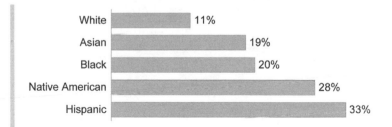

White	11%
Asian	19%
Black	20%
Native American	28%
Hispanic	33%

7.8 African American and Native American Children at Greater Risk

NOTHING HIGHLIGHTS RACIAL INEQUALITIES IN THE U.S. more starkly than disparities in children's life chances. The ratio of African American to white infant mortality rates declined in the late 1960s but began to worsen in 1974 and grew to more than double white rates in recent years. Native American children also suffer significantly higher infant mortality than whites.

In 2001, the infant mortality rate was 13.5 per 1,000 live births for black infants and 9.7 for Native Americans, compared to 5.7 for whites. Black infants face a higher risk of death than infants in much poorer countries including Bulgaria and Costa Rica. Some inner-city neighborhoods face even bleaker prospects.

Not all minority groups endure such grim statistics. In 2001, Asian, Pacific Islander, and Hispanic Americans had infant mortality rates slightly below those of whites.

Limited access to health insurance and prenatal care accounts for a large part of the problem. In 2002, 89% of all white mothers received prenatal care during the first trimester, compared to 75% of black mothers and 70% of Native American mothers.

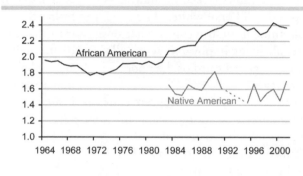

Ratio of African American and Native American infant mortality rates to white rates, 1964–2001 (broken line indicates missing data)

A NATIONAL ACADEMY OF SCIENCE'S INSTITUTE OF MEDICINE REPORT FINDS MINORITIES ARE LESS LIKELY TO RECEIVE PROPER MEDICAL CARE THAN WHITES.

...BACK OF THE AMBULANCE, BUB!...

U.S. HEALTH CARE SYSTEM

AMBULANCE

www.cagle.com ©2002

JEFF PARKER, FLORIDA TODAY

7.9 The Poor Pay More

UNLIKE LIPOSUCTION AND face-lifts, most medical procedures are necessities. When people get sick, they need help, regardless of their income. Many workers fear losing their insurance if they get laid off, and private insurers often refuse to cover individuals with "preexisting conditions."

Treatment costs about the same for rich and poor alike, and individuals lacking insurance are often forced to resort to emergency room visits because they cannot afford preventative care. As a result, poor families spend a larger part of their income on health care than affluent families do.

In 2003, the poorest fifth of earners spent 17% of their after-tax income on medical care, but the top fifth paid only 3%. Such inequality in medical spending exacerbates differences in living standards.

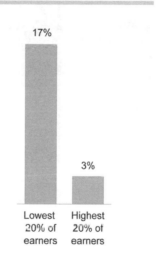

Health care spending as a percentage of after-tax income in 2003

17% — Lowest 20% of earners

3% — Highest 20% of earners

R. Jay Magill

119

7.10 Can't Afford a Kid

NOTHING STIRS UP POLITICAL DEBATE IN THE U.S. like abortion. The legality of the procedure has been under constant attack since it was first established nationwide in 1973. The number of legal abortions has declined significantly since 1990. Still, almost a quarter of all pregnancies ended in abortion in 2002.

There are many factors contributing to the decline. Women seem to be having fewer unintended pregnancies, perhaps because new contraceptives are available and concern about sexually transmitted infections has increased condom use. But new legal restrictions and a 37% drop in the number of providers between 1982 and 2000 are making it more difficult for women who want an abortion to obtain one.

Over half the women undergoing abortions in 2000 had incomes below or close to the poverty line. In 2004, 73% of women having abortions said they couldn't afford to have a child at that time—23% were in such dire straits they said they couldn't even afford the basic necessities of life.

AMPERSAND BY B. DEUTSCH

Percentage of women reporting "can't afford a baby now" as a reason for abortion in 2004, by income level

200% of poverty line or more — 60%

Below poverty line — 81%

7.11 **Mental Health**

POP ARTIST ROZALLA SANG "EVERYBODY'S FREE TO FEEL GOOD," but that's hard to do when you're suffering from a mental illness. In 2004, nearly 7 million noninstitutionalized adults experienced serious psychological distress in a given month. In 2002, there were 2.5 million hospitalizations for mental disorders.

In addition to suffering from the symptoms themselves, people with mental illness have difficulty holding a job, and the stress of dealing with their illness can affect their whole family. An estimated 20–25% of all homeless individuals suffer from serious mental health troubles.

Insurance companies often provide limited coverage for mental illness, and social stigma can prevent people from seeking help. Mental illness is unevenly distributed. The likelihood that a person will suffer from an anxiety or depressive disorder is highest at the bottom of the income distribution. Women are more likely than men to experience serious psychological distress, and blacks and Hispanics are more vulnerable than whites.

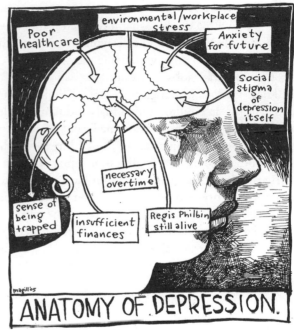

R. JAY MAGILL

Probability of an individual having an anxiety or depressive disorder, by quintile of family income

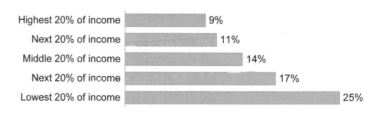

Highest 20% of income	9%
Next 20% of income	11%
Middle 20% of income	14%
Next 20% of income	17%
Lowest 20% of income	25%

7.12 Medical Bankruptcy

WHEN ILLNESS OR INJURY STRIKES, PEOPLE CAN GET HIT with a double whammy. Even if they have insurance, they face deductibles and co-payments that cost thousands of dollars. On top of that, some who miss work while they recover or care for a sick family member may lose their jobs as a result.

These medical expenses push many people into unmanageable debt. In 2001, nearly 1.5 million individuals and families filed for bankruptcy. In approximately half those cases, medically related expenses helped push debtors over the line. Three-quarters of those filing for medically related bankruptcy had health insurance when illness or injury struck.

By the time these people filed for bankruptcy, their circumstances were extreme. Twenty-two percent had gone without food at some point in the previous two years. Sixty-one percent had gone without a needed doctor or dental visit. Half had failed to fill a prescription for medicine.

Financial recovery can be difficult. People who have filed for bankruptcy at some time in their lives are often turned down for new jobs, mortgages, apartment rentals, or car loans.

JEN SORENSEN, SLOWPOKECOMICS.COM

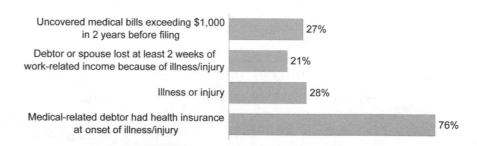

Percentage of all personal bankruptcies with various medical-related causes in 2001

Uncovered medical bills exceeding $1,000 in 2 years before filing — 27%

Debtor or spouse lost at least 2 weeks of work-related income because of illness/injury — 21%

Illness or injury — 28%

Medical-related debtor had health insurance at onset of illness/injury — 76%

7.13 Selling Sickness

THE FOUR MOST COMMON KILLERS IN THE U.S.—RESPONSIBLE FOR over 60% of all deaths—are heart disease, cancer, stroke, and chronic lower respiratory disease (like emphysema). Together, they resulted in over 9 million years of potential life lost (before age 75) in 2002.

These diseases are mostly preventable. Tobacco is well known as a cause of various diseases and is responsible for 18% of all deaths. Poor diet and lack of physical activity lead to 15% of all deaths, and alcohol consumption adds another 3.5%.

Large industries encourage unhealthy habits. From automobile- and TV-centered lifestyles to junk food sold in schools that can't afford physical education programs, negative influences on health are pervasive. Industry spent over $2.4 billion advertising alcohol, candy, and snacks in 1999—$15 of advertising for every $1 spent promoting fruit and vegetables. In 2003, tobacco companies alone spent over $650 million touting their products.

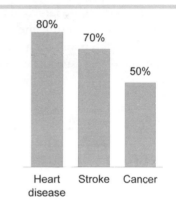

Minimum percentage of cases that are preventable, by disease

- Heart disease: 80%
- Stroke: 70%
- Cancer: 50%

SCHOOL BEVERAGE CONTRACTS

BEVERAGE COMPANIES

SINGER

ANDY SINGER

7.14 Rx = Big Bucks

THERE'S A LOT OF MONEY IN the drug trade, enough to make pharmaceuticals the most profitable industry in the U.S. for eight of the years between 1995 and 2003. The industry's huge profits are largely the result of aggressive marketing and government lobbying to maintain high prices. Though TV ads suggest otherwise, drug company revenues are more likely to pay for marketing and administration or to be counted as profits than they are to be spent on research and development (R&D) for new drugs.

Congressional investigations in 2005 found that the industry's addiction to profits was so serious that some companies continued to heavily promote high-profit drugs even after finding evidence that the drugs were unsafe.

Expensive drugs have a human cost. In 2001, high prices forced nearly 25% of seniors to go without medications prescribed to them by their doctors. In countries with universal health care, the government negotiates directly with drug companies, allowing them to earn a profit but keeping a lid on prices. In the world's poorest countries, international trade laws protecting drug company patents reduce the availability of affordable generic drugs.

"This one shows great promise...
It keeps the patient alive until their money runs out."

CAROL SIMPSON

Selected allocations of revenues for major drug companies in 2001

R & D	Profits	Marketing, advertising and administration
11%	18%	27%

7.15 HIV/AIDS

IV, THE HUMAN IMMUNO-deficiency virus, continues to plague the world. While the virus can strike anyone, it mostly infects the young and the poor. Sub-Saharan Africa has been hit worst, with an estimated 25.4 million people suffering from HIV/AIDS in 2004. Worldwide, over 3 million people died from the disease that year.

Since the disease usually strikes people in their most productive years, the economic consequences are enormous. When one family member falls ill, another must often stay home to provide care. Children are pulled out of school. Already-poor families become desperate and are less able to withstand economic slumps or natural catastrophes.

Poor people suffer most from the epidemic. High-priced patented drugs allow people with good health care coverage to live longer. But drug companies have fought the introduction of cheaper generic versions of these drugs: in poor countries in 2005, only 15% of those in need of anti-retroviral therapy were receiving it. In the U.S. in 2002, the death rate from AIDS was 8.6 times higher for blacks than for whites.

OLLE JOHANSSON, SWEDEN

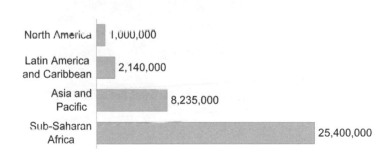

Number of people
living with HIV/AIDS
in 2004

North America	1,000,000
Latin America and Caribbean	2,140,000
Asia and Pacific	8,235,000
Sub-Saharan Africa	25,400,000

DISEASES THAT HAVE BEEN STAMPED OUT IN developed nations still ravage poorer countries, killing millions each year. Malaria, diarrhea, and dysentery run rampant in the less developed world. Each year almost 2 million children die from diarrhea and another 2 million from respiratory illnesses. Many adults also die from these diseases.

Getting basic medical care poses huge challenges for people living in poor countries. For every 100,000 people, high-income countries have 380 doctors, while low-income nations have 40. This disparity partly reflects a "brain drain": many doc-

tors and nurses from poor countries migrate to rich countries, taking with them not only their skills but thousands of dollars' worth of training their home countries had invested in them.

More than 1.1 billion people worldwide lack access to safe drinking water and over 2.3 billion lack adequate sanitation. Such underdevelopment is deadly, since many diseases are spread through contaminated water.

The news isn't all bad. For example, between 1990 and 2000, the proportion of people in low-income countries with adequate sanitation increased by 13%. A real commitment from the world community could finish the job.

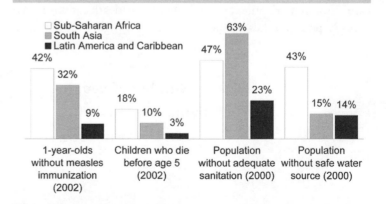

R. Jay Magill

Health conditions in 2000/2002

Legend:
- ☐ Sub-Saharan Africa
- ▨ South Asia
- ■ Latin America and Caribbean

	Sub-Saharan Africa	South Asia	Latin America and Caribbean
1-year-olds without measles immunization (2002)	42%	32%	9%
Children who die before age 5 (2002)	18%	10%	3%
Population without adequate sanitation (2000)	47%	63%	23%
Population without safe water source (2000)	43%	15%	14%

CHAPTER 8: **The Environment**

RUSSELL CHRISTIAN

FROM SEA TO POLLUTED SEA, ENVIRONMENTAL hazards have become a perennial feature of our economic landscape. Clean air, good water, and stable ecosystems don't have obvious price tags, and it's difficult to measure their deterioration. Companies under pressure to maximize profits are tempted to ignore the pollution they create if they aren't forced to pay for cleaning it up. But the future of our economy depends heavily on the well-being of our global ecosystem.

Chart 8.1 shows that the value of sustainable harvesting and ecosystem services provided by forests and wetlands in their natural state is often much greater than the cash generated by converting them to agriculture. Protecting the environment can also be a source of jobs. Chart 8.2 points out that employment in the U.S. environmental industry has more than tripled in the past generation.

The release of toxic wastes threatens public health. New data on both the levels and dangers of specific emissions make it possible to name the worst polluters in Chart 8.3. These emissions have pervasive and long-lasting effects. Chart 8.4 reports some of the toxins discovered in the umbilical cord blood of newborn babies.

When choosing where to locate polluting industries, politicians and business leaders frequently discount the effects on low-income neighborhoods. Chart 8.5 offers evidence that people of color are especially likely to live in communities with high pollution levels and associated risks of cancer. Democratic participation can counter environmental abuses as long as communities have enough political clout to challenge corporate influence. Chart 8.6 shows that in U.S. states where political power is more unequal, environmental protection tends to suffer.

The government's commitment to maintaining a healthy environment has wavered. Chart 8.7 documents that funding for the Environmental Protection Agency has fallen steeply as a share of the federal budget over the past generation. Meanwhile, concerned people continue to search for creative ways to deal with environmental problems. Chart 8.8 shows the potential economic results of a proposal to control greenhouse gas emissions using a surcharge-and-rebate plan called the Sky Trust.

Forests in most of the world are in decline, in part because demand for wood products has risen. Growth in the consumption of paper and paperboard is tracked in Chart 8.9. As forests are harvested at unsustainable rates, millions of different species are being driven toward extinction. Chart 8.10 offers a sobering look at the varieties of life that are most at risk.

The environment includes wilderness habitat as well as cultivated land. The world's population requires a steady supply of affordable food, but modern methods for increasing agricultural production have many negative side effects. Chart 8.11 tracks the unequal distribution of government farm subsidies, which exacerbate the decline of small, family farms. Poor land use planning leads to ever-worsening sprawl, which gobbles up high-quality farmland and reinforces America's reliance on automobiles. Chart 8.12 shows that more and more people commute to work by car, adding

to greenhouse gas emissions and encouraging an unhealthy lack of physical activity.

The sports utility vehicle has become a symbol of addiction to oil. Chart 8.13 identifies the sources of oil used by the U.S., emphasizing our reliance on imports for more than half of overall consumption. Our dependence on oil and other fossil fuels is not the inevitable consequence of high average living standards, because it reflects extraordinary waste. Chart 8.14 shows that even a country with high living standards, like Germany, can get by on half the fossil fuels per person that we consume in the U.S.

Burning fossil fuels is expensive. It also contributes to global warming. Chart 8.15 measures the emissions of the primary greenhouse gas, carbon dioxide, in the second half of the 20th century. Some have responded to the problem of global warming by calling for more reliance on nuclear energy. But safe disposal of nuclear waste remains an unsolved problem, and Chart 8.16 warns that this problem is likely to intensify in the future.

8.1 Gifts of Nature

OUR MARKET-BASED ECONOMY RELIES HEAVILY on gifts of nature, including ecosystem services such as natural water purification processes in wetlands. Markets take these services for granted because they are not bought and sold. But the benefits of maintaining natural ecosystems can far exceed the value of the market revenues that alternative uses would generate.

For instance, turning Canadian marshes into farms nets $2,400 per hectare, expressed in current dollars. The estimated benefits of keeping the wetlands intact are over twice as high: $5,800 per hectare. Similarly, intact mangrove forests in Thailand produce a stream of benefits worth a minimum of $1,000 per hectare. Converting the mangroves to shrimp farming yields just $200 per hectare.

Putting a price on the environment may seem like a scary idea. But people put price tags on nature every day when they choose to harvest a forest or dam a river. They assume that the benefits automatically outweigh the costs. Unless we develop new ways of accounting for the real cost of human activities, we might not discover the true story until it's too late.

MATT WUERKER

Total economic value of alternative resource management (in $U.S. per hectare, net present value)

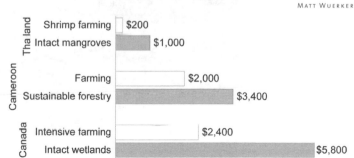

Thailand	Shrimp farming	$200
	Intact mangroves	$1,000
Cameroon	Farming	$2,000
	Sustainable forestry	$3,400
Canada	Intensive farming	$2,400
	Intact wetlands	$5,800

129

8.2 **Jobs and the Environment**

MANY BELIEVE THAT AN ECONOMY CAN EITHER PROTECT THE environment or create jobs, but not both. U.S. employment numbers paint a different picture. Workers in environmental industries help to manage waste, control pollution, and recycle materials. Between 1980 and 2003, the number of jobs in these industries more than tripled.

These numbers don't include the large number of jobs in recreation and ecotourism. Without protected wilderness areas, these opportunities would shrink.

Globally, billions of people directly depend on renewable natural resources: 44% of the world's population earns a basic living from farming, fishing, or forest products. Without sustainable management of the world's natural resources, their livelihoods will be undermined.

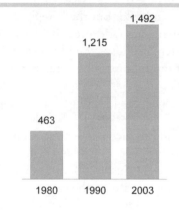

U.S. environmental industry employment (in thousands)

- 1980: 463
- 1990: 1,215
- 2003: 1,492

8.3 Toxic Neighbors

HOLD YOUR BREATH. SOME U.S. businesses are filling the air with dangerous chemicals. In 2000, General Electric was the worst corporate polluter in the U.S., taking into account the volume of pollution, its toxicity, and the risk of human exposure.

Not all pollution is the same. Some toxins are more deadly than others, and chemicals spread through the environment in different ways. Analysts at the Environmental Protection Agency (EPA) assign a score to toxic releases by multiplying the amounts released by their levels of toxicity and by the number of people likely exposed. Matching the score of particular facilities to the corporations that own them makes it possible to calculate overall company scores.

The EPA's Toxics Release Inventory was established after the Union Carbide chemical disaster killed hundreds and injured thousands 20 years ago in Bhopal, India. After the tragedy, activists argued that the public has a right to know how much pollution is coming into their communities.

"That looks awful...we'd better fund a PBS nature show or something."

CAROL SIMPSON

Top five corporate air polluters in the U.S. in 2000, by toxic release score

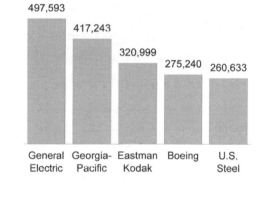

General Electric	Georgia-Pacific	Eastman Kodak	Boeing	U.S. Steel
497,593	417,243	320,999	275,240	260,633

8.4 Environmental Health

CARBON MONOXIDE IS A colorless, odorless gas produced by burning gasoline and other fossil fuels. Many people are unaware of their levels of exposure to it, which can be affected by local weather conditions as well as proximity to traffic. A recent statistical analysis used data on air quality in California collected through the 1990s. It measured the impact of variations in exposure to air pollution on infant mortality.

The study found that high levels of exposure to carbon monoxide, in particular, were associated with a significantly higher risk of death among infants. What's more, decreases in carbon

monoxide levels brought about largely through environmental regulation probably saved the lives of about 1,000 children in California in the 1990s.

Other forms of pollution are also worrisome. Some 75,000 chemicals are licensed for production in the U.S., with hundreds of new compounds introduced each year. Few have undergone thorough safety studies. Recent tests found, on average, 200 pesticides, car emissions, and other industrial chemicals in the umbilical cord blood of newborn babies. Many are known carcinogens.

Average number of different chemicals found in umbilical cord blood of tested newborns in 2004, by potential health effect or body system affected

Cancer	133
Birth defects/developmental delays	151
Stomach or intestines	194

8.5 Environmental Racism

RACIAL INEQUALITY HAS MANY DIMENSIONS, including unequal exposure to industrial waste. New facilities producing toxic emissions are more likely to be located in neighborhoods where many of the residents are people of color.

A study in California found that census tracts with higher levels of airborne pollution were home to higher proportions of people of color. As the risk for exposure to carcinogenic pollution rose, so did the percentage of Hispanic, African American, or Asian American/Pacific Islander residents.

Because polluted neighborhoods tend to have lower housing costs, many poor people can't avoid living with the pollution. Yet income alone doesn't explain environmental disparities. Even when blacks, Hispanics, and whites of equal income are compared, nonwhites are more likely to live in the most polluted sections of American cities. Discrimination in bank loans and housing may contribute to this pattern.

These injustices have become an issue only because activists in communities of color pushed them onto the radar screen of politicians and mainstream environmentalists. Environmental justice activists insist that every person has an equal right to a healthy environment.

(TH)INK BY KEITH KNIGHT

Composition of census tracts in California (in 2000) by estimated cancer risk from ambient air toxins (in 1996)

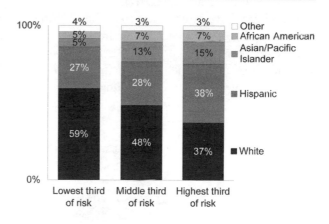

8.6 Upper-Class Benefit Analysis

THE POORER YOU ARE, THE HIGHER YOUR RISK OF exposure to pollution. Industries that pollute create profits for their owners and lower prices for consumers. When the industries' owners and consumers live in clean areas, they don't realize or don't care that other people suffer negative environmental side effects.

If polluters have more power than their victims, government is less likely to protect the environment. In the U.S., states with a more equal political participation tend to have lower levels of environmental stress (measured, in part, by the strength of state environmental policies).

Inequalities in the sharing of benefits and burdens can be masked by cost-benefit analysis. Cost-benefit analysis assumes that a policy is a good idea if estimated benefits outweigh estimated costs. Government agencies often ask economists to use this technique to judge a project or regulation. When the analysis is oversimplified, the fact that some people pay the costs (dollar, health, and so on) while others receive the benefits is ignored.

R. JAY MAGILL

Equality of power distribution vs. environmental stress within U.S. states

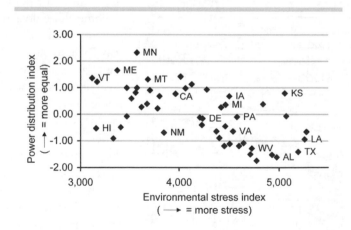

8.7 EPA SOS

THE U.S. ENVIRONMENTAL PROTECTION AGENCY (EPA) COULD USE some protection itself. Understaffed and underfunded, the EPA has difficulty enforcing existing regulations, much less developing new ones. In 1980, the EPA's total budget was just under 1% of the total federal budget. By 2004, it had dropped to 0.35%.

When companies are tempted to put private profits ahead of public health, government regulation to protect the public interest becomes especially important. But regulations are hampered when EPA administrators are more concerned with keeping politicians happy than safeguarding the environment. Also, regulatory agencies can be "captured" by the industries they regulate when political appointees spin through a revolving door between an agency and lucrative industry jobs. Their ties to industry may cloud appointees' judgment on implementing or enforcing strong regulations.

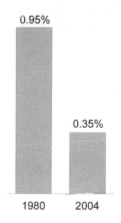

Environmental Protection Agency budget as a percentage of total federal budget

0.95% — 1980

0.35% — 2004

CLAY BENNETT / © 2002 THE CHRISTIAN SCIENCE MONITOR (WWW.CSMONITOR.COM). ALL RIGHTS RESERVED.

8.8 Environmental Markets

IN ADDITION TO TRADITIONAL ENVIRONMENTAL REGULATIONS, like strict limits on pollution that apply to everyone, governments are trying market-based alternatives. One successful example is the tradable permit system used to reduce sulfur dioxide (SO_2) emissions that cause acid rain. The government sets a limit on total SO_2. Facilities that produce it can buy and sell emission permits within the government's limit. If a company can easily reduce emissions, it is allowed to make money by selling its permits to another company that can't.

Some people have proposed using this type of plan to control greenhouse gas emissions that lead to global warming. One version is the Sky Trust. Producers of greenhouse gases would have to pay into the trust, creating an incentive to reduce emissions. All residents would receive an equal payment from the trust. Most people, especially those with middle and lower incomes, would receive more than they pay, because they produce less than the average share of greenhouse gases. Because higher-income households, on average, consume more energy-using goods and services, they would pay more into the fund than they received.

R. JAY MAGILL

Estimated average annual net gain (right side) or loss (left side) to households in proposed Sky Trust plan, by income group

-$1,821	Richest 20%
Middle 60%	$984
Poorest 20%	$808

8.9 When a Tree Falls...

FORESTS ARE CRUCIAL TO THE GLOBAL ECOSYSTEM, producing oxygen and providing habitat for innumerable species. Trees also stabilize the climate and soil. But the marketplace values forests based on the commodities they produce. The average American used almost 700 pounds of paper and paperboard in 2002. World consumption is growing as economies develop.

Globally, forestland shrank by 232 million acres between 1990 and 2000. Today, only about half the world's original forestland remains. The most frequent motives for deforestation are the expansion of agriculture, the creation of new roads, and the commercial wood and paper trade. In the critically important Brazilian rainforest, deforestation makes room for cattle ranches that sell beef internationally.

Increasingly, mangrove forests in Asia and Central America are being cleared to raise shrimp for U.S. and European markets. Left in their natural state, these forests foster biodiversity and provide millions of people with food, medicine, and other necessities.

Pounds of paper and paperboard used per person each year, 1961–2002

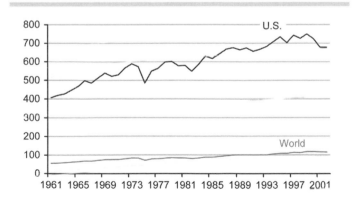

ANDY SINGER

JAWS II

HUMAN OVERFISHING

www.caglecartoons.com

MIKE LANE, CAGLE CARTOONS

ZOOS SHOWCASE ONLY THE TINIEST TIP OF THE BIODIVERSITY iceberg. Every species of plant and animal depends on other species. Bacteria help animals digest food and help plants pull nutrients from the soil. Worms, fungi, insects, and microorganisms convert materials into soil, the basis for life on land. Insects fertilize flowers so that plants can reproduce.

When species disappear, the whole system can be thrown out of whack. That's why environmentalists are concerned about high rates of extinction. The main culprit is habitat destruction. As forests are cut, species that live among the trees have nowhere to go. In the oceans, overfishing and destruction of coral reefs reduces populations below sustainable levels.

Around the world, 15,500 species were listed as threatened with extinction in 2004, about 41% of all species that have been evaluated. Some biologists believe that as many as 50,000 species disappear every year.

Percentage of those species that have been evaluated that were threatened in 2004

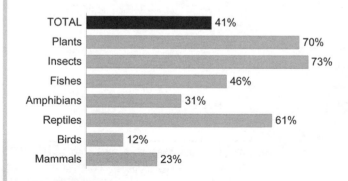

TOTAL	41%
Plants	70%
Insects	73%
Fishes	46%
Amphibians	31%
Reptiles	61%
Birds	12%
Mammals	23%

8.11 **Down on the Farm**

AMERICA HAS BEEN CALLED THE "WORLD'S BREADBASKET." Food is one of our biggest exports, bringing in over $61 billion in 2004. But this bounty is heavily dependent on environmentally damaging technologies and misdirected government subsidies.

Over-reliance on mechanization, chemical fertilizers, and pesticides is dangerous. Each year, U.S. farms lose over 1 billion tons of topsoil and use over 500 million pounds of pesticides.

In 2000, farmers got only 19¢ for each dollar spent on food purchases. The federal government provides huge subsidies that primarily benefit larger farms. While only 3% of farms had incomes of $500,000 or more in 2002, they received 27% of all government farm payments. Smaller farms received far less. Such policies endanger the future of family farms, with negative consequences for rural communities.

The same subsidies also undermine farmers in other countries who compete with artificially low-priced U.S. exports. Millions of corn farmers in Mexico have been driven out of business, forced to move to urban slums or to cross the U.S. border illegally in search of work.

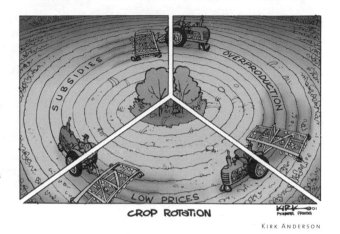

CROP ROTATION

KIRK ANDERSON

Percentage of total government farm payments going to categories of farms in 2002, by annual income of farm

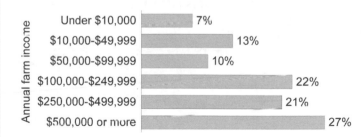

Annual farm income

Under $10,000	7%
$10,000-$49,999	13%
$50,000-$99,999	10%
$100,000-$249,999	22%
$250,000-$499,999	21%
$500,000 or more	27%

139

8.12 **Sprawl**

ONCE, THERE WERE CITIES, towns, and farms. Then came suburbs, and then exurbs. As fewer people live in rural towns and city centers, American metropolitan areas are spreading out—way out. Over 1 million acres of farmland are converted to suburban development each year.

People are attracted to new homes with nice lawns, homes that are often cheaper than existing housing in already built-up areas. But this process of relentless sprawl comes with hidden costs. Living in suburbs and exurbs requires reliance on cars for transportation. More and more people use cars to get to work, while fewer walk or use public transportation. Between 1985 and 2003, the U.S. added over 6,000 miles of new roads every year, and the average number of vehicle miles traveled per person rose 33% overall.

All that driving increases the need for oil imports and adds greenhouse gases and other pollution to an already overburdened atmosphere. Many housing developments don't even include sidewalks. This contributes to sedentary lifestyles, increasing the risk of heart disease, strokes, and obesity.

MONOCULTURE

KIRK ANDERSON

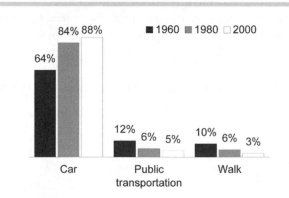

Percent of people commuting to work, by method, 1960–2000

■ 1960 ■ 1980 □ 2000

Car: 64%, 84%, 88%
Public transportation: 12%, 6%, 5%
Walk: 10%, 6%, 3%

8.13 Black Gold

OIL HAS BEEN CALLED "BLACK GOLD," AND THOSE who control it enjoy enormous wealth and power. In 2003, the world's oil workers pumped 1 trillion gallons of petroleum from the earth. Americans consumed 25% of the total. Since the U.S. only produced about one-third of what it used, it had to spend over $130 billion importing the difference from other countries.

The struggle to control oil reserves shapes many global political conflicts, often leading to war. Major oil-producing countries restrict production in order to keep prices high. Reliance on imported oil leaves American consumers vulnerable to unpredictable political events as well as natural disasters such as hurricanes.

Multinational oil companies have enormous political influence in the U.S. In 2005 they received billions of dollars in tax breaks and exemptions from laws that protect clean water. For years they have been lobbying for permission to drill in the Arctic National Wildlife Refuge in Alaska. The native Gwich'in people and environmentalists fear this could undermine local culture and disrupt the fragile ecosystem.

Sources of oil consumed in the U.S. in 2003 (thousands of barrels per day)

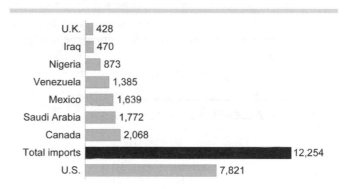

U.K.	428
Iraq	470
Nigeria	873
Venezuela	1,385
Mexico	1,639
Saudi Arabia	1,772
Canada	2,068
Total imports	12,254
U.S.	7,821

WILL YOU SIGN THIS PETITION AGAINST OIL DRILLING IN ANWR?

THOSE RAPACIOUS THUGS WON'T LOOK TWICE AT YOUR PETITION. IT'S POINTLESS.

NO, WE HAVE A GOOD STRATEGY. WE'RE GOING TO COLLECT MILLIONS OF SIGNATURES, GATHER A HUGE STACK OF PETITIONS...

...AND USE THEM TO FILL IN ALL THE HOLES THEY DRILL.

STEPHANIE McMILLAN, MINIMUMSECURITY.NET

141

8.14 **Dinosaurs on Our Backs**

AMERICANS HAVE AN ENERGY ADDICTION. WE CAN'T SEEM TO imagine life without unlimited fossil fuels. We rely heavily on oil for transportation, coal for electricity generation, and natural gas for home heating. In 2003, the average American consumed energy from fossil fuels equivalent to 24,325 pounds of coal, more than five times the world average of 4,788 pounds.

Most of the energy contained in our fuels is wasted due to inefficient use and substandard technology. In 2002, only 20% of the energy burned in automobiles, trucks, and airplanes actually helped them travel. Replacing inefficient devices like incandescent lightbulbs with the best existing technologies could cut America's electricity needs in half.

Other countries tax energy consumption in order to encourage conservation. Countries like Germany, with living standards comparable to those in the U.S., use half as much fossil fuel per person. Poor countries like China currently use far less than we do, but their appetite will increase along with economic growth.

ANDY SINGER

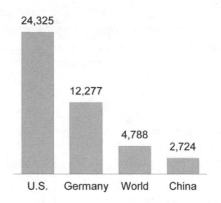

Average consumption of fossil fuels per person in 2003 (in equivalent pounds of coal)

U.S.	Germany	World	China
24,325	12,277	4,788	2,724

8.15 Hot! Hot! Hot!

MODERN INDUSTRIAL SOCIETY IS ADDING extra greenhouse gases to the atmosphere, and most scientists agree that this is causing average temperatures to rise. The climate shift is predicted to produce an increase in the number and severity of weather extremes, like hurricanes and droughts. Already the polar ice caps have shrunk and the oceans have risen. Tens of millions of people are likely to be adversely affected.

The main culprits are carbon dioxide (CO_2) and other greenhouse gases released by burning fossil fuels, cement production, some agricultural practices, and deforestation. Over the last half century, the U.S. has released a large share of all cumulative CO_2 emissions, but less than other regions of the world. In 2003, however, we released 7 billion metric tons, more than all of Africa and Latin America combined.

The U.S. government, influenced by industry lobbyists, has strongly resisted seriously addressing the problem. As of August 2005, the U.S. remained one of only six countries in the world that had failed to ratify the Kyoto Protocol, the main international effort to reduce global warming.

Cumulative net CO_2 emissions, 1950–2000 (billions of metric tons)

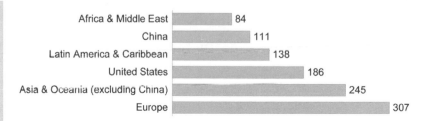

Africa & Middle East	84
China	111
Latin America & Caribbean	138
United States	186
Asia & Oceania (excluding China)	245
Europe	307

8.16 Radiation to the Rescue?

THE ANTINUCLEAR MOVEMENT OF THE 1970S AND 80S BROUGHT construction of new nuclear plants to a halt by focusing the nation's attention on safety problems. However, growing concern over global warming has led some environmentalists to reconsider nuclear power as a necessary evil, because nuclear power plants don't directly produce greenhouse gases. This gives hope to an industry that's been stagnating for years.

But nukes are still controversial. Radioactive wastes and security risks are the biggest concerns. The U.S. has 149 nuclear reactors generating over 2,000 tons of highly radioactive spent fuel each year. The U.S. government plans to bury high-level waste at Yucca Mountain, Nevada, but critics worry the site will leak. Meanwhile, the waste sits in temporary storage at facilities around the country.

Terrorists could use nuclear waste in a bomb and are suspected of targeting nuclear facilities for attack. If a nuclear waste pool near a major city were set on fire, more than 100,000 people could die of radiation-induced cancer, with evacuation and other costs totaling over $500 billion.

STEPHANIE McMILLAN, MINIMUMSECURITY.NET

Recent and projected total quantity
of high-level nuclear waste
in the U.S. (metric tons)

CHAPTER 9: **Macroeconomics**

ACROECONOMICS ("MACRO" FOR SHORT) focuses on factors that affect average incomes, employment, and economic growth. Macroeconomic forces can be formidable, since their influence permeates the economy. Powerful institutions, such as the Federal Reserve banking system, attempt to steer the economy by influencing interest rates and inflation. But stock market crashes, trade imbalances, and skittish investors can knock the economy off course. This chapter looks at the path we've traveled and where we may be heading.

The growth of gross domestic product (GDP) is seldom smooth. Chart 9.1 traces the ups and downs of the economy's business cycles since the 1950s. During a recession, the value of output falls; during a recovery it increases. However, GDP reflects only the market value of what gets bought and sold, ignoring the value of work and assets outside the marketplace. Chart 9.2 presents an alternative measure of the health of our economy—the Genuine Progress Indicator (GPI)—which incorporates nonmarket indicators, such as the value of household work, the benefits of volunteerism, and the cost of pollution.

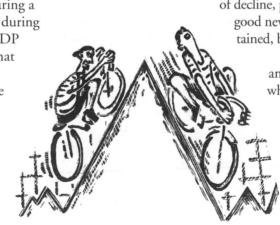

RUSSELL CHRISTIAN

Chart 9.3 documents long-run patterns of economic growth and shows that the boom economy of the 1990s wasn't remarkable by historical standards. Investment in new productive resources supports long-run economic performance. But, as Chart 9.4 demonstrates, rates of investment have declined, on average, since the 1960s.

The 1990s taught us that productivity improvements contribute to faster growth, but average living standards don't keep up when the benefits aren't widely shared. Chart 9.5 illustrates trends in productivity and employee compensation. Productivity improvements support higher profits when wages don't increase proportionately. Chart 9.6 points out that, after many years of decline, profit rates have indeed improved. This is good news for business if profitability can be sustained, but workers may be left behind.

Inflation is the scourge of bankers and financiers. It can also lower living standards when improvements in family incomes fail to compensate for higher prices. Chart 9.7 traces the history of inflation in the U.S. The Federal Reserve attempts to keep inflation under control by influencing interest rates. Chart 9.8 explains how "the Fed" works.

Interest rates affect economic growth and employment. Chart 9.9

shows how the cost of borrowing has evolved since the 1950s and points out limits to the Federal Reserve's influence. Chart 9.10 offers another perspective on interest rates, examining the differences between short-run and long-run rates and the impact of investors' expectations.

American banks have been consolidating since the mid-1980s, with small banks incorporated into larger ones, as Chart 9.11 illustrates. At the same time, household borrowing has climbed to record levels. Chart 9.12 documents the steady rise in household debt. The powerful banking sector, along with credit card companies, has pushed through reforms to personal bankruptcy laws, making it hard for ordinary people to endure a sudden job loss or medical emergency.

Asset prices have an enormous impact on the economy, and the most important asset for many Americans is their home. Chart 9.13 shows how housing prices have been rising throughout the country, increasing the wealth of those who own their home, but excluding others from the bounty. Changes in the average price of stocks also have far-reaching implications. Chart 9.14 traces the dot-com boom and bust of the 1990s through the rise and fall of the NASDAQ Composite Index.

The U.S. consumes more of the world's output than it produces, resulting in record trade deficits, as Chart 9.15 documents. The value of the dollar influences how much we're willing to buy from the rest of the world. Chart 9.16 points out that the value of the dollar was strong during much of the 1990s, allowing Americans to purchase products from abroad at bargain prices but making U.S. exports less competitive. This situation may not be sustainable in the long run.

9.1 The Ups and Downs of GDP

WE PRODUCE A LOT OF STUFF IN THE U.S.: over $11 trillion worth each year. That's much more than we produced in the 1950s, but the increase hasn't been steady. Growth speeds up and then slows down, in a pattern known as the business cycle. Periods of expansion are followed by periods of recession in which growth falls significantly and the amount produced can actually shrink. The National Bureau of Economic Research determines the dates for business cycles by deciding when recessions begin and end.

During a slump, businesses have trouble selling their products. They hire fewer new workers and lay off others; some businesses go bust. The result is rising unemployment. Things turn around during a recovery. Unemployment falls and sales increase, but rapid expansion often fuels inflation. Policy makers try to influence the business cycle by changing interest rates and government spending. However, their efforts don't always produce predictable results.

R. JAY MAGILL

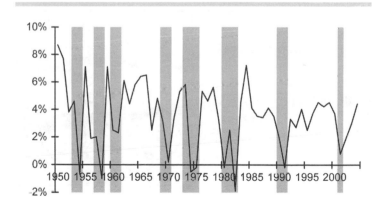

GDP growth rate, 1950–2004
(gray bars indicate recession years)

9.2 GDP Is Misleading

THE MARKET KNOWS THE PRICE OF EVERYTHING and the value of nothing. Economists measure our well-being by changes in the value of everything that is bought and sold divided by the population (the per capita gross domestic product, or GDP). But this measure can be misleading. It ignores the value of nonmarket work such as unpaid child care and elder care, which add to overall economic activity. It also ignores the depreciation and destruction of environmental assets such as forests, which should be subtracted.

The Genuine Progress Indicator (GPI) provides an alternative measure of economic well-being. It adds the value of nonmarket activities such as household and volunteer work and subtracts the costs of pollution, resource depletion, and loss of leisure time.

This indicator paints a very different picture of the amount of progress we've made in recent years. While per capita GDP tripled between 1950 and 2002, per capita GPI has been stagnating for decades.

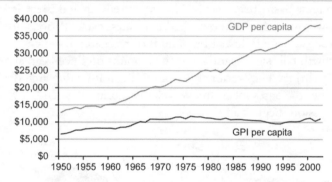

Gross domestic product and genuine progress indicator, 1950–2002 (in $2004)

STEPHANIE McMILLAN, MINIMUMSECURITY.NET

9.3 The Growth Record

N THE 1990S, THE MEDIA CELEBRATED THE BOOM-
ing "new economy," which promised to deliver unprece-
dented prosperity. The economy did experience the longest
period of sustained growth since the end of World War II. But
the rate of growth achieved did not set any records.

Over the last full business cycle, 1991–2001, growth averaged 3.3%. The first cycle of the 1950s boasted average growth
rates of 5.4%. During the country's second longest expansion,
1961–1971, growth averaged
4.4%.

A stock market bubble and
unusually low interest rates
helped prop up growth in the
1990s. These factors are probably unsustainable in the long
run. Even the modest boom of
the last decade could prove
hard to replicate in the
future.

R. Jay Magill

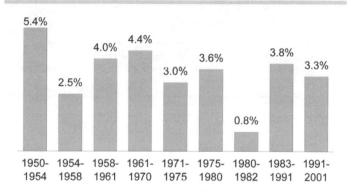

Average annual GDP growth rates across business cycles, 1950–2001

Period	Growth
1950-1954	5.4%
1954-1958	2.5%
1958-1961	4.0%
1961-1970	4.4%
1971-1975	3.0%
1975-1980	3.6%
1980-1982	0.8%
1983-1991	3.8%
1991-2001	3.3%

9.4 Investing for the Future

TODAY'S INVESTMENTS DETERMINE TOMORROW'S standard of living. Americans can improve the economy's productive capacity by setting aside resources for investment. Adopting new technologies and updating equipment pay off in the long run. In order to invest in the future, we cannot consume everything we produce. We must save.

Net investment refers to investment above the amount needed to maintain the current stock of capital. Although net investment fluctuates from year to year, on average it has been declining as a share of GDP.

In the past, savings kept pace with investment. In recent years, the two have parted company. Investment has exceeded savings, which is possible only because of the availability of resources from abroad. Without this foreign boost, net investment would fall even further.

SPUD AND BARRY DEUTSCH

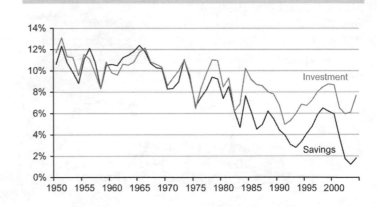

Investment and savings as a
percentage of GDP, 1950–2004
(net domestic investment and savings)

9.5 Working Hard for Your Money

IT'S ALWAYS A GOOD IDEA TO GET the most out of what you have. New technology, better equipment, more skills, and improved ways of organizing production all help to increase labor productivity, the value of what workers produce for each hour worked.

Average gains in U.S. labor productivity began to decline after the 1960s. This trend reversed itself in recent years. During the last full business cycle of the 1990s, labor productivity growth averaged 2.3% per year, a level last seen in the early 1970s.

If everyone gets a fair share, the living standards of working people will improve. However, the growth of compensation lags behind productivity gains. Workers receive only a fraction of the rewards from producing more. The remaining benefits are captured as higher profits or lower prices.

JEN SORENSEN, SLOWPOKECOMICS.COM

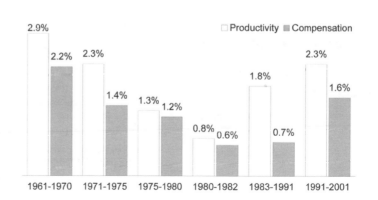

Growth of labor productivity and real hourly compensation across business cycles, 1961–2001 (nonfarm business sector)

9.6 **Profits in America**

O NE MEASURE OF BUSINESS'S RETURN ON ITS INVEST-
ments is the profit rate, total profits expressed as a percent of the
capital invested. After drifting downward for years, the corporate
profit rate rebounded in the 1990s, reaching about 8% in 1997, not long
before the stock market boom went bust. Have the good times stopped
rolling or are they just taking a temporary detour?

High interest rates, low productivity growth, and more global competition took their toll on corporate performance in the late 1970s and
much of the 1980s. Cheerleaders for the U.S. economy say that recent
technological advances have allowed companies to retool and emerge as
global leaders. But retooling can cause a lot of pain for those left behind
due to outsourcing and downsizing.

R. JAY MAGILL

Corporate profit rate,
1950–2003 (after-tax profits
as a percent of nonresidential
capital stock)

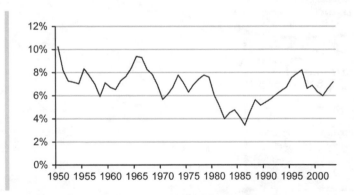

9.7 Inflation

A DOLLAR TODAY DOESN'T BUY NEARLY AS MUCH as it did a generation ago. That's because the price level has been increasing since the 1950s. Inflation is defined as the rate at which average prices grow each year. Changes in the consumer price index (CPI), a measure of the cost of buying a standard bundle of goods and services, are often used to determine the inflation rate.

Inflation rates reached their highest levels in the 1970s, when oil price increases rocked the economy. More recently, inflation has been lower. Rising prices reduce living standards when incomes don't keep pace. Owners of financial assets generally hate inflation. It erodes the value of their wealth over time.

Policy makers frequently raise interest rates to reduce inflation, even if this leads to higher unemployment. However, the trade-off between fighting inflation and creating more jobs isn't iron-clad. In the 1990s, the U.S. economy enjoyed both low inflation and low unemployment. Cheap imports from abroad, low labor costs at home, and a strong dollar helped keep prices in check.

AND IF THE ECONOMY KEEPS BOOMING, I SHOULD BE ABLE TO GET RAISES THAT NEARLY KEEP UP WITH INFLATION!

THE NEW OPTIMISM

Rate of consumer price inflation, 1950–2004 (CPI-U)

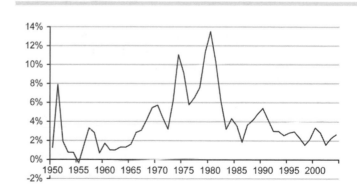

9.8 The Story Behind the Fed

TOM TOMORROW

Who determines interest rates?

The Fed, aka the Board of Governors of the Federal Reserve System, a group of bankers nominated by the president and appointed for 14-year terms, makes decisions that influence interest rates and economic performance. Ben S. Bernanke became chair of the Fed in 2006. Alan Greenspan had held the position for 18 years before that.

What does the Fed do?

The Fed uses interest rates to influence the economy, raising them to stop inflation and lowering them to encourage growth. As the "bankers' bank," the Fed changes the rate of interest it charges other banks, and influences the growth of the money supply in various ways.

What determines the Fed's decisions?

The Fed is supposed to curb the extremes of the business cycle and help the economy grow. But many critics argue that the Fed is more worried about inflation than employment. They claim that higher interest rates benefit bankers and bond owners more than workers.

How does the Fed influence economic performance?

If the Fed gets worried about inflation, it raises the interest rate that banks pay when they borrow money. This usually pulls up rates throughout the economy. Higher interest rates discourage consumer spending and make long-run investments more costly. The resulting slowdown limits wage and price increases and can help restore profitability. Unfortunately, it also increases unemployment.

9.9 The Cost of Borrowing

BECAUSE INTEREST RATES determine the cost of borrowing, they influence economic performance. But there are many different interest rates, and they don't always do as they are told.

In the 1950s and '60s, interest rates, adjusted for inflation, remained low, supporting strong economic growth. That changed in the 1980s when interest rates soared. Borrowing rates have fallen significantly since then but have not returned to their previous low levels.

A number of factors contributed to the jump. Most importantly, in 1979 the Federal Reserve dramatically raised the rate it charges banks, called the federal funds rate, to combat inflation. The aftermath of this hike was one of the worst economic downturns in decades.

During the 2001 recession, the Fed reduced the federal funds rate to some of the lowest levels in history. However, corporate lending rates have responded slowly. Accounting scandals, uncertain profits, and the bursting of the stock market bubble raised perceptions of risk and helped keep the cost of corporate borrowing relatively high.

SPUD AND BARRY DEUTSCH

The federal funds rate and the cost of corporate borrowing (real yield on corporate Aaa bonds), 1955–2004, adjusted for inflation

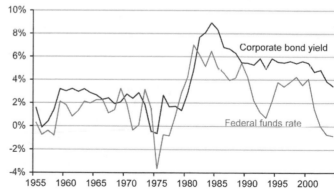

155

9.10 Long Run, Short Run

LIKE MOST PEOPLE, FINANCIERS would love to have a working crystal ball. They spend a lot of time assessing future possibilities. Different perceptions of financial risk cause interest rates to vary, since creditors demand higher returns for riskier loans.

Time is also a factor. Unexpected inflation and the possibility of default affect the value of a loan. Lenders have a better sense of economic trends in the near future than in the long run. Therefore, loans paid back over a long period of time generally have higher interest rates than short-term credit. When financiers get antsy about economic performance in the years to come, the gap between long-run and short-run rates widens.

Long-term and short-term interest rates tend to move together, but they occasionally part ways. The Federal Reserve directly influences short-term rates. If long-term rates are slow to follow, the Fed's policies are less effective.

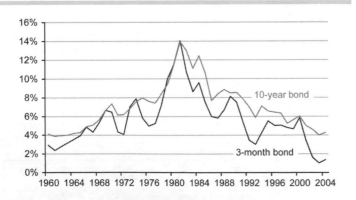

Long-run and short-run interest rates, 1960–2004 (yields on 10-year and 3-month government bonds)

156

9.11 Disappearing Banks

EVER GET THE FEELING THAT BANKS IN YOUR community are vanishing, either changing names or being swallowed up by bigger banks? No, you aren't imagining things. Since 1984, the number of commercial banks has plummeted.

Access to services has not declined. Many of the remaining banks have increased the number of branches they operate. However, as banking becomes more concentrated, competitive pressures get weaker. Banks find it easier to impose new fees or increase old ones without losing customers.

Huge corporate mergers in the financial sector accelerate this concentration of economic clout. In 2003, Bank of America bought FleetBoston for $47 billion, and in 2005, it snatched up credit card giant MBNA for $35 billion. Bank of America had already become the nation's largest depository bank in 1998 when it acquired NationsBank for $57 billion.

Number of commercial banks, 1950–2003

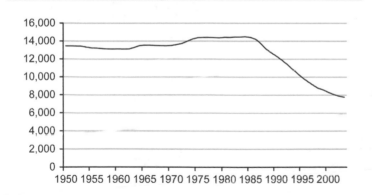

R. JAY MAGILL

9.12 **Deeper in Debt**

I F SLOW-GROWING WAGES HAVE got you down, maybe the credit card offers in your junk mail can cheer you up. Credit card companies are always looking for new customers, and people are borrowing more and more.

In 1950, the total debt of households amounted to about a third of their income. By 2004, it had risen to over 100%.

Some people borrow excessively just in order to keep up with the Joneses. Others land in debt as a result of an unexpected illness or job loss. Large debts squeeze household resources. A sudden setback such as unemployment can lead to default and loss of a car or a home.

Things aren't getting any easier. The 2005 bankruptcy reform bill, backed by banks and the credit card industry, makes it harder for ordinary Americans to keep their heads above water after experiencing a personal calamity.

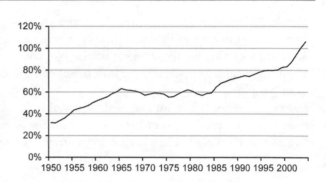

Household debt as a percent of personal income, 1950–2004

BOB THE ANGRY FLOWER BY STEPHEN NOTLEY

9.13 Housing Bubble?

INFLATION IS USUALLY DEFINED IN TERMS OF THE PRICE OF A BASKET OF consumer goods and services. But changes in the prices of assets people own also affect their standard of living.

In recent years, housing prices have skyrocketed. From 2000 to 2004, national housing prices grew at three times the rate of consumer prices. For many cities, the growth differential has been more extreme. Over this period, housing prices grew at an average annual rate of over 13% in the Washington, D.C., area and over 15% in Los Angeles.

Higher prices benefit those who already own houses. As wealth grows, at least on paper, some wealth holders consume more and save less. Others accumulate new assets. In 2004, second homes accounted for one-third of all housing sales.

Those without existing assets have a harder time. When prices are high, many first-time home buyers can't get their foot in the door. Often those who do buy homes struggle with mortgage payments. Recently, foreclosure rates have risen in most states across the country.

Average annual inflation rates for housing and consumer prices

□ Housing price index
■ CPI-U

	1990-1994	1995-1999	2000-2004
Housing price index	1.9%	4.0%	7.9%
CPI-U	3.6%	2.4%	2.5%

FOR SALE $385,000

HOUSING PRICES IN THE COUNTRY REALLY ARE GETTING OUT OF CONTROL...

BRIAN FAIRRINGTON, CAGLE CARTOONS

9.14 NASDAQ Boom and Bust

IN THE 1990s, THE SPECULATIVE FRENZY AROUND high-tech and telecom companies lifted stock prices into the stratosphere. Poor performance and unfulfilled hopes knocked them back to earth. The rise and fall of the dot-com bubble is best captured by the NASDAQ Composite Index, an indicator of price trends for more than 5,000 different stocks. Other stock price indices, such as the Dow Jones Industrial Average, include fewer companies.

NASDAQ (the National Association of Securities Dealers Automated Quotation system) represents a new breed of stock exchange. In contrast with staid old institutions like the New York Stock Exchange, NASDAQ forgoes the formality of a trading floor. Instead, trades happen electronically, in cyberspace.

The growth of electronic trading has certain advantages for dealers. Increased competition and improvements in efficiency have lowered the costs of buying and selling shares. However, huge volumes of electronic trades can contribute to financial instability.

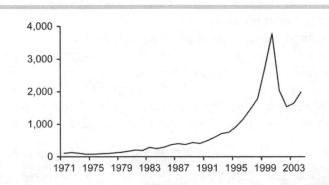

NASDAQ Composite Index, 1971–2004

TOM TOMORROW

9.15 **Unbalanced Trade**

AMERICA IS IMPORT-CRAZY. EVERY YEAR SINCE 1975, the U.S. has run a trade deficit, importing more from other countries than it exports. The trade balance, the gap between imports and exports, has reached alarming levels in recent years.

In 2004, nearly 70 percent of the deficit came from trade with developing countries in Latin America, the Caribbean, Africa, and Asia. American businesses and consumers benefit from the cheaper consumer goods that low-wage workers produce. But most people in these countries are too poor to buy many U.S. products.

Does the trade deficit really matter? By consuming more of the world's goods and services than we make, we are living beyond our means, and it's not clear what the costs might be if these debts come due.

Balance of trade (exports less imports) as a percentage of GDP, 1960–2004

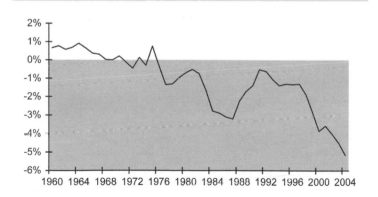

SPUD AND BARRY DEUTSCH

9.16 **The Value of the Dollar**

PRICES OF GOODS AND SERVICES FROM OTHER countries are often expressed in the local currency. The purchasing power of a U.S. dollar depends on its value relative to other currencies. How many euros or yen can a dollar buy?

The U.S. exchange rate is the price of the dollar relative to other currencies. The Federal Reserve uses an index to track shifts in the dollar exchange rate relative to other major currencies. A higher index value means a stronger dollar. The exchange rate increased sharply in the 1980s when high inter-est rates attracted financial investors and kept the dollar strong. The stock market boom of the 1990s also encouraged money to flow in and raised the dollar's value.

An increase, or appreciation, of the exchange rate makes imports cheaper for Americans. But U.S. exports become harder to sell. In the 1990s, inexpensive imports from abroad helped keep inflation down. The trade deficit, the difference between imports and exports, grew to record levels. This situation can't go on unless the dollar loses value or other countries continue to pour their money into the American economy.

ARCADIO ESQUIVEL (BEST OF LATIN AMERICA, CAGLE CARTOONS, LA PRENSA, PANAMA)

Index of the real value of the dollar relative to the currencies of major trading partners, 1973–2004

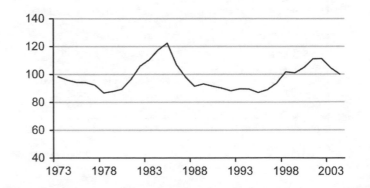

CHAPTER 10: **The Global Economy**

THE GLOBAL ECONOMY ENCOMPASSES A LAND-scape of extremes. Billions of dollars change hands on currency markets 24/7 while hundreds of millions of people scrape by on less than a single dollar each day. The terrain is unstable. Today's stock market booms create overnight millionaires and tomorrow's financial crises push thousands into poverty.

It's a high-stakes arena in which many countries try to please investors rather than meet the needs of their citizens. This chapter looks at developments in the world economy, including trends in trade, migration, finance, and indicators of human well-being.

Chart 10.1 shows that the engine of global growth has slowed down in recent years, constraining progress in many regions. But growth alone is not enough to improve well-being. As Chart 10.2 illustrates, some relatively well-off countries actually have higher infant mortality rates than poorer but more egalitarian regimes.

About 1.1 billion people, a significant fraction of the world's population, survive on less than the equivalent of a dollar per day. Using the dollar-a-day poverty line, Chart 10.3 documents poverty rates for representative countries around the world. Differences in standards of living in poor and rich countries are enormous, as Chart 10.4 points out. The richest 20% of countries consume 50 times more marketed goods and services than the poorest 20%.

International migration has increased in recent years, with the bulk of movement from poor countries to rich ones, as described in Chart 10.5. Such migration imposes costs on poorer countries, which lose high-skilled workers and professionals. Chart 10.6 examines some of the costs of the global brain drain.

RUSSELL CHRISTIAN

People frequently move in search of better employment opportunities. As Chart 10.7 shows, unemployment has been increasing the world over. With more people than jobs, multinational companies can often find bargains in the form of cheap labor. But low-wage competitors don't always have the edge over high-income countries. Chart 10.8 shows that the U.S. still imports a large share of its goods from high-wage regions, such as the European Union and Japan.

Once upon a time, most developing countries specialized in exporting agricultural products and raw materials. Times have changed and manufacturing has spread. Chart 10.9

reveals that manufactured goods account for similar fractions of exports in both high-income and developing countries. Some of this new economic activity comes from outsourcing, in which U.S. companies subcontract out a portion of their business activities, displayed in Chart 10.10.

The current global trading system has built-in inequalities that tilt the balance in favor of wealthier nations. Chart 10.11 describes one of the policy areas contributing to this unevenness: trade-related aspects of intellectual property rights (TRIPS) provisions. Other policies distort the playing field further and have led to the collapse of high-level trade talks, as Chart 10.12 explains.

Charts 10.13 and 10.14 look at international flows of capital. Firms expand abroad for many reasons: cheap wages, lower taxes, less regulation, and bigger markets. Foreign direct investment, or FDI, provides funds to finance job-creating activities and boost economic growth. However, most FDI goes to rich, industrialized countries.

Developing countries often attract short-term financial investment instead of long-run productive investments. The rapid movement of short-term funds can destabilize entire regions and trigger disastrous financial crises. Chart 10.15 presents trends in the movement of short-term investment, or "hot money." Some of the options countries have to protect themselves from speculators are described in Chart 10.16.

Huge external debts have crippled the economies of many poor countries, making it hard for them to move forward. Chart 10.17 traces the history of the debt buildup in the developing world. The affluent nations of the world aren't as generous as they used to be with overseas development assistance, as Chart 10.18 points out. More help is needed.

10.1 Global Slowdown

THE WHEELS OF THE WORLD ECONOMY aren't spinning as fast as they used to. In the 1960s, world gross domestic product (GDP) grew at over 5% per year; between 1991 and 2002 the average slipped to just 2.8%.

Average growth in the large industrialized economies has slowed, pulling global performance down. Economies in sub-Saharan Africa and many parts of Latin America have also lagged behind. Eastern Europe and Central Asia had a rough time after the collapse of the Soviet Union in the early 1990s, but in many of these countries economic performance has recently improved.

Asia produced most of the economic superstars over the past two decades, with many countries growing 2 to 3 times faster than the world average. India and China currently carry the banner for fast economic growth. However, the devastating East Asian financial crisis of 1997–1998, which pushed much of the region into recession, reminds us that fast-growing economies can spin out of control.

R. JAY MAGILL

Average growth rate of world GDP, 1961–2002

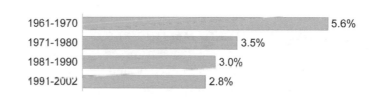

1961-1970	5.6%
1971-1980	3.5%
1981-1990	3.0%
1991-2002	2.8%

Does Economic Growth Deliver?

Infant mortality vs. GDP per capita in 2002

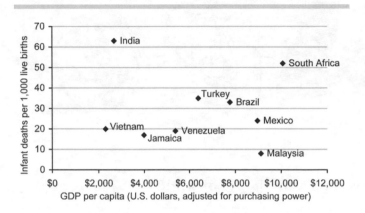

Infant deaths per 1,000 live births vs. GDP per capita (U.S. dollars, adjusted for purchasing power)

AMPERSAND BY B. DEUTSCH

WHEN IT COMES TO MEETING BASIC NEEDS, higher per capita GDP doesn't necessarily do the job. The distribution of income and the provision of public services have a more direct impact.

Vietnam, with less than one-fourth of the GDP per capita of South Africa, outranks that country in terms of human development indicators such as infant mortality rate, adult literacy, and life expectancy. Mexico's infant mortality rate is three times that of Malaysia's, but both countries have nearly identical per capita GDPs.

When the benefits of economic expansion are broadly shared, basic indicators of human well-being tend to improve with growth. If the distribution of income becomes more unequal or public services fail to improve, signs of meaningful progress are harder to find.

10.3 World Poverty

AT THE UNITED NATIONS MILLENNIUM SUMMIT in 2000, member countries pledged to bring down the percentage of people living on less than the equivalent of $1 a day to 14% by 2015. It's an ambitious goal. Currently, an estimated 21% of the world's population (1.1 billion people) live below this global poverty line.

The poverty rates of countries in sub-Saharan Africa are among the highest in the world, but enormous numbers of extremely poor families live in populous countries like China, India, and Brazil. Despite strong economic growth in recent years, 35% of the population in India and 17% in China live below the dollar-a-day threshold.

The level of development only partly explains differences in poverty rates. The distribution of resources also matters. Poverty rates are five times higher in Mexico than in Costa Rica even though average incomes are comparable. Less income inequality and more generous social policies in Costa Rica help account for the difference.

SERGIO LANGER (BEST OF LATIN AMERICA, CAGLE CARTOONS, FI CLARIN, ARGENTINA)

Percentage of population living on less than $1 a day

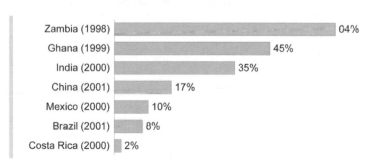

Zambia (1998)	64%
Ghana (1999)	45%
India (2000)	35%
China (2001)	17%
Mexico (2000)	10%
Brazil (2001)	8%
Costa Rica (2000)	2%

10.4 **The Consumption Gap**

GLOBAL INEQUALITY IN STANDARDS OF LIVING FAR surpasses the disparity within any individual nation. The richest fifth of all countries accounts for 58% of worldwide consumption of goods and services sold in the market, while the poorest fifth barely gets 1%.

The world economy has become more polarized. In the ten years from 1993 to 2002, per capita consumption in the U.S. grew at an average yearly rate of 2.6%, compared to a world average of 2.2%. In contrast, consumption per person in Latin America and the Caribbean grew at just 1%. Sub-Saharan Africa lagged behind at 0.4%.

Some developing countries are catching up to the richest nations while others are left behind. Between 1993 and 2002, consumption per capita grew at an average rate of 5.2% in East Asian countries and 4.7% in South Asia. Narrowing the gap by creating new consumer economies has its downside. The world's affluent consumers place pressures on the environment and the earth's resources.

SERGIO LANGER (BEST OF LATIN AMERICA, CAGLE CARTOONS, EL CLARIN, ARGENTINA)

World consumption

expenditures in 2002

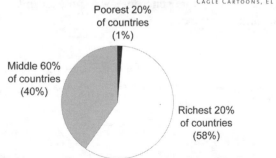

Poorest 20% of countries (1%)

Middle 60% of countries (40%)

Richest 20% of countries (58%)

10.5 Cross-Border Migration

AROUND THE GLOBE, PEOPLE ARE ON THE MOVE. In 2000, an estimated 175 million individuals worldwide were living outside of their country of birth. About 158 million of these were international migrants, 16 million were refugees, and 0.9 million were asylum seekers.

People generally flow from poor countries to rich ones. In 2000, international migrants constituted 9% of the population in developed countries, up from 3% in 1960. For less developed regions, migrants made up only 1% of the population in 2000, down from 2% in 1960.

Most migrants contribute to their host country's economy by working for pay. Overseas jobs generate sizeable flows of money back into poorer countries. In 2002, developing countries received a total of $79 billion in annual remittances.

International migrants as a percentage of total population

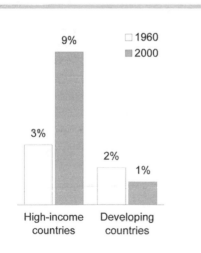

- 1960
- 2000

9%

3%

2%

1%

High-income countries

Developing countries

SORRY FOLKS.. IT READS A LITTLE DIFFERENTLY FOR YOU...

THEY LEFT OUT THE PART THAT READS "AND THEN GO BACK"..

MIGRANT WORKERS

GIVE ME YOUR TIRED, YOUR POOR, YOUR HUDDLED MASSES YEARNING TO WORK FOR NEARLY FREE

JEFF PARKER, FLORIDA TODAY

10.6 **Brain Drain**

INTERNATIONAL MIGRANTS FROM DEVELOPING countries are often skilled workers, trained and educated in their home countries. When they leave home, the costs are significant.

* A recent study of immigrants who moved to high-income countries found that they had 7.2 more years of education, on average, than was typical back in their home countries.

* According to recent estimates, each professional emigrating from Africa represents a loss of investment in training and education valued at $184,000. This is over 300 times the average GDP per capita in sub-Saharan Africa.

* Emigration of skilled workers generates indirect costs. For example, the migration of skilled Indian workers to the U.S. has meant an estimated loss of 12 percent of the revenue that India could otherwise expect from its personal income tax system.

* High-income countries like Canada, Australia, and the U.S. have developed systems to attract skilled immigrants from poorer countries because of the benefits these workers bring with them.

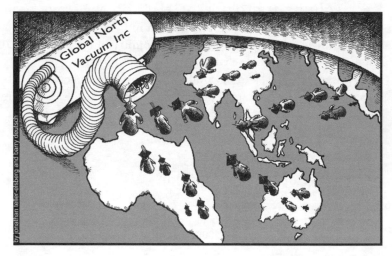

SPUD AND BARRY DEUTSCH

10.7 **Global Unemployment**

APPROXIMATELY 186 MILLION PEOPLE WERE JOBLESS WORLDWIDE IN 2003, the highest level of unemployment ever recorded by the International Labor Organization. This represents a 34% increase from 1993, when 141 million people were unemployed. The world's population grew by 14% over this same period. If these trends keep up, an increasing number of people will lack paid employment and the differences between the haves and have-nots will intensify.

Unemployment figures understate the extent of the problem. In many countries around the world, an increasing number of people are employed in precarious jobs and informal activities, with unstable earnings, few protections, and no guarantees for the future.

By itself, access to employment won't keep people out of poverty. An estimated 550 million people worldwide are employed but still live in households surviving on less than a dollar a day per person.

SPUD AND BARRY DEUTSCH

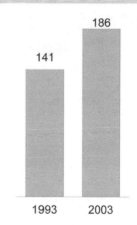

Global unemployment in 1993 and 2003 (millions of people)

1993	2003
141	186

Cheap Labor and Imports

DOES OUR OBSESSION WITH EVERYDAY LOW PRICES push employers to move production to low-wage countries? Maybe, but many high-wage countries successfully compete in global markets.

Many retailers purchase their inventory from factories located in countries with rock-bottom wages. But the U.S. currently gets over half its imports of manufactured goods from Canada, the European Union, and Japan. In fact, the average hourly wage for manufacturing workers in these countries was $18.29 in 2002, not much lower than in the U.S.

High levels of education, good public infrastructure, and productivity improvements can be more important than wages in decisions about locating a factory. As developing countries begin providing these amenities, they will make greater inroads into the world market.

MATT WUERKER

Hourly compensation costs for manufacturing workers in the U.S. and major trading partners in 2002

China	$0.62
Mexico	$2.60
Korea	$9.00
Canada	$16.68
Japan	$18.49
European Union	$19.80
U.S.	$21.11

10.9 Trade Transformation

THE BANANA REPUBLICS OF the past are fast becoming the manufacturers of the future. For years, developing countries depended on exporting raw materials and unprocessed commodities to rich countries. Today, manufactured goods from many of these countries are flodding world markets.

In 1980, manufactured goods accounted for only 19% of total merchandise exports from developing countries. By 2001, manufacturing constituted 65% of the total, approaching the same proportion as in industrialized countries.

Rapid growth in manufacturing in developing nations creates much-needed jobs, but it also unleashes more competition. Pressures mount to keep wages low, to limit worker protections, and to avoid environmental regulations. Countries can end up running a "race to the bottom" in which many of the gains from export growth simply vanish.

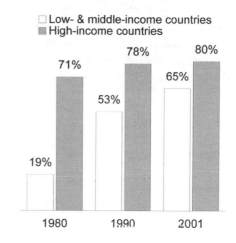

Manufacturing exports as a percentage of total exports, 1980–2001

☐ Low- & middle-income countries
■ High-income countries

1980: 19%, 71%
1990: 53%, 78%
2001: 65%, 80%

R. JAY MAGILI

10.10 Outsourcing

MOST AMERICANS HAVE FIRSTHAND KNOWLEDGE of outsourcing. The worker at the other end of a customer service call often is speaking from Bangalore or Delhi instead of Birmingham or Detroit. Outsourcing has been grabbing headlines as U.S. companies subcontract out an increasing share of their business activity.

A recent study estimates that approximately 406,000 U.S. jobs shifted abroad in 2004, up from 204,000 in 2001. The three most important destination countries have been China, Mexico, and India. Labor costs are significantly lower in these countries than in the U.S.

Outsourcing frequently means new job opportunities for workers in poor countries lucky enough to get them. However, the same competitive pressures that cause jobs to relocate also keep wages low and workdays long. Many of the benefits of outsourcing are captured elsewhere—as lower prices for U.S. consumers or higher profits for American firms.

STEPHANIE McMILLAN, MINIMUMSECURITY.NET

Number of jobs shifted out of the U.S. in 2001 and 2004

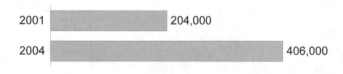

10.11 Tripped Up

KNOWLEDGE IS POWER AND CORPORATIONS ARE eager to control the world's intellectual property in the form of copyrights, trademarks, brand names, and patents. The trade-related aspects of intellectual property rights (TRIPS) agreements of the World Trade Organization (WTO) aim to safeguard intellectual property in the global economy.

Rich countries own the bulk of the world's intellectual property rights. Since patented products and brand-name goods cost more than generic merchandise, poorer nations often operate at a disadvantage in world trade.

Protections for intellectual property may be essential to reward innovation, but some patent applications border on theft. For example, multinationals have patented genetic material from crops that indigenous communities have maintained for centuries.

Intellectual property rights can be a matter of life or death. Many developing countries cannot afford to purchase patented drugs to treat devastating diseases such as HIV/AIDS.

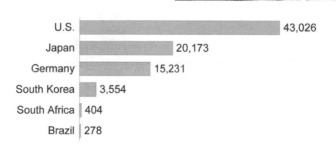

STEPHANIE MCMILLAN,
MINIMUMSECURITY.NET

Number of international patent applications filed in 2004 (under the Patent Cooperation Treaty)

U.S.	43,026
Japan	20,173
Germany	15,231
South Korea	3,554
South Africa	404
Brazil	278

10.12 Cancún Collapse

RECENT HIGH-LEVEL MEETINGS OF THE WORLD Trade Organization (WTO) have dramatized dissent over global trade policies. In 1999, protestors nearly shut down its ministerial meeting in Seattle. In 2003, representatives from developing countries pulled out of negotiations in Cancún. At stake are a number of existing and proposed policies that favor corporations and rich countries.

AGRICULTURAL SUBSIDIES. High-income countries legally subsidize agricultural production in ways that give them an advantage in world markets, hurting poorer nations. For instance, the U.S. gives its cotton farmers a $3.9 billion boost each year, shutting many small-scale producers in regions like West Africa out of the American market.

TRADE-RELATED INVESTMENT MEASURES (TRIMs). These measures could force governments to treat all investors equally, from large multinationals to local producers. Some proposed measures would outlaw policies that encourage specific types of investment and help achieve development targets.

GOVERNMENT PROCUREMENT RULES. Developing countries fear that new rules would prohibit governments from favoring certain companies, including local firms and socially responsible businesses, when awarding contracts. Supporters of the proposed changes consider such preferences unfair to international corporations.

DARRIN DRDA

176

10.13 **Have Profits, Will Travel**

FOR DECADES, U.S. CORPORATIONS HAVE BEEN scouting the earth in search of profit opportunities. They've been very successful. In 1950, foreign profits made up only 3% of all before-tax profits. In 2003, 20% of U.S. corporate profits came from overseas.

Expanding international operations may help businesses stay competitive, but it also makes them footloose. Further downsizing at home and outsourcing abroad could put American communities at risk of losing their economic base.

Companies can use their international status to reduce taxes and dodge regulations. By manipulating the prices one corporate division charges another, they can lower their reported profits and avoid paying taxes. The loss of those tax revenues makes it harder for the government to improve the public infrastructure and education that contributes to U.S. competitiveness.

Foreign profits of U.S. corporations as a percentage of all before-tax profits, 1950–2003

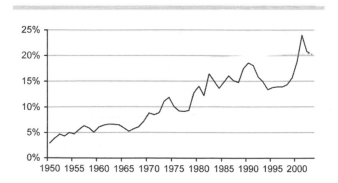

ANDY SINGER

177

IN THEORY, THE SEARCH FOR HIGHER PROFITS should propel investment to poor countries where capital is scarce. In reality, the opposite happens. Rich countries attract most of the foreign investment.

To qualify as foreign direct investment, or FDI, the investor must own at least 10% of the value of a business. Unlike shorter-term capital flows, FDI usually comes with a willingness to set up shop in another country. For developing countries receiving investments, it can mean more stable sources of finance and less borrowing.

High-income countries attract nearly three-quarters of all FDI inflows thanks to affluent consumers, well-educated workers, and quality infrastructure. Developing countries often compete for FDI by cutting government spending and promising lower wages, strategies that undermine the benefits FDI is supposed to deliver.

"The last step says to dismantle the whole thing and ship all the jobs overseas."

Distribution of foreign direct investment inflows, 2000–2003

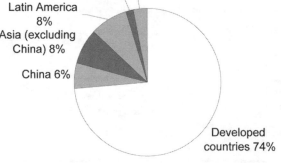

Eastern Europe 3%

Africa 2%

Latin America 8%

Asia (excluding China) 8%

China 6%

Developed countries 74%

10.15 **Hot Money**

"HERE TODAY, GONE TOMORROW" WOULD MAKE a good slogan for today's financial investors. Since the 1990s, the amount of short-term money flowing into and out of developing countries has grown enormously. When financiers take flight, they often leave behind a mess: failed banks, currency crises, and depressed economies.

Such short-term investments in stocks and bonds are called portfolio investments, or "hot money." A buildup of portfolio investments spells trouble. A sudden reversal can throw an entire country or region into chaos.

Not surprisingly, over the past 10 to 15 years financial crises have plagued many countries, including Mexico, East Asia, Russia, Brazil, Turkey, and Argentina. These crises pushed millions of people into poverty. Without more attention directed at monitoring and managing short-term flows, the risk of future crises remains high.

R. JAY MAGILL

Net portfolio investment, low- and middle-income countries, 1970–2002 (in $ billions)

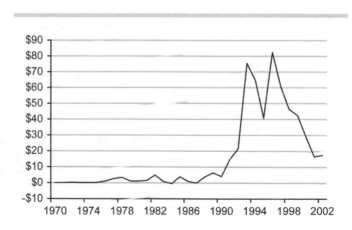

10.16 **Managing Capital**

A NUMBER OF POLICIES CAN BE USED TO REGU-late volatile capital flows and minimize the damage they cause.

Speed bumps slow down short-term money flows into or out of an economy. For example, foreign investors could be required to deposit a fraction of their money in an interest-free account for a fixed period of time before being allowed to move the cash back out of the country.

Trip wires would automatically introduce controls on capital flows whenever a country's risk of financial crisis entered a danger zone. For example, restrictions on capital flows could be activated if the available supply of foreign currency needed to meet payments to other countries fell too low.

The **Tobin tax**, named after economist James Tobin, would place a small tax on buying or selling currencies. The idea is to discourage speculative investors who make large numbers of trades over a short period of time.

A **securities transaction tax** is similar to the Tobin tax, except it taxes the sale of stocks and bonds. In addition to dampening speculative investment, a securities transaction tax would generate additional government revenue that could be used for education, health care, or basic infrastructure.

10.17 The Debt Trap

IT'S HARD FOR A COUNTRY TO MAKE PROGRESS WHEN large interest payments drain its resources. The overseas debts of many developing countries grew to record levels in the 1970s and 1980s. Current repayments to high-income creditors limit the ability of governments to invest in infrastructure, improve health care, or raise the level of education.

During the debt buildup, lenders continued to supply credit even when they knew that the loans were often misused. In many cases, the cash enriched political elites, funded projects with few social benefits, or simply left the country again. The benefits, if any, were fleeting, but the burden of debt has remained.

Recently, the World Bank, the International Monetary Fund, and lenders from affluent countries have agreed to provide some relief by reducing required payments or even canceling existing obligations. Such help is available only to those poor countries that lenders consider worthy. Many others remain trapped under mountains of debt.

Total external debt as a percentage of GDP, 1970–2002

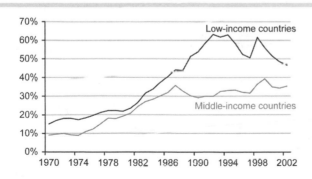

Stephanie McMillan, minimumsecurity.net

181

10.18 Global Assistance

WHEN IT COMES TO HELPING OUT THEIR poorer neighbors, affluent countries have become less generous. The average amount that high-income countries contributed to overseas development assistance fell from $77 per capita in 1990 to $69 in 2002 (2004 dollars). Some countries have increased their spending, but not by enough to keep the average from falling.

Countries vary in the amount they are willing to give. In 2002, the U.S. provided an average of $49 per person in foreign aid. Norway supplied $355.

Funds don't always go where they are most needed. Badly designed projects can generate unintended consequences, driving out domestic producers or funding imported goods. Overseas assistance alone won't solve the problem of uneven development and global poverty. But more help from the world's richest nations can make a difference.

Development assistance per person in donor country (in $2004)

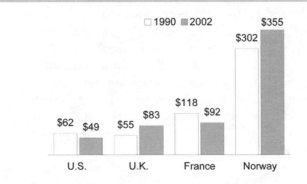

□ 1990 ■ 2002

	U.S.	U.K.	France	Norway
1990	$62	$55	$118	$302
2002	$49	$83	$92	$355

STEPHANIE McMILLAN, MINIMUMSECURITY.NET

182

Toolkit

T.1 A Guide to General Sources

This section provides a guide to sources of data and analysis that are useful in economic research. It begins with an overview of general sources, then provides further information for each chapter topic. Use the detailed references in the Sources and Notes section of this book to track down or update specific facts and figures.

The Internet has made a wealth of economic information more accessible than ever. This section includes addresses for a number of the most useful sites providing the type of economic information presented in the pages of this book. In many cases, statistics and entire publications will be available online. In other cases, the websites only provide ordering information.

* The two best sources of general economic data are the *Statistical Abstract of the United States,* http://www. census.gov/statab/www, published by the U.S. Bureau of the Census, http://www.census.gov, and the *Economic Report of the President,* http://www.gpoaccess.gov/eop, published by the President's Council of Economic Advisors. Both can be downloaded from the Web. New editions of the *Economic Report of the President* usually become available in February from the Government Printing Office, http://www.gpoaccess.gov.

* FedStats, http://www.fedstats.gov, is an extremely useful Web site with links to a large number of federal agencies and departments. Also see the Department of Commerce site, Stat-USA, http://www.stat-usa.gov.

* Short, interesting, and useful articles about current economic events are published bimonthly in *Dollars & Sense* magazine, 29 Winter Street, Boston, MA 02108, http://www.dollarsandsense.org. More academic yet still accessible articles are published bimonthly in *Challenge: The Magazine of Economic Affairs,* M. E. Sharpe, Inc., 80 Business Park Drive, Armonk, NY 10504, http://www.mesharpe.com/mall/results1.asp? ACRCHA.

* The major publications of the business press, including the *Wall Street Journal, Fortune, Forbes,* and *Barron's,* are all useful, but *BusinessWeek,* http://www.businessweek .com, usually offers the most systematic analysis of economic trends. For a distinctly anticorporate approach, see *The Left Business Observer,* 38 Greene Street, 4th floor, New York, NY 10013, http://www.leftbusiness observer.com.

* For more in-depth reading, *The State of Working America 2004/5,* produced by the Economic Policy Institute,

offers a comprehensive analysis of the way economic trends affect working Americans. 1660 L Street NW, Suite 1200, Washington, DC 20036, http://www.epinet.org, 202-775-8810.

* The National Priorities Project provides helpful information and analysis on the government's budget priorities. 17 New South Street, Northampton, MA 01060, http://www.nationalpriorities.org, 413-584-9556.

* United for a Fair Economy has developed a range of publications, educational materials, and workshops that focus on wealth and income distribution. 29 Winter Street, 2nd Floor, Boston, MA 02108, http://www.faireconomy.org, 617-423-2148.

* The Center for Popular Economics provides workshops on economic literacy and international economics. Contact us at PO Box 785, Amherst, MA 01004, http://www.populareconomics.org, 413-545-0743.

Chapter 1: Owners

Every year, usually in September, *Forbes* magazine publishes a feature article describing the richest 400 people in the U.S., http://www.forbes.com/400richest. In late spring or early summer, *Fortune* ranks the top industrial corporations of the year and provides considerable information about their performance. In April or May, *Business Week* usually publishes a list of the highest-paid corporate executives.

For an abundance of information on money in politics and its effects on electoral outcomes, contact the Center for Responsive Politics, 1101 14th Street NW, Suite 1030, Washington DC 20005, http://www.opensecrets.org, 202-857-0044.

Chapter 2: Workers

The Bureau of Labor Statistics (BLS), http://www.bls.gov, provides a wealth of information on employment, wages, occupations, and prices, among other topics. The bureau also publishes the *Monthly Labor Review,* http://www.bls.gov/opub/mlr/mlrhome.htm, which often includes articles on special topics such as displaced workers. The American Federation of Labor (AFL-CIO) also maintains a useful Web site at http://www.aflcio.org.

Chapter 3: Women

The Bureau of the Census periodically publishes special reports on women. A recent compendium based on the 2000 census is entitled *We the People: Women and Men in the United States,* available at http://www.census.gov/prod/2005pubs/censr-20.pdf. A useful source for political and economic analysis is the Institute for Women's Policy Research, 1400 20th St. NW, Suite 104, Washington, DC 20036, http://www.iwpr.org, 202-785-5100. For more scholarly research and networking information, see the International Association for Feminist Economics (IAFFE) Web site, http://www.iaffe.org. The United Nations recently released a compendium of statistical information on women around the world, at http://unstats.un.org/unsd/demographic/products/indwm/. For a recent report on global gender issues, see the United Nations Research Institute for Social Development (UNRISD) report *Gender Equality: Striving for Justice in an Unequal World,* at http://www.unrisd.org. Columbia University maintains an excellent clearinghouse of information on international family policies at http://www.childpolicyintl.org/policies.html.

CHAPTER 4: PEOPLE OF COLOR

For a good overview of issues facing African Americans see *African Americans in the U.S. Economy,* edited by James Steart, Patrick Mason, John Whitehead and Cecilia Conrad (Rowman and Littlefield, 2005). The Bureau of the Census maintains a special Web page with citations to publications on race at http://www.census.gov/population/www/socdemo/race.html. A recent summary Census report is *We the People: Blacks in the U.S.,* http://www.census.gov/prod/2005pubs/censr-25.pdf. For a good discussion of race issues in a global context, see the United Nations Research Institute for Social Development (UNRISD) report *Racism and Public Policy* at http://www.unrisd.org.

CHAPTER 5: GOVERNMENT

Every January, the president proposes a budget for the next fiscal year to Congress, detailed in *The Budget of the U.S. Government* and summarized in *The Budget in Brief.* The best source for historical data on revenue and taxation is *The U.S. Budget, Historical Tables.* Look at the Office of Management and Budget Web site, http://www.whitehouse.gov/omb, for easy access to many of these publications. They are also available through the Government Printing Office, http://www.gpoaccess.gov/usbudget/index.html.

The Center on Budget and Policy Priorities publishes regular reports on government spending, particularly as it affects low-income Americans. 820 1st Street NE, Suite 510, Washington DC 20002, http://www.cbpp.org, 202-408-1080. Citizens for Tax Justice focuses on tax issues,1311 L Street NW, Washington, DC 20005, http://www.ctj.org, 202-626-3780.

CHAPTER 6: EDUCATION AND WELFARE

In March of every year, the Bureau of the Census, http://www.census.gov, conducts a survey of U.S. families to determine trends in income and poverty. The results are published annually in the *Current Population Reports* (CPR) Series P-60, often under the title *Money Income of Households, Families, and Persons in the United States.* Recently, the Bureau of the Census began to conduct a survey of income and program participation that includes information about who receives public assistance. Some of the results are published in the CPR Series P-70, *Economic Characteristics of Households in the United States*. Expenditures per recipient in social programs such as Temporary Assistance for Needy Families are provided by the Social Security Administration in its annual Statistical Supplement, available at http://www.ssa.gov/policy/docs/statcomps/supplement. Another important source of information on government programs are the publications of the House Ways and Means Committee, especially the *Green Book,* available at http://www.gpoaccess.gov/wmprints/index.html.

The Condition of Education and the *Digest of Educational Statistics,* both published by the National Center for Educational Statistics, http://www.nces.ed.gov, a division of the U.S. Department of Education, http://www.ed.gov, are good primary sources on the state of education. For statistics and articles on higher education, see *The Chronicle of Higher Education*, published on a weekly basis. Information is available online at http://chronicle.com.

CHAPTER 7: HEALTH

Primary sources on the health of Americans are *Health, United States* and *Vital Statistics of the U.S.*, both published annually by the National Center for Health Statistics at the U.S. Centers for Disease Control, http://www.cdc.gov/nchs. Information on health care costs and expenditures can be found in the *Health Care Financing Review*, published by the

Centers for Medicare and Medicaid Services, http://www.cms.hhs.gov/review/default.asp. Additional information is at http://www.cms.hhs.gov/researchers. The Henry J. Kaiser Family Foundation, http://www.kff.org, is another good source for analysis and statistics relating to health care.

CHAPTER 8: ENVIRONMENT

Many different sources are useful here, but a publication that provides an international overview of the state of the environment is *World Resources,* a joint publication of several international organizations. The 2005 edition is available online at http://population.wri.org/worldresources2005-pub-4073.html. One of the contributors is the World Resources Institute, 10 G Street NE, Suite 800, Washington, DC 20002, http://www.wri.org, 202-729-7600. Another contributing organization is the United Nations Environment Programme, http://www.unep.org. The Energy Information Administration, a part of the U.S. Department of Energy, provides data on sources and usage of energy in the U.S. and around the world, http://eia.doe.gov. The U.S. Environmental Protection Agency is also a good source of information, http://www.epa.gov. The Pew Center on Climate Change, http://www.pewclimate.org, is a good source regarding climate change (aka global warming). Environmental groups, like the Natural Resources Defense Council, http://www.nrdc.org, also compile information in an activist context.

Chapter 9: Macroeconomics

The Bureau of Economic Analysis (BEA), a division of the U.S. Department of Commerce, is the best source of current data on the national accounts, such as gross domestic product (GDP), investment, and the trade balance. An online database, http://www.bea.gov, lets you download the information you need. The tables published in the back of *The Economic Report of the President* each year are an excellent source of statistics, http://www.gpoaccess.gov/eop. The Department of Commerce maintains a Web site with current data on many facets of the U.S. economy, http://www.stat-usa.gov. The Board of Governors of the Federal Reserve posts timely information, both data and research reports, on topics such as the banking sector, interest rates, consumer credit, and exchange rates, http://www.federalreserve.gov/rnd/htm. The Financial Markets Center Web site contains a wealth of accessible information on monetary and financial trends and policies, http://www.fmcenter.org. Data on inflation can be found at the Bureau of Labor Statistics, http://www.bls.gov.

Cross-national macroeconomic data for high-income countries can be found in the *Main Economic Indicators*, published by the Organization for Economic Cooperation and Development, http://www.oecd.org. Databases with worldwide coverage include *International Financial Statistics*, published by the International Monetary Fund, http://www.imf.org, and *World Development Indicators*, published by the World Bank, http://www.worldbank.org.

Chapter 10: The Global Economy

A wide range of statistics on economic performance and socioeconomic indicators for countries around the world can be found in the *World Development Indicators* database, published each year by the World Bank, http://www.worldbank.org. The World Bank also publishes *Global Development Finance,* which contains detailed country-by-country information on debt. The International Labor Organization, http://www.ilo.org, collects information on the global employment situation. Three useful publications from the ILO are the *World Employment Report, Global Employment Trends,* and *Yearbook of Labor Statistics.*

For a different approach that emphasizes human needs and potential, see the *Human Development Report,* published each year by the United Nations Development Programme, http://www.undp.org. The United Nations Conference on Trade and Development (UNCTAD), http://www.unctad.org, makes statistics on global trade available on its Web site. The United Nations, http://www.un.org, publishes the annual *World Economic and Social Survey,* http://www.un.org/esa/policy/wess, which analyzes thematic challenges facing the world economy. Every two years the UN also publishes the *Report on the World Social Situation,* http://www.un.org/esa/socdev/rwss/ rwss/htm, which covers emerging trends of global concern.

T.2 How to Read and Write Graphs

Despite the fact that we are bombarded daily by graphs and graphics, it's easy to be intimidated, confused, or misled by them. The best way to learn to read graphs is to make a few. Once you have a sense of how to make them by hand, experiment with computer software. Here are some basic guidelines for reading graphs.

1. *Understand the title.* Chart titles often sound very technical, and that is because the people producing them want to be sure that readers understand what information the chart is presenting. Small differences in a title can mean large differences in what the chart shows. For example, a chart showing poverty rates among all Americans will be quite different from a chart showing the poverty rate only among Americans below the age of 65, because Social Security protects many elderly from poverty.

Also make sure you understand the technical shorthand included in many charts—things like "($2004)" or "($U.S.)" or "($ billions)." The first of those indicates that all dollar amounts in the chart have been adjusted for inflation and are being presented in their equivalent value as of the year 2004. The second of those indicates that all the money values in the chart have been converted to U.S. dollars. The third example indicates that dollar values in the chart are presented without all their zeros and should be multiplied by 1,000,000,000 to represent their full size.

2. *Figure out what the variables are.* A graph usually displays a relationship between the values of two or more variables. In bar and line graphs, the value of one variable is usually represented on a horizontal axis that starts at zero and increases to the right. The values of the other variable are represented on a vertical axis that usually starts at zero and increases upward. For instance, look at Chart 2.3. Along the horizontal axis, time increases from 1950 to 2004 (not all years are labeled). Dollar values are shown along the vertical axis. In this case, the values shown don't start at $0, but range from $2 up to $10.

Note that sometimes one of the axes is not shown explicitly. Chart 1.11 is an example. While the years are seen along the horizontal axis, ranging from 1983 to 2004, the vertical axis is not numbered. You are still able to see the values measured vertically by looking at the height of the line at each point and reading the numbers in the label alongside that point.

Pie charts picture the relationship between a whole and its parts, as in Chart 1.2. The pie as a whole represents $20 trillion. Each portion of it represents a fraction of that whole, and is labeled accordingly.

Column and bar charts follow a similar logic. Chart 2.10 shows columns that are displaying information similarly to a line graph (just imagine that instead of the gray columns, you saw a line that touched the top of each column as it moved from left to right). Chart 1.9 has three columns, each of which functions like a different pie. The column on the right-hand side, labeled "Single-issue and other," represents a total value of $857 million. Each section of the column is color-coded to indicate the source of a fraction of the total. However, a stacked column does not always have to add up to 100% of the values being measured (while a pie should). The right-hand column in Chart 5.3 is an example.

Finally, a scatterplot shows a number of dots spread out against vertical and horizontal axes, for example in Chart 1.8. Here, each dot represents two values that exist at the same time. One value is the murder rate in a U.S. state or Canadian province (measured along the horizontal axis). The other value is a numerical measure of income inequality in that state or province (measured along the vertical axis). By looking at the way the dots are arranged, you can see if there appears to be a meaningful pattern. But be careful when judging scatterplots (and all graphs)—patterns that seem obvious may be the result of coincidence. Also, sometimes the most interesting thing about a chart is that there is no pattern perceivable when you might have expected one. Chart 10.2 is an example.

3. Look at the range of values of the variables.

Sometimes they start not at zero but at a higher value, as in Chart 2.3. Often, they are multiples of the numbers indicated, such as thousands or millions. The scale of measurement used largely determines the visual impact of a graph. Also, be sure you understand the units being used. Numbers may represent dollar amounts or physical amounts like gallons of a fluid. One more complicated example is Chart 7.8, where the vertical axis is showing a ratio scale. The ratio shows the infant mortality rate being charted, as compared to an uncharted value, which has a constant value of 1 across the entire chart. In other words, each point on the African American line represents an infant mortality rate that is a multiple of the white infant mortality rate from the same year. Although the white rate does change from year to year, it is transformed into a value of 1. After the same transformation is applied to the black rate, you can see how much higher the black rate remains.

4. Determine rounding and accuracy. Many of the

values portrayed in our charts have been rounded up or down to the nearest whole number. So, for example, instead of labeling a bar as "30.2%" or "$284.95," we print "30%" and "$285." When the extra information of .2% or 95¢ doesn't seem to add anything important, rounding the number makes the chart friendlier to look at. Sometimes this can make the results seem a little off. For instance, the overall pie chart on page 10.4 includes 100% of consumption expenditures, but because of rounding, the numbers shown with the slices only add up to 99%.

However, values should not be rounded too much. For instance, we report unemployment rates including a decimal value. Every month, when the government releases its new economic reports, newspapers and other media may report on shifts in unemployment of "a tenth of a percent" (that is, a shift of 0.1%). For this issue, even small percentages are considered important.

5. *Ask yourself what you expect the relationship to be.* Graphs display patterns. Only a critical, attentive reader can decide whether those patterns really represent important trends.

When you set out to make graphs, follow a similar line of reasoning.

1. Choose the variables whose relationship you want to explore or display; let them determine the type of graph.
2. Decide upon the range and the units you want to use. Experiment with some alternatives, and expect a fair amount of trial and error.
3. Choose the length of your horizontal and vertical axes (or the diameter of your pie). Allow enough space for the variation you want to show. Note that the relative length of the two axes will determine how the graph looks. Increasing the height of the vertical axis will exaggerate differences in the values; increasing the length of the horizontal axis will minimize them.

A computer can do much of the trial-and-error part of this work, though you still have to make the decisions and enter the numbers. The specifics depend almost entirely on the hardware and software that you have access to. In general:

1. You need a computer, a printer, and some kind of graphing software. Since most computers come with a suite of business applications preinstalled, chances are good that you already have the software you need. The best place to start is with a spreadsheet program, like Microsoft Excel or Calc, part of the free OpenOffice software suite, http://www.openoffice.org. You may be able to access a graphing module directly from your word-processing program. Business presentation programs like Microsoft PowerPoint or OpenOffice Impress can create graphs and combine them with text, illustrations, and a variety of effects to make slideshows.
2. You may find that you need more than one program to do what you need to do. For example, you might use Excel or Calc to generate graphs, then copy and paste them into a word-processing document as part of a report, or into a Web page authoring program for publishing on the Internet.

The software we've been talking about is getting easier and easier to use. But the more powerful a software package is, the longer it takes to learn how to make all of its features work for you. So ask for help from somebody who knows how to use it. Read the manual if you have it, or check in a library for guides to the programs. Give yourself time to play around.

T.3 Means, Medians, and Other Measures

Sometimes empirical data is wrapped up in a bewildering variety of statistical lingo, such as "means" and "medians." You can look up their definition in a dictionary or glossary, but the best way to learn what they mean is to apply them yourself. One way of summarizing information about a large number of cases is to ask what's happening to the "typical" case. For instance, you might want to know the income of the typical American family. There are two common ways of estimating this.

The simplest and most common way is to calculate the average, also called the "mean." To do so, add up all the different family incomes and then divide this sum by the number of families. Another way to define "typical" is by the median, rather than the mean. To find the median, line up all the relevant cases from the lowest value to the highest, then choose the one that is closest to the middle. This is the family whose income is greater than the bottom half of all families and less than the top half of all families.

Sometimes the mean and the median are the same or very similar. More often, they diverge. The reason is that extreme cases affect the mean much more than they affect the median. An example will help show this best. If you are measuring five families and their incomes are $100, $110, $120, $150, and $500, the average is $196 [calculated as ($100 + $110 + $120 + $150 + $500) ÷ 5], which is higher than the income for all but the richest family. However, the median is the value of the middle family, $120.

The overall distribution of income, like the distribution of both earnings and wealth, has many more extreme cases on the high side than on the low side. For this reason, the mean overestimates the income of the typical family, and the median is a better measure.

T.4 Real vs. Nominal: How to Use Price Indices

In everyday language, "real" is the opposite of "imaginary." In the economist's world, however, "real" describes a number that has been adjusted to take inflation into account. A real value is one that is expressed in "constant" dollars, or dollars with the same purchasing power. By contrast, a "nominal" value reflects the value or purchasing power current at the time it occurred and is therefore described as being in "current" dollars.

You can use estimates of the rate of inflation to convert nominal values (expressed in current dollars of purchasing power) to real values (expressed in constant dollars of purchasing power). First, you must decide what estimate of the rate of inflation to use. The most commonly used measure is the consumer price index for urban consumers, or CPI-U, which is produced by the Bureau of Labor Statistics. This index calculates the number of dollars required to buy a certain "basket of goods" (including food, clothing, and housing) in a certain benchmark year or an average of several years, such as

1982–1984, and determines how many dollars would have been required to purchase that same basket of goods in another year, such as 2004. The ratio between the two determines the CPI-U.

For instance, in 2004, the CPI-U was 189 relative to the benchmark years 1982–1984 = 100. That means that $1.89 in 2004 had the same purchasing power as $1 did over the years 1982 to 1984. To calculate the value of your 2004 salary of $22,000 in 1982-1984 dollars (and determine if your real wages increased), set up this formula and plug in the appropriate numbers:

$$\frac{2004 \text{ CPI-U}}{1982\text{--}1984 \text{ CPI-U}} = \frac{\text{Your salary in 2004 dollars}}{\text{Your salary in 1982--1984 dollars}}$$

$$\frac{189}{100} = \frac{\$22,000}{x}$$

Using a little algebra (cross-multiply and divide—multiply the 1982–1984 CPI-U by the 2004 salary, then divide by the 2004 CPI-U), you can determine that your 2004 earnings had the same purchasing power as $11,640.21 had, on average, in the years 1982–1984.

Suppose you want to compare your real earnings in 2000 with your real earnings in 2004. As long as you can consult an estimate of the CPI-U for the range of years you are interested in, you can use any year as a base year. The 2000 CPI-U is 172. You can use the figure you just used for the 2004 CPI-U

to convert your 2004 salary (say, $22,000 again) to 2000 dollars as follows:

$$\frac{189}{172} = \frac{\$22,000}{x}$$

A few calculations show that x, your 2004 salary in 2000 dollars, is $20,021.16. Did you earn more or less than that in 2000? If you earned more than that, then your real ("inflation adjusted") salary went down over those four years.

There are a variety of consumer price indices, and the method used to construct them has changed over time. In particular, the BLS adjusted the CPI index in 1998, creating a new series. There are a number of reasons for the update, including changes in the quality of goods and services in the basket of goods, the need to account for new products that never existed before, and changes in patterns of consumer spending. For more details on the CPI and these changes, see the CPI Web site, http://www.bls.gov/cpi/home.htm.

No index is a perfect measure of the purchasing power of your dollars, because the goods and services you spend your money on may be different from those included in the basket of goods the BLS uses for its calculations.

Another complication is that the composition of the average basket of goods people buy varies over time. The rates of price increase vary considerably—in some years, food prices may increase faster than the cost of other commodities, in other years more slowly. In addition to the consumer price index for all items (CPI), the BLS publishes indices for many separate items.

Many important economic data, such as measurements of gross domestic product or investment, pertain to sums of money that are not really spent by consumers. To convert these sums to real terms, you should use a different index, the implicit price deflator, which is calculated for this purpose. You can use it exactly the same way as the CPI, using either the overall index or an index of one of its separate components. The implicit price deflator is calculated by the U.S. Department of Commerce, Bureau of Economic Analysis, and is available through the St. Louis Federal Reserve Bank at http://research.stlouisfed.org/fred2/data/GDPDEF.txt.

T.5 The Census Vocabulary: Families, Households, Persons, and Heads

In the language of the Census Bureau, "person" means just what we expect it to—an individual human being. The official Bureau terms "families" and "households," however, mean something a little different from their everyday definitions. A family is any group of people related by blood, marriage, or adoption living at the same residence. If you don't live with your parents, you are not considered part of their family (and the census would not consider your income part of their family income). People who live alone are not considered members of families. By official definition, they represent single-person households.

A household consists of all the people living in one residence, whether or not they are related. Individuals, unrelated roommates, and families all qualify, but people living in "institutions" such as prisons, army barracks, and hospitals are not considered part of households. Here's one way to keep the distinction straight: according to the Census Bureau, all families are households, but not all households are families.

People who compile statistics should choose their units of analysis carefully. Sometimes the choice is obvious. You wouldn't want to ask what percentage of households experience a divorce because many household members aren't even married. On the other hand, you wouldn't want to ask what percentage of families receive Social Security because you would be excluding all people living alone, many of whom are elderly.

At other times, the choice is not so obvious. The percentage of all households that includes children is arguably just as interesting a fact as the percentage of families that includes children. But the two percentages mean different things and should not be confused.

Beyond the household/family distinction lies the question of "headship." Until 1980, the bureau always classified a husband as the head of his family if he lived in the same household with them. A female-headed household was, by definition, a family household lacking a husband. Now, the census designates the person in whose name the home is owned or rented as the householder. If the home is owned or rented jointly by a married couple, either the husband or the wife may be listed first. The families once termed "female-headed" are now termed "families with female householders, no husband present." The Bureau of Labor Statistics has a nicer way of putting it: "families maintained by women."

T.6 What They Call Us: Racial and Ethnic Labels in Economic Data

Everyone who works with economic statistics about people should pay attention to the implications of racial and ethnic labels. The categories that government agencies such as the Bureau of the Census and the Bureau of Labor Statistics use to define and gather economic data reflect the unspoken assumptions and biases of the larger society. Sometimes these categories are politically offensive or simply outdated. Sometimes agencies change and improve the racial and ethnic labels but introduce problems of comparability between data collected in different years. Take, for instance, the category "nonwhite," which government agencies once used to describe African Americans, Asians, and Native Americans as a group. This category accurately reflects conventional English usage of that period, a usage defined by a white population that automatically considered its own race as the standard. It's a bit like defining women as "non-men."

The conventional racial categories "white" and "nonwhite"

also overlooked the distinctive character and sense of community shared by people whose origins lay in Spanish-speaking countries. In 1979, many government agencies responded to widespread criticism by changing their categories to white, black, and Hispanic, providing data for these three groups and largely discontinuing the white/nonwhite distinction. There is no data predating 1979 for blacks and Hispanics as separate groups, and there is very little data after 1978 for Asians, Native Americans, and people of color taken together.

As a result it is difficult to construct long-run comparisons based on comparable categories. For instance, until 1978 the Handbook of Labor Statistics provided data on average earnings for "Black and other" workers. Beginning in 1979, the category changed to "Black." One might be tempted to splice the two series together. But this would be misleading; "Black and other" included people of Asian origin, whose relatively high incomes raised the average earnings of the group significantly above those of African Americans alone.

Official terminology underwent further evolution in the 1990s. Objecting to a description based on skin color, many argued that the term "African American" better conveys ethnic heritage. The concept of "race" itself has no true biological meaning, and definitions based on skin color simply represent a particular cultural interpretation of ethnicity. The term "African American" is now widely used, but the term "black" remains common. Many government statistical agencies use the two terms interchangeably, and this edition of the *Field Guide* follows this convention as well.

The term "Hispanic" has been criticized because it misleadingly implies Spanish, and thereby European, origin. Some prefer the term "Latino." The Census Bureau now uses both terms interchangeably, but many other statistical agencies use the term "Hispanic." In order to avoid confusion, this edition of the *Field Guide* uses the term "Hispanic" (previous versions used the term "Latino").

Because we think there is an important political and cultural boundary between whites and a group that includes African Americans, Hispanics, Asians, and Native Americans, we use the term "people of color" as an alternative to "nonwhite." It is an alternative, not a synonym, because it includes Hispanics, which "nonwhite" does not. We use the term "Native Americans" to refer to the group the Bureau of the Census currently labels "American Indians and Alaska Natives."

In the year 2000, the racial and ethnic classifications used by all government agencies underwent a fundamental shift. People were allowed to identify with one or more racial categories (but not allowed to describe themselves as simply "multiracial"). Relatively few people chose to identify themselves as having more than one race in the 2000 census, but this category may grow in the future. For an interesting discussion of this issue, see the Census Bureau's 2005 publication *We the People of More than One Race in the United States*, available at http://www.census.gov/prod/2005pubs/censr-22.pdf.

It is easy to overlook the implications of racial/ethnic distinctions. For instance, you might think that you could arrive at the total number of families in poverty by adding together white families in poverty, African American families in poverty, and Hispanic families in poverty. Not so. Hispanic is an ethnic, not racial, designation. Hispanics can be of any race; if you add their numbers to the numbers of black and white families, you will overcount the total. At the same time, you will overlook those Asian and Native American families living in poverty.

Since the Census Bureau invites people to define their own race and ethnicity, there are no hard-and-fast rules for people to follow. For instance, Native Americans became more assertive of their cultural pride and political rights in the 1970s, and many people who had never done so before identified themselves as such. If you didn't know this, you might infer incorrectly from census publications that Native Americans had an extraordinarily high rate of population growth. Cultural trends are also likely to affect the number of people who identify themselves in the future as having more than one racial identity.

T.7 Measuring Growth: What's Gross About Gross Domestic Product?

When economists use the word "gross," they usually mean "total." Gross domestic product (GDP) is simply the total value of all the final goods and services produced for sale within a country (usually in a given year). But there is something a little gross, even downright vulgar, about using GDP as a measure of total production or economic welfare. None of the many goods and services produced in households is included in GDP because they aren't sold. And GDP doesn't reflect changes in the quantity or quality of goods that don't have a price tag, such as clean air or good health. But unless and until a better summary of production is widely adopted, GDP will remain central to the national income accounts that government agencies use to track the growth of the economy over time.

Until recently, the Bureau of Economic Analysis (BEA), http://www.bea.gov, emphasized the gross national product (GNP), which is the value of all goods and services produced for sale by U.S. businesses or U.S. citizens (whether inside or outside the country). In 1991, it began to use GDP instead for two reasons: first, to make U.S. national accounting figures compatible with those of other countries, and, second, because GDP, in contrast with GNP, emphasizes production located in the United States, no matter who gets the income from it. In other words, income earned by foreigners on economic activities taking place in the U.S. is included in GDP, while it is not in the GNP. Similarly, income earned by Americans on investment in foreign countries is not included in GDP but is a component of GNP. As the U.S. becomes more and more integrated into the global economy, the GDP gives a more reliable picture of economic activity taking place in the country.

The national accounts break GDP down into four components:

1. Personal consumption expenditures: total purchases of goods and services by households and individuals
2. Gross private domestic investment: total purchases by businesses, excluding investment in inventories
3. Net exports: total exports minus total imports (which has been negative in recent years)
4. Total government purchases

Estimates of the value of these items in the national accounts are usually released quarterly by the BEA, often seasonally adjusted and converted to an annual rate to make them more easily comparable. A detailed explanation of the national accounts system is provided in *The U.S. Economy Demystified: What the Major Economic Statistics Mean and Their Significance for Business,* by Albert T. Sommers (Lexington, MA: D.C. Heath and Company, 1985).

T.8 Uppers and Downers: The Business Cycle

Economic growth fluctuates, and its ups and downs are usually described as part of a cycle of recession and recovery. Economists typically declare a recession when GDP declines for two quarters of a year in a row (whether or not these quarters are in the same calendar year). A decline in GDP means that economic activity is shrinking and that economic growth is negative. A recession year is one in which GDP is lower than it was in the previous year. "Depression" is a word with no technical definition, generally reserved for prolonged recessions. There is no technical definition for "recovery" either, but the term usually refers to the period immediately after recession, when positive growth is restored.

Why is the economy plagued by a business cycle? At least a dozen explanations have been offered, including one that blames sunspots. But most economists agree that the business cycle is closely related to fluctuations in the level of business investment. That level is determined by expected costs and expected profits, which shift in both predictable and unpredictable ways.

Because the business cycle has such an important impact on virtually all economic indicators, it's important to keep it in mind when interpreting economic statistics and to distinguish between short-run and long-run trends. Imagine, for instance, a beach at the ocean. If the water is calm and there are no waves, it's easy to tell whether the tide is moving in or out. But a lot of waves can disguise the movement of the tide. To see which way it's going, you might need to compare the distance from peak to peak (or from trough to trough) of several succeeding waves. Economists use the word "secular" to describe trends that continue through multiple business cycles.

T.9 A Guide to the Federal Budget

Early every year, the president presents a proposed budget for the next fiscal year (FY) to Congress. For example, in February 2005, President Bush transmitted his budget for fiscal year 2006, which runs from October 1, 2005, to September 30, 2006. This budget presents the administration's proposals for all the different programs of the federal government, including national defense, Social Security, Medicaid, and education. It explains and defends the spending required to meet the administration's objectives in all these areas. It also projects government revenues for the fiscal year and, consequently, estimates the size of the federal deficit (or surplus, if revenues are expected to be larger than expenditures).

The president's budget is only a proposal until it is passed by Congress and signed into law by the president. Congressional work on the budget originates in the spring in the House of Representatives. After lengthy work by the House Appropriations Committee, the House votes on an appropriations bill. The approved budget proposal is sent to the Senate, which comes up with its own version. A House and Senate conference committee then works out the differences between the two proposals, and the final bill is sent to the president. The president then has the option of either signing the bill into law or vetoing it, but he cannot amend it.

The federal budget process has a terminology (as well as a logic) of its own. For instance, there is an important difference between budget authority and outlays. The term "budget authority" describes an amount of money that is authorized for a particular program, which might last for several years. "Outlays" refers to the amount of money spent out of the budget authority "checking account" during a particular fiscal year. When calculating the budget deficit, it is important to focus on budget outlays. Budget authorities often extend over several budget years; in a given fiscal year, most federal spending is, in a sense, predetermined by previous budgets. Given the existence of both budget authority and entitlements (such as Social Security, veterans' benefits, and Medicare), only a small component of the federal budget is discretionary in a given budget year.

Economists disagree over the correct definition of the federal deficit. One issue is a component of the budget known as the Social Security trust fund, money accumulated to help pay future Social Security claims. This fund currently has a large surplus, which makes the deficit look much smaller. But since it is money that must be spent at some future date, Congress decided it should not be included. The Omnibus Budget Reconciliation Act of 1990 enshrined Social Security as an "off-budget" item, which means it is not counted when calculating the deficit.

For a good discussion of this and other issues surrounding the definition of the deficit, see Robert Eisner's *The Misunderstood Economy: What Counts and How to Count It* (Boston, MA: Harvard Business School Press, 1994).

T.10 Poverty, the Poverty Line, and Quintiles

Feeling poor in the U.S. is not the same thing as officially being poor. The U.S. government includes a person or family among the poor if their income falls below an officially designated poverty line or "threshold" that varies according to family size.

In 2004, the poverty threshold for a single person under 65 years old was $9,827; for a family of four including two children, it was $19,157. Every year, these thresholds are adjusted for inflation. A list of the different thresholds can be found at http://www.census.gov/hhes/www/poverty/threshld.html.

This definition of poverty is problematic for a number of reasons. First, the original threshold was set in a somewhat arbitrary way that has become increasingly inaccurate over time. Second, it is misleading to define poverty entirely in absolute rather than relative terms. In 1960, the poverty line for a family of four amounted to about 54% of median family income. By 2004, it had fallen to less than a third. In relative terms, officially poor families are much poorer today than they were in the past.

These are good reasons to raise the poverty line, but, of course, doing so would increase the poverty rate (the percentage of people living in households with income below the poverty line). Revisions that would decrease the official poverty rate have received more recent attention.

Since the mid-1970s, government transfer programs have

provided large amounts of noncash or in-kind assistance, such as food stamps, Medicaid, and subsidized housing. It's difficult to estimate the market value of such benefits. For instance, if the value of services received through Medicaid were counted as if it were cash income, a person could escape official poverty simply by getting very sick. Still, the failure to include some estimate of noncash transfers in calculations of family income biases the official poverty rate upward. This compensates to some extent for the effect of setting the poverty line very low. Changes in the definition of the poverty line affect calculations of trends as well as levels of poverty. If the full value of noncash transfers is included in calculations of family income in the 1990s and no other revisions are made, estimates of the poverty rate are lower. However, the estimated increase of the poverty rate between 1990 and 1998 is even greater because cuts in social spending diminished the relative size of noncash transfers to poor people.

For a good discussion of these issues, see Patricia Ruggles, *Drawing a Line: Alternative Poverty Measures and Their Implications for Public Policy* (Washington, DC: The Urban Institute Press, 1990).

Throughout this book, we frequently refer to groups of Americans by their income. Most often, the grouping is by "quintile." A quintile is one fifth of the total, and so the same as 20% of the total. You may be curious to know where you and your family stand in the rankings of income in the U.S. In 2004, the Census Bureau ranked the U.S. population in the following way (see section T.5 for definition of "household"):

Lowest-income **20%** of households:
annual income less than **$18,500**

Lower-middle **20%** of households:
annual income between **$18,500** and **$34,737**

Middle **20%** of households:
annual income between **$34,738** and **$55,330**

Upper-middle **20%** of households:
annual income between **$55,331** and **$88,029**

Highest-income **20%** of households:
annual income **$88,030** and above

We also sometimes refer to the very top of the income ladder. In 2004, the highest-income 5% of households had annual income of $157,176 and above.

For details, alternative breakdowns by family or individual, and yearly updates, visit the Census Bureau's "Detailed Income Tables from the CPS" Web page at http://www.census.gov/hhes/www/income/dinctabs.html. Historical changes are tracked at http://www.census.gov/hhes/www/income/histinc/histinctb.html.

Glossary

Note: words in *italics* are defined separately in the Glossary.

401(k) plan. Arrangements that allow employees to make a tax-deferred contribution into a trust in order to finance *investments*. Employees get their money back when they depart from the plan or upon retirement.

Affirmative action. A plan or program designed to remedy the effects of past racial or sexual discrimination in employment, and to prevent its recurrence. Unlike antidiscrimination or equal-opportunity laws, which forbid unequal treatment, affirmative action requires positive corrective measures.

Aggregate. A total that is made up of smaller amounts added together.

Aid to Families with Dependent Children (AFDC). Financial aid provided under the assistance program of the Social Security Act of 1935 for families of children who lack adequate support but are living with one parent or relative. In 1996, AFDC was replaced by *Temporary Assistance for Needy Families (TANF)*.

Apartheid. Literally meaning "separateness" in the Afrikaans language, a policy of strict racial segregation, legal and economic discrimination, and political rule by the minority white population in South Africa between 1948 and 1990.

Asset. Anything of value that is owned. See *financial assets*.

Balance of payments. The difference between the total payments into and out of a country during a period of time. It includes such items as all merchandise trade, tourist expenditures, capital movements, and interest charges.

Black ink. Slang accounting term for a *budget surplus* or other money account that is running a surplus or profit. Opposite of *red ink*.

Bond. An IOU or promissory note from a *corporation* or government. A bond is evidence of a debt on which the issuer (borrower) usually promises to pay a specified amount of interest for a specified period of time and also to repay the principal on the date of expiration, or maturity date.

Bond yield. The implicit *interest rate* earned by holding a *bond,* given the prevailing market price of that bond.

Budget deficit. The amount by which government expenditures exceed government tax revenues. The difference must be borrowed.

Budget surplus. The amount by which government tax revenues exceed government expenditures.

Business cycle. The pattern of medium-term economic fluctuations in which expansion is followed by recession, which is followed by expansion, and so on. See Toolkit section T.8.

Business equity. The total value of a *firm's assets*, less the amount that is owed to *creditors*. For *corporations,* the *stock* of a company represents a significant portion of its equity.

Capital. Accumulated *assets* that are used to produce goods and services or to generate income. The term "capital" can refer to many different types of assets, depending on the context, including *capital goods,* financial capital (see *financial assets*), or intangible assets possessed by an individual or group (e.g., a person's education and skills, or cooperation and communication within a community).

Capital gain. The difference between the purchase price of an *asset* and its resale price at some later date. It is called a "capital loss" if the resale price is less than the purchase price.

Capital goods. Machinery, equipment, and structures used in the production of goods and services.

Capital stock. The value of the sum of *capital goods* in an economy at a given time.

Caring labor. Work, both paid and unpaid, that involves face-to-face personal care for other people, including children, elderly individuals, and disabled or sick persons.

Census tract. The U.S. Census Bureau defines tracts as "small, relatively permanent statistical subdivisions of a county. . . . Designed to be relatively homogeneous units with respect to population characteristics, economic status, and living conditions, census tracts average about 4,000 inhabitants." The tract is one of several geographical units used by the Census. From broadest to narrowest, they are: United States, Region, Division, State, County, County subdivision, Place (or part), Census tract (or part), Block group (or part), and Census block. Additional information on Census geographic terms and concepts is available at http://www.census.gov/geo/www/tiger/glossry2.pdf.

Commercial banks. Privately owned banks that receive deposits and make loans. Commercial banks issue time deposits and savings deposits, operate trust departments, act as agents in buying and selling *securities,* and underwrite and sell new security issues for state and local governments.

Commons. Resources for which it is difficult to exclude people from accessing and using them. Examples include fishing areas, forests, water sources, air, and the Internet. They can be used in a sustainable manner, or they can be overused, polluted, or otherwise reduced in quality. They may be privately or publicly owned; governed by an alternative, nonproperty arrangement; or left as "open access" to all. No one system of control works to sustainably maintain all commons.

Comparable worth. A method for establishing a wage and salary structure across occupations whereby an occupation's wage rate or salary is based on certain characteristics, such as responsibility and working conditions, in comparison with other occupations. Also called "pay equity."

Conglomerate. A *corporation* that competes in multiple, not necessarily related, *industries*. A conglomerate often acquires its large, diversified holdings through *mergers* and/or buyouts.

Consumer price index (CPI). A measure of the average change in prices over time in a fixed "market basket" of goods and services purchased by consumers. The most common CPIs used focus on purchases either by urban wage earners and clerical workers (CPI-W) or by all urban consumers (CPI-U). See Toolkit section T.4.

Consumption. Spending on goods and services for current use, not for *investment* purposes. (Home purchases are an exception—they are counted as investment even though the owner may live in the home.) Income that is not consumed becomes *savings*.

Corporate income tax. A tax imposed on the annual *net* earnings of a *corporation*. In the U.S. such taxes are levied by the federal government and by most states on all incorporated business.

Corporation. A form of business organization consisting of an association of owners, called "stockholders" or "*shareholders*," who are regarded as a single entity (person) in the eyes of the law.

Cost-of-living allowance (COLA). An increase in wages, based on a *consumer price index*, intended to keep them in line with changing costs of living.

Creditor. A lender. A person, group, or business that has lent money or other *assets* to a *debtor*.

Debtor. A borrower. A person, group, or business that owes a debt of money or other *assets* to a *creditor*.

Default. Failure to make good on a debt. A *debtor* who cannot pay what he/she owes to his/her *creditor* is "in default."

Deficit. See *budget deficit* and *trade deficit*.

Depreciation. The cost, due to wear and tear, aging, and/or technological obsolescence, of restoring the *capital goods* used in producing last year's output.

Depression. A prolonged *recession*. Production is greatly reduced, there is little or no new capital *investment,* income is sharply lowered, there is massive unemployment, many businesses fail, and banks are slow to create credit.

Deregulation. The lessening of government supervision and oversight over the operations of various industries.

Devaluation. A reduction in the value of a country's currency relative to foreign currencies.

Discouraged workers. Workers who have become so disheartened by their unsuccessful search for employment that they give up and withdraw from the *labor force.*

Dividends. A payment to *shareholders* in a company, in the form of cash or additional shares of *stock,* in proportion to their fraction of ownership.

Dow Jones Industrial Average (DJIA). A daily index, based on the prices of 30 industrial *stocks,* that serves as a barometer of the stock *market* as a whole.

Downsizing. A reduction in the size of a *firm*'s workforce.

Employee stock ownership plan (ESOP). Also called "employee stock purchase plan," an ESOP permits employees to purchase *stock* in the company which employs them, often at a discount from the current *market* price, by means of payroll deductions. While giving employees partial ownership of the *firm*'s *assets,* ESOPs usually confer little or no control over them.

Equal Employment Opportunity Commission (EEOC). An independent federal agency established by the Civil Rights Act of 1964 to help end racial and sexual discrimination in employment practices and promote voluntary *affirmative action.*

Equal Pay Act. The 1963 labor law that prohibits discrimination in pay on the basis of race or gender.

Et al. "And others." Used in citing a source that has multiple authors without listing every author's name.

Exchange rate. The price of one currency expressed in terms of another currency, usually the U.S. dollar.

Excise tax. A tax on the sale of goods. Includes general sales taxes plus other taxes on specific commodities (for example, a cigarette or alcohol tax).

Export. Any good or service sold to customers in a foreign country. See *import.*

External debt. Debt owed to *creditors* located in other countries. Most external debt is denominated in major international currencies, such as the dollar, yen, or euro.

Extinction. Elimination of a species of life-form. A species may become extinct within a particular region, or throughout the entire world.

Federal funds rate. The *interest rate* U.S. banks charge on overnight loans to other banks that need cash to meet their regulatory obligations.

Federal Reserve Bank. The central bank of the United States. Its main purpose is to maintain and enhance the viability and stability of the monetary system. The Fed operates under a system of 12 regional Federal Reserve banks owned by the member banks in their respective districts.

Financial assets. *Assets* that are monetary in character or easily converted to money, such as cash, checking and savings accounts, *stocks, bonds,* or government *securities.*

Financial wealth. The total value of *financial assets* less any outstanding financial obligations, such as loans.

Firm. A business or company.

Fiscal policy. The policy of using government spending and taxation to affect some aspect of the economy, especially levels of unemployment and *inflation.*

Food Stamp Program. A welfare program to improve nutrition in low-income households. The food stamp program is administered by the Department of Agriculture through state and local welfare agencies, which establish eligibility, issue food stamps, and maintain controls.

Foreign direct investment (FDI). *Investment* from abroad that represents a significant degree of managerial influence (usually meaning at least 10% ownership of the voting *stock* of a *firm*). FDI is often assumed to be more long-term and less volatile in nature than other types of foreign investment. See *portfolio investment.*

Gini coeffecient. The Gini coeffecient is the most commonly used gauge of how equally income (or whatever is being measured) is distributed across the population. The Gini score represents an overall measure of the cumulative income share against the share of households in the population. The higher the Gini score, the greater the inequality. For a more thorough explanation see http://william-king. www.drexel.edu/top/prin/txt/factors/dist4.html.

Greenhouse gases (GHG). A group of gases that, as part of the atmosphere, hold in the heat that comes from the sun. The concentration of greenhouse gases has been increasing and this appears to be causing global warming. The primary greenhouse gases are carbon dioxide, methane, nitrous oxide, and CFC-12.

Gross. A value before final applicable subtractions have been calculated. See *net*.

Gross domestic product (GDP). A measure of the total value of *market* goods and services produced within the borders of a country over a specified time period, normally a year. Income arising from *investments* abroad is not included. See Toolkit section T.7.

Gross national product (GNP). A measure of the total value of *market* goods and services produced by the businesses and citizens of a country (regardless of where the businesses or citizens are located) over a specified time period, normally a year. It includes income from *investments* made outside the country. See Toolkit section T.7.

Householder. The person (or one of the persons) in whose name the housing unit is owned or rented. The U.S. Census Bureau describes other members of the household in terms of their relationship to the householder. See Toolkit section T.5.

Import. Any good or service purchased from producers in a foreign country. See *export*.

Industry. All of the *firms* producing similar goods and/or services, for example, all automobile makers or all providers of health care.

Infant mortality rate. The number of infants, per 1,000 born, that die within the first year of life.

Inflation. A general increase in prices, usually measured by an increase in the *consumer price index*. See Toolkit section T.4.

Informal employment. Employment in unregulated activities, in unregistered enterprises, or in jobs without enforced social protections.

Interest rate. A percentage rate applied to borrowed money, resulting in an amount of interest. The interest is owed by the borrower to the lender as payment for the loan. The higher the interest rate, the more expensive the loan. There are many different interest rates used throughout the economy, depending on who is making the loan and to whom, and what the money is being borrowed for. Interest rates available at any given time can change depending on circumstances in the economy. See *mortgage*.

International Monetary Fund (IMF). An institution affiliated with the United Nations, set up at the Bretton Woods Conference in 1944 to promote international monetary cooperation, facilitate the growth of international trade, and make the fund's resources available to members. The IMF's headquarters are in Washington, DC.

Inventories. Goods produced by businesses but not yet distributed and sold to final consumers.

Investment *(capital)*. A purchase of *capital goods* that will be used directly in production of goods and services.

Investment *(financial)*. The purchase of *financial assets,* such as a *stock* or *bond*. Distinguished from the purchase of productive *capital goods,* such as a *plant* or equipment.

Jobless recovery. A situation in which the economy begins to grow again, after a recession, but the increase in employment—if any—is too small to bring the unemployment rate down.

Labor force. Those persons who have jobs or are actively looking for jobs.

Labor force participation rate. The proportion of the working-age population that is part of the *labor force*.

Labor productivity. The amount of goods and/or services produced by a worker in a given time period (for example, goods produced per hour of work).

Liabilities. The claims of a *creditor*. The *assets* of a *debtor* are subject to payment of these claims.

Liberalization. The reduction or removal of government regulations and controls over the exchange of goods, services, and *assets,* for both domestic and international transactions. Examples of such regulations include *tariffs* on *imports* and controls on financial flows.

Living wage. There is no technical definition of a living wage, but it generally refers to a wage high enough that a full-time worker paid that level would earn enough to maintain a household of two adults and two children above the poverty line. Some proposed living wages are based on different household structures. See *minimum wage*.

Lobbying. Seeking to influence the development of new policy or to maintain existing policy. Lobbyists are hired to promote a client's interests either directly, by meeting with lawmakers to convince them to write or vote for legislation favorable to the client, or indirectly, by trying to change public opinion in a way that leads to favorable legislation.

Macroeconomics. The study of the behavior of the economy as a whole, focusing on variables such as employment, *inflation,* growth, and stability.

Market. Economists usually use "market" to refer to one of two things, depending on context. It can refer to a particular *stock exchange* or all stock exchanges as a group. For example, "the market fell in 2000" refers to the fall in price of many *stocks*. More broadly, it refers to a system of exchange in which things are sold for money. For example, the "labor market" is the system in which people are hired as workers by employers. Any part of the economy that affects hiring and firing of employees is part of the labor market.

Mean. See Toolkit section T.3.

Means-tested. Describes any government-aid program that is available only to persons with income below a certain threshold (usually at or slightly above the official poverty line).

Median. See Toolkit section T.3.

Medicaid. A federal program, managed in conjunction with the states, that pays for medical services for some low-income households.

Medicare. A health insurance program enacted in 1965 as an amendment to the Social Security Act to provide medical care for the elderly.

Merger. The fusion of two or more separate companies into one.

Microeconomics. The study of individual decision making in response to changes in prices and incomes.

Minimum wage. The lowest wage that can legally be paid to an employee. Generally refers to the national minimum wage established by federal law; some states also have minimum wage laws. See *living wage.*

Monetary policy. The use of monetary controls, such as restrictions or expansion of the money supply and manipulation of *interest rates,* in order to achieve some desired policy objective, such as the control of *inflation,* an improvement in the *balance of payments,* a certain level of employment, or growth in the *gross domestic product.*

Monopoly. Strictly speaking, a monopoly exists when a *firm* or individual is the sole producer and seller of a particular commodity. The lack of competition confers *market* power on the monopolist. The term is sometimes used more casually to refer to a firm that has a very large share of the market in a particular commodity, even if it does not have a 100% share.

Mortgage. A loan most often used to purchase or improve property. With a mortgage, a house, building, or other real estate serves as collateral. Over the life of the mortgage, the borrower repays the amount of the original loan, called the principal, as well as interest on the loan. The amount of interest paid depends on the *interest rate* and the length (in years) of the loan.

Multinational corporation. A company that has operation centers in many countries, as opposed to an international company, which *imports* and *exports* goods but has its operation centered in one country.

Mutual fund. A financial institution that manages financial *investments* on behalf of its *shareholders*. Many individuals contribute to the mutual fund, which then directs the pool of money into different investments. The shareholders receive a portion of the total investment income.

NASDAQ. National Association of Securities Dealers Automated Quotation system. The largest electronic *stock exchange* in the U.S.

NATO. The North Atlantic Treaty Organization. An association of 26 countries from North America and Europe sharing a mutual defense treaty.

Net. A value after final applicable subtractions have been calculated. See *gross*.

Net domestic investment. *Investment* in *capital goods,* such as buildings and machinery, adjusted for the *depreciation* of the current *capital stock.*

Net domestic product. *Gross domestic product* minus *depreciation.*

Net domestic savings. Total national savings, the portion of domestic income not spent on consuming goods and services, adjusted for *depreciation.*

Net national product. *Gross national product* minus *depreciation.*

Net present value. The sum of a stream of future benefits less the sum of a stream of associated future costs, expressed in current dollars. It is a method for estimating the lifetime value of an object or process, as perceived from the point of view of the current day.

Net worth. The total value of the *assets* of a person or business less the total *liabilities* (amounts due to *creditors*).

Nonfinancial corporate assets. Physical *assets* (such as *plant,* equipment, and *inventories*) and other assets (such as accounts receivable) owned by a corporation.

Nonmarket work. Work that takes place outside the money

economy, such as housework, care of family members or friends, and volunteer work.

OASDI. See *Social Security*.

OECD. Organization for Economic Cooperation and Development. A 30-member international, intergovernmental agency founded in 1961 to promote policies leading to optimum economic growth, employment, and living standards in member countries while maintaining financial stability. The OECD reviews economic problems of members, conducts research, collects and disseminates statistics on its member countries, and issues publications. It includes 23 European nations, Canada, Mexico, the U.S., Japan, Korea, Australia, and New Zealand.

Outsourcing. The contracting out of business activities to other *firms,* often located abroad.

Pay equity. See *comparable worth*.

Pension fund. Sums of money laid aside and normally invested to provide a regular income in retirement or in compensation for disablement.

Per capita. A Latin term meaning "for each person," and used as a synonym for "per person."

Plant. Buildings used for production of *market* goods or services.

Political action committee (PAC). A group of people, usually professionals, that lobbies Congress or state legislatures. PACs raise substantial amounts of money for political candidates of their choice. See *lobbying*.

Portfolio investment. Foreign *investment* in *financial assets*. Portfolio investment is often assumed to be short-term and highly mobile. See *foreign direct investment*.

Poverty line. See Toolkit section T.10.

Poverty rate. The percentage of the population with incomes under the poverty line. See Toolkit section T.10.

Private sector. All economic activities that are independent of government management (thus outside the *public sector*), carried on principally for profit but also including non-profit organizations directed at satisfying private needs, such as private hospitals and private schools. Included are enterprises owned individually or by groups, and the self-employed.

Productive capacity. The potential output of a business given its existing *plant,* workers, and equipment.

Profit rate. The ratio of a company's profits to the value of its *capital stock*.

Progressive tax. A tax in which the tax rate rises with income. The federal income tax is a good example—rates go up (to a certain point) along with the "tax bracket" one is in. See *regressive tax*.

Protectionism. The policy of imposing import restrictions, such as *tariffs* or *quotas* on imported goods and/or services in order to protect domestic industries. See *import*.

Quota. A maximum or minimum limit on a quantity. With regard to trade, a quota is a form of *protectionism* that sets a maximum limit on the amount of a good or service that may be *imported*. With regard to some forms of *affirmative action*, a quota is a requirement to hire or admit at least a minimum number of persons from groups that have historically been discriminated against.

Real. Monetary values that have been adjusted to take the effects of *inflation* into account. See Toolkit section T.4.

Real earnings. Earnings after the effects of *inflation* have been taken into account.

Real interest rate. The *interest rate* minus the anticipated rate of *inflation*; what a borrower is actually paying for the use of money. See Toolkit section T.4.

Recession. That part or phase of the *business cycle* in which total output falls; during a recession *investment* usually declines and the demand for labor is reduced, so unemployment rises. See Toolkit section T.8.

Red ink. Slang accounting term for a *budget deficit* or other money account that is running a loss. Opposite of *black ink*. Derived from the fact that accountants traditionally used red ink to identify deficits in their financial books.

Regressive tax. A tax that takes a larger proportion of low incomes than of high incomes. Many taxes on basic goods, such as gasoline, are regressive because poor people spend a larger percentage of their income on these goods. See *progressive tax*.

Remittance. Money sent back home by individuals who work and reside away from the household, often overseas.

Renewable sources of energy. Energy sources, such as solar energy, that are not depleted by use.

Return *(financial)*. The income received from an *investment*.

Revenue. Money flowing into the accounts of a business or government, resulting from sales of goods and services or from taxation.

Revenue-neutral. A revenue-neutral tax bill is one that does not affect overall tax *revenues*. For example, if the bill promises to reduce one tax, it simultaneously proposes an increase in another tax (or the creation of a new tax) so that the total amount of tax revenue is unchanged.

Savings. All income not spent on goods and services used for current consumption. Both *firms* and households can save.

Security. Any paper *asset*. Securities include corporate or government *bonds* and company *stock*.

Shareholder. A person or organization that owns one or more shares of *stock* in a *corporation*.

Single-payer health insurance. A system in which the government provides health insurance covering all people. Providers of medical services are not employees of the government, but payment for their services is made through the government's insurance plan. The government may fund the plan through general revenues or a special tax specifically for that purpose. See *universal health care*.

Social Security. Officially named Old Age, Survivors, and Disability Insurance (OASDI), its major purposes are to provide retirement income for the elderly, assistance for workers who are totally disabled, income for spouses and children of deceased wage earners, and *Medicare*. All eligible workers are required to contribute a certain percentage of their earnings, to be matched by their employer.

State Children's Health Insurance Program (SCHIP). It is funded jointly by the federal and state governments and administered by each state within guidelines set by federal law.

Stock. A certificate or claim of ownership interest in a *corporation*. Stocks entitle the owner to *dividend* payments from the corporation.

Stock exchange. The location or electronic system through which corporate *stocks* are bought and sold.

Stock option. An agreement allowing a person to purchase a company's *stock*, often at a favorable price. Usually offered as part of a salary-and-benefits package.

Stockholder. See *shareholder*.

Surplus. More than is needed to fulfill current obligations. See *budget surplus*.

Tariff. A tax on *imported* goods or services. See *protectionism*.

Tax loophole. A legal provision that can be used to reduce one's tax *liabilities*. Such provisions may be unintentional discrepancies, or may be provisions intended to benefit an *industry* or group.

Temporary Assistance for Needy Families (TANF). A government program to provide short-term aid to low-income families. The program includes term limits on the total length of time assistance can be provided. TANF also requires that participants find employment or be placed in unpaid jobs. TANF replaced *Aid to Families with Dependent Children* (AFDC) in 1996.

Terms of trade. The purchasing power of a country's *exports* in terms of the *imports* that they will buy.

Trade deficit. The amount by which a nation's *imports* exceed its *exports* over a given period of time.

Trade-related aspects of intellectual property rights (TRIPS). Provisions in trade agreements that aim to protect intellectual property, such as patents and copyrights.

Trade-related investment measures (TRIMS). Provisions in trade agreements that govern *investment* behavior.

Underemployment. A situation in which an individual who would like to secure full-time work is employed only part time or temporarily.

Universal health care. Any health care system that provides care to all people in a country. Health care providers might be employees of the government, or the government might provide *single-payer health insurance* that pays nongovernment providers for their services. In almost all countries with universal health care, people also have the option of paying for additional private care and/or additional private insurance.

World Bank. An institution affiliated with the United Nations and set up at the Bretton Woods Conference in 1944, whose chief purpose is to assist in the reconstruction and development of its poor members by facilitating capital *investment*, making loans, and promoting foreign investment. The World Bank's headquarters are in Washington, DC.

World Trade Organization (WTO). An international institution established in 1995 to govern trade agreements, regulatory standards, *tariff* levels, and intellectual property rights. The WTO renders decisions regarding disputes between member countries. The WTO's headquarters are in Geneva, Switzerland.

Sources and Notes

For a general guide to sources, see Toolkit T.1. This list uses the following abbreviations:

AER   *Annual Energy Review* (Energy Information Administration, U.S. Department of Energy), http://www.eia.doe.gov/emeu/aer/contents.html

BJS   Bureau of Justice Statistics, http://www.ojp.usdoj.gov/bjs

BLS   Bureau of Labor Statistics, http://www.bls.gov

BUSG   *Budget of the United States Government,* http://www.gpoaccess.gov/usbudget

CBPP   Center on Budget and Policy Priorities, http://www.cbpp.org

CDC   U.S. Centers for Disease Control and Prevention, http://www.cdc.gov

Census   U.S. Census Bureau, http://www.census.gov

CMS   Centers for Medicare and Medicaid Services, http://www.cms.hhs.gov

CPR   Current Population Reports, http://www.census.gov/main/www/cprs.html

CPS   Current Population Survey, http://www.bls.census.gov/cps/cpsmain.htm

CRP   Center for Responsive Politics, http://www.opensecrets.org

CTJ   Citizens for Tax Justice, http://www.ctj.org

DOL   U.S. Department of Labor, http://www.dol.gov

EE   *Employment and Earnings,* http://www.bls.gov/ces/home.htm#ee

ERP   *Economic Report of the President,* (President's Council of Economic Advisors, annual) http://www.gpoaccess.gov/eop

HDR   *Human Development Report,* (United Nations Development Programme, annual) http://hdr.undp.org/statistics

HUS   *Health, United States* (NCHS, annual), http://www.cdc.gov/nchs/hus.htm

IEA   *International Energy Annual* (Energy Information Administration, U.S. Department of Energy), http://www.eia.doe.gov/iea/contents.html

ITEP   Institute on Taxation and Economic Policy, http://www.itepnet.org

IWPR   Institute for Women's Policy Research, http://www.iwpr.org

MLR   *Monthly Labor Review* (BLS), http://www.bls.gov/opub/mlr/welcome.htm

MMWR   *Morbidity and Mortality Weekly* (CDC), http://www.cdc.gov/mmwr

NCES   National Center for Education Statistics (U.S. Department of Education), http://nces.ed.gov

NCHS   National Center for Health Statistics (CDC), http://www.cdc.gov/nchs/Default.htm

NPP   National Priorities Project, http://www.national

priorities.org

NYT   *New York Times* (daily), http://www.nytimes.com

OECD   Organization of Economic Cooperation and Development, http://www.oecd.org

PERI   Political Economy Research Institute, http://www.umass.edu/peri

SA   *Statistical Abstract of the U.S.* (Census, annual/biannual), http://www.census.gov/statab/www

SIPRI   Stockholm International Peace Research Institute, http://www.sipri.org

SWA   *State of Working America* (Mishel et al., Economic Policy Institute, biannual), http://www.epi.org/content.cfm/books_swa2004

USDA   U.S. Department of Agriculture, http://www.usda.gov

WDI   *World Development Indicators* (World Bank, annual), http://www.worldbank.org

WHO   World Health Organization, http://www.who.int/en

WP   *Washington Post* (daily), http://www.washingtonpost.com

WRI   World Resources Institute, http://www.wri.org

CHAPTER 1: OWNERS

1.1   Edward Wolff, "Changes in Household Wealth in the 1980s and 1990s in the U.S.," Table 2, Levy Economics Institute of Bard College, Working Paper No. 407 (May 2004), http://www.levy.org/pubs/wp/407.pdf; Joel Friedman and Ruth Carlitz, "Estate Tax Reform Could Raise Much-Needed Revenue," CBPP, Mar. 16, 2005, http://www.cbpp.org/3-16-05tax.htm; CBPP, "The Estate Tax: Myths and Realities," http://www.cbpp.org/pubs/estatetax.htm.

1.2   Wolff, pp. 5 and 9 and Tables 2 and 5; Wolff, personal communication. Note: the households in each wealth category are not necessarily the same in the different years.

1.3   Wolff, p. 10 and Tables 5, 6, and 12b.

1.4   Wolff, p. 16 n. 11 and Tables 7 and 8; Wolff, personal communication regarding the 1989, 1992, 1995, 1998, and 2001 Survey of Consumer Finances.

1.5   *BusinessWeek,* "A Payday for Performance," Apr. 18, 2005; BLS, "May 2004 National Occupational Employment and Wage Estimates," Tables 41-2031 and 29-1062, http://www.bls.gov/oes/current/oes_nat.htm; *BusinessWeek*, "Executive Compensation," Apr. 18, 2005, and "Executive Pay," Apr. 15, 2002; Penelope Patsuris, "Layoff Tracker Archive," Forbes.com, Mar. and Dec. 2001.

1.6   Chuck Collins et al., "I Didn't Do It Alone: Society's Contribution to Individual Wealth and Success," United for a Fair Economy, Aug. 2004, http://www.responsiblewealth.org/press/2004/notalo

nereportfinal.pdf; *Forbes*, "The Forbes 400," Oct. 11, 2004, http://www.forbes.com/free_forbes/ 2004/1011/103.html&rl04.

1.7   Census, "Historical Income Tables-Households," Tables H1 and H3, http://www. census.gov/hhes/ income/histinc/h01ar.html and h03ar.html.

1.8   Martin Daly et al., "Income Inequality and Homicide Rates in Canada and the United States," *Canadian Journal of Criminology*, Vol. 43, No. 2 (Apr. 2000), Figure 4, http://psych.mcmaster.ca/dalywilson/ iiahr2001.pdf; Richard Wilkinson, *The Impact of Inequality* (New York: The New Press, 2005); Dimitri Landa and Ethan Kapstein, "Inequality, Growth, and Democracy," *World Politics*, Vol. 53, No. 2 (Jan. 2001); Ichiro Kawachi et al., "Social Capital, Income Inequality, and Mortality," *American Journal of Public Health*, Vol. 87, No. 9 (Sept. 1997), Figure 1.

1.9   CRP, "Business-Labor-Ideology Split," http://www.opensecrets.org/overview/blio.asp?Cycle= 2004&display=Total; "527 Committee Activity," http://www.opensecrets.org/527s/527cmtes.asp?level=S &cycle=2004; "Top Industries," http://www.open secrets.org/overview/industries.asp?cycle=2004; "Industry Profiles," http://www.opensecrets.org/ industries/index.asp; and "Donor Demographics," http://www.opensecrets.org/overview/DonorDemo graphics.asp?cycle=2004. Note: The graph does not show the $5 million given by business through 527s or the $1 million given by labor through individuals and firms.

1.10   CRP, "Winning vs. Spending," http://www.open secrets.org/overview/bigspenders.asp?cycle=2004, and "Incumbent Advantage," http://www.opensecrets. org/overview/incumbs.asp?cycle=2004. Note: Values in the chart have been rounded off to the nearest 1,000. The calculation showing winners in the House of Representatives spending 3.7 times more than the losers includes those races in which the winner's opponent spent nothing. This calculation is also shown in the graph. In some of these races, there may truly have been no opponent. However, in many cases, there was an opponent—who may have been either a write-in candidate or officially listed on the ballot—and yet that opponent did not report any campaign spending to the Federal Elections Commission. We therefore thought it reasonable to include those races in the calculations. If those races are excluded from the calculations, the ratio of winners' spending to losers' is 2.7 to 1, and the losers' bar on the graph should read $370,000.

1.11   Corporate Accountability Project, "Media Reform Information Center," http://www.corporations .org/media; Ben Bagdikian, *The New Media Monopoly* (Boston: Beacon Press, 2004); Time Warner, "Businesses," http://www.timewarner .com/corp/businesses/index.html. Note: Different categories of media use different methods to measure size and rank. For instance, some calculate it based on the percentage of audience reached, others base it on the number of outlets providing media content, and others—like book publishers—take into account the percentage of new titles produced. Professor Bagdikian's measure of media consolidation aggregates the different media according to the internal standard of measure of dominance of each.

1.12   Gregg Fields, "No Business as Usual After 'Perfect Storm' of Enron Scandal," *Seattle Times,* July 11, 2004, http://seattletimes.nwsource.com/html/businesstechnology/2001976669_enron11.html; BJS, "Criminal Victimization in the United States, 2002 Statistical Tables," Table 82, http://www.ojp.usdoj.gov/bjs/abstract/cvusst.htm.

1.13   *Fortune,* "World's Largest Corporations," July 26, 2004, p. 163; World Bank, "Total GDP 2003" and "Population 2003," http://www.worldbank.org/data/quickreference/quickref.html.

1.14   *Forbes,* "The Forbes Global 2000: 2005 Edition," p. 172; Wal-Mart, "About Wal-Mart / Timeline," "About Wal-Mart / The Story of Wal-Mart," and "About Wal-Mart / Student Research Information / Quarterly Sales Report / Wal-Mart Reports January 2000 Sales," http://www.walmartstores.com/wmstore/wmstores/HomePage.jsp; Kenneth Stone, "Impact of the Wal-Mart Phenomenon on Rural Communities," http://www.econ.iastate.edu/faculty/stone/10yrstudy.pdf; Jerry Useem, "Should We Admire Wal-Mart?" *Fortune,* Mar. 8, 2004; Arindrajit Dube and Ken Jacobs, "Hidden Cost of Wal-Mart Jobs," UC-Berkeley Labor Center briefing paper, Aug. 2, 2004, http://laborcenter.berkeley.edu/lowwage/walmart.pdf; Charles Fishman, "The Wal-Mart You Don't Know," *FastCompany*, December 2003, http://www.fastcompany.com/magazine/77/walmart.html; Liza Featherstone, "Letters: Featherstone Replies," *The Nation,* Feb. 28, 2005.

1.15   Social Investment Forum, "2003 Report on Socially Responsible Investing Trends in the United States," http://www.socialinvest.org/areas/research/trends/sri_trends_report_2003.pdf; Standard & Poor's, "S&P 500," http://www2.standardandpoors.com/servlet/Satellite?pagename=sp/Page/IndicesIndexPg&r=1&l=EN&b=4&s=6&ig=48&i=56&si=138&xcd=500; William Greider, *The Soul of Capitalism* (New York: Simon & Schuster, 2004). Note: Market capitalization values for the S&P 500 are as of Dec. 31 of each year.

1.16   National Center for Employee Ownership, "A Statistical Profile of Employee Ownership," http://www.nceo.org/library/eo_stat.html; National Cooperative Business Association, "About Cooperatives: Worker-owned Cooperatives," http://www.ncba.coop/abcoop_work.cfm.

Chapter 2: Workers

2.1 BLS, *Handbook of Labor Statistics 1980,* p. 118, Table 60; *Handbook of Labor Statistics 1985,* p. 94, Table 41; EE, January issues, 1985–1994, Table 54; EE, January issues, 1995–2005, Table 37; OECD, *OECD Employment Outlook: Statistical Annex,* p. 255, Table F, http://www.oecd.org/dataoecd/36/30/3502 4561.pdf.

2.2 CPS, "Employment Status of the Civilian Noninstitutional Population, 1940 to Date," http://www.bls.gov/cps/cpsaat1.pdf; MLR, "Nearly 7.2 Million Working Poor in 1998," Sept. 20, 2000; BLS, "A Profile of the Working Poor [various years]," Reports 936, 944, 957, 968, 976, and 983; CPS, "2004 Annual Social and Economic Supplement," Table HI03, http://pubdb3.census.gov/macro/032004/health/h03_001.htm; Peter Gottschalk, "Work as a Stepping Stone for Low-Skilled Workers: What Is the Evidence?" in *The Low-Wage Labor Market: Challenges and Opportunities for Economic Self-Sufficiency,* Kelleen Kaye and Demetra Smith Nightingale, eds. (Washington, DC: Urban Institute Press, 2000), http://aspe.hhs.gov/hsp/lwlm99/gottschalk.htm; William Carrington and Bruce Fallick, "Do Some Workers Have Minimum Wage Careers?" MLR, May 2001, http://www.bls.gov/opub/mlr/2001/05/art2full.pdf.

2.3 SA 2004/5, Table 626; DOL, "Minimum Wage Laws in the States—January 1, 2005," http://www.dol.gov/esa/minwage/america.htm; EE, Jan. 2005, Table 44; Census, "Poverty Thresholds 2004," http://www.census.gov/hhes/poverty/threshld/thresh04.html.

2.4 Association of Community Organizations for Reform Now (ACORN), "Living Wage Wins," http://www.livingwagecampaign.org/index.php?id=1959; ACORN, "Living Wage Impact Research Summaries and Citations," http://www.livingwage campaign.org/index.php?id=1953; DOL, "Minimum Wage Laws in the States—January 1, 2005."

2.5 SWA 2004/5, pp. 158 and 162, Tables 2.21 and 2.22; Robert Frank and Philip Cook, *The Winner-Take-All Society* (New York: Penguin Books, 1996); BLS, Occupations Employment Statistics, "May 2004 Occupational Employment and Wage Estimates" and "1999 Occupational Employment and Wage Estimates," http://www.bls.gov/oes/oes_dl.htm. Note: The pay difference between high- and low-paid college educated workers was calculated as the difference between the wage at the 90th percentile and at the 10th percentile of all workers who are college graduates. (The wage at the 90th percentile is the wage that is greater than that of the lowest-paid 90% of college-graduate workers and less than that of the top-paid 10% of college-graduate workers. The wage at the 10th percentile is the wage that is greater than that of the lowest-paid 10% of college-graduate workers and less than that of the top-paid 90% of college-graduate workers.)

2.6   SA 2004/5, Tables 214 and 215; SWA 2004/2005, p. 158, Table 2.21; NCES, "Digest of Education Statistics, 2003," Table 108, http://nces.ed.gov/ programs/digest/d03/tables/pdf/table108.pdf; Katharin Peter and Laura Horn, "Gender Differences in Participation and Completion of Undergraduate Education and How They Have Changed Over Time," NCES Publication #2005169, Feb. 2005, p. 12, http://nces.ed.gov/pubs2005/2005169.pdf.

2.7   William Wiatrowski, "Documenting Benefits Coverage for All Workers," BLS, Compensation and Working Conditions Online, Table 2 (see note below), http://www.bls.gov/opub/cwc/cm2004051 8ar01p1.htm; BLS, "National Compensation Survey: Employee Benefits in Private Industry in the United States, March 2004," Tables 1, 2, 3, 4, 8, and 13, http://www.bls.gov/ncs/ebs/sp/ebsm0002.pdf; BLS, National Compensation Survey statistics series EBUFAMAVE00000ML and EBUSELFAVE0000ML, http://data.bls.gov/cgi bin/srgate. Note: Table 2 of William Wiatrowski's article contains data that were subsequently updated. The values for medical coverage in 2003 should be ignored in that table. See instead Table 1 from the BLS news release "New Estimates for March 2003 Health Care Benefit Access and Participation," http://www.bls.gov/ncs/ebs/notice112004.htm.

2.8   BLS, "Employee Benefits in Medium and Large Private Establishments, 1995," Table 1, http://www.bls.gov/ncs/ebs/sp/ebbl0015.pdf; BLS, "National Compensation Survey: Employee Benefits in Private Industry in the United States, March 2004," Table 2; Robin Blackburn, "The Great Pension Crunch," *The Nation,* Feb. 17, 2003; AFL-CIO, "Pensions," http://www.aflcio.org/issues politics/pensionsavings/pensions.cfm.

2.9   CPS, "Household Data—Annual Averages—Table 10. Employed Persons by Occupation, Race, Hispanic or Latino Ethnicity, and Sex," ftp://ftp.bls.gov/pub/special.requests/lf/aat10.txt; BLS, "National Census of Fatal Occupational Injuries in 2003," http://www.bls.gov/news.release/ pdf/cfoi.pdf; BLS, "Lost-Worktime Injuries and Illnesses: Characteristics and Resulting Days Away from Work, 2003," Table 10, http://www.bls.gov/ iif/oshwc/osh/case/osnr0022.pdf; BLS, "Workplace Injuries and Illnesses in 2003," http://www.bls.gov/ iif/oshwc/osh/os/osnr0021.pdf; David Barstow, "U.S. Rarely Seeks Charges for Deaths in Workplace," NYT, Dec. 22, 2003, p. A1; National Institute for Occupational Safety and Health, "Occupational Cancer," http://www.cdc.gov/niosh/topics/cancer.

2.10   BLS, "Mass Layoffs in December 2004 and Annual

Averages for 2004," Table B, ftp://ftp.bls.gov/pub/
news.release/History/mmls.01262005.news; SWA
2004/5, p. 275, Table 3.22; Hans De Witte, "Job
Insecurity and Psychological Well-being: Review of
the Literature and Exploration of Some Unresolved
Issues," *European Journal of Work and Organizational
Psychology*, Vol. 8, No. 2 (1999), pp. 155–77; Mika
Kivimäki et al., "Factors Underlying the Effect of
Organisational Downsizing on Health of Employees:
Longitudinal Cohort Study," *British Medical Journal*,
Vol. 320 No. 7240 (Apr. 8, 2000), pp. 971–75.

2.11   BLS, "Employment Status of the Civilian
Noninstitutional Population by Age, Sex, and Race,"
ftp://ftp.bls.gov/pub/special.requests/lf/aat3.txt; BLS,
"Employment Status of the Hispanic or Latino
Population by Age and Sex," ftp://ftp.bls.gov/pub/
special.requests/lf/aat4.txt; BLS, "Employment
Situation News Release," Table A-9, http://www.bls
.gov/cps/cpsatabs.htm; Bill Gillham et al.,
"Unemployment Rates, Single Parent Density, and
Indices of Child Poverty: Their Relationship to
Different Categories of Child Abuse and Neglect,"
Child Abuse and Neglect, Vol. 22, No. 2 (1998), pp.
79–90; Katrin Barkow et al., "Risk Factors for
Depression at 12-Month Follow-up in Adult Primary
Health Care Patients with Major Depression: An
International Prospective Study," *Journal of Affective
Disorders*, Vol. 76 (2003), pp. 157–69.

2.12   ERP 2005, Table B-35; BLS, "Employment
Situation," Table A-1, http://www.bls.gov/news
.release/empsit.toc.htm.

2.13   BLS, "The Employment Situation," Jan.-Dec. 2004,
http://www.bls.gov/schedule/archives/empsit_nr.htm;
J. Buckley and R. VanGiezen, "Federal Statistics on
Medical Benefits and Cost Trends: An Overview,"
MLR, Nov. 2004; D. Dooley and J. Prause, *The
Social Costs of Underemployment* (New York:
Cambridge University Press, 2003).

2.14   BLS, "Contingent and Alternative Employment
Arrangements, February 2001," http://www.bls.gov/
news.release/conemp.nr0.htm; Steven Hipple,
"Contingent Work in the Late-1990s," MLR, Mar.
2001; Steven Hipple, "Contingent Work: Results
from the Second Survey," MLR, Nov. 1998; Sharon
Cohany, "Workers in Alternative Employment
Arrangements," MLR, Oct. 1996; Anne Polivka,
"Into Contingent and Alternative Employment: By
Choice?" MLR, Oct. 1996; Sharon Cohany,
"Workers in Alternative Employment Arrangements:
A Second Look," MLR, Nov. 1998; Marissa
DiNatale, "Characteristics of and Preference for
Alternative Work Arrangements, 1999," MLR, Mar.
2001.

2.15   BLS, "Union Members in 2004," Tables 1 and 3,
http://www.bls.gov/news.release/pdf/union2.pdf;
Peter D. Hart Research Associates for the AFL-CIO,

"Labor Day 2005: The State of Working America," Aug. 2005, p. 6, http://www.aflcio.org/aboutus/laborday/upload/ld2005_report.pdf; Gerald Epstein, "Threat Effects and the Impact of Capital Mobility on Wages and Public Finances: Developing a Research Agenda," PERI Working Paper #7, 2000; B. Luthje and Christoph Scherrer, "Race, Multiculturalism, and Labour Organizing in the United States: Lessons for Europe," *Theory and Society*, Vol. 25, No. 4 (Aug.) 1996; BLS, "Gender Gap in Unionization Closing," MLR, Editor's Desk, Mar. 3, 2004.

2.16   BLS, "National Compensation Survey: Employee Benefits in Private Industry in the United States, March 2004," Tables 2, 4, 7, 8, 9, and 12; BLS, "Union Members in 2004," Tables 2, 3, and 4.

CHAPTER 3: WOMEN

3.1   David Cotter et al., "Gender Inequality at Work" (Washington, DC: Population Reference Bureau, 2004), p. 3, Figure 1.

3.2   Estimates for May 2004, based on CPS Household Data, Table A-6, ftp.bls.gov/pub/suppl/empsit/cpseea6.txt.

3.3   EE, Jan. 1981, Table A-77; EE, Jan. 1990, Table A-73; EE, Jan. 2005, p. 248, http://www.bls.gov/cps/cpsaat37.pdf; BLS, "Highlights of Women's Earnings in 1999," Report 943 (1999), Table 1.

3.4   Stephen Rose and Heidi Hartmann, "Still a Man's Labor Market: The Long-Term Earnings Gap," IWPR, 2004.

3.5   CPS, "Characteristics of the Employed," Table 11, http://www.bls.gov/cps/cpsaat11.pdf.

3.6   BLS, "May 2004 National Occupational Employment and Wage Estimates," http://www.bls.gov/oes/current/oes_nat.htm.

3.7   Catalyst, 2000 and 2002 "Catalyst Census of Women Corporate Officers and Top Earners in the Fortune 500," http://www.catalystwomen.org/press_room/factsheets/factscote00.htm and http://www.catalystwomen.org/press_room/factsheets/COTE%20Factsheet%202002.pdf.

3.8   On Federal Express, http://usgovinfo.about.com/cs/consumer/a/fedexpays.htm; on Merrill Lynch, http://www.epexperts.com/news_index1468.html; on United Airlines, http://www.epexperts.com/news_index831.html; on Wal-Mart, "No Way to Treat a Lady," *BusinessWeek,* Mar. 3, 2003; Liza Featherstone, *Selling Women Short: The Landmark Battle for Workers' Rights at Wal-Mart* (New York: Basic Books, 2004).

3.9   Carmen DeNavas-Walt et al., *Income, Poverty, and Health Insurance Coverage in the United States: 2003* (CPR P60-226), p. 40, Table B-1, http://www.census.gov/prod/2004pubs/p60-226.pdf.

3.10 Child Trends Data Bank, http://www.childtrends databank.org.

3.11 BLS, "American Time Use Survey," http://www/bls.gov/tus.

3.12 Michael Hout and Caroline Hanley, "The Overworked American Family: Trends and Nontrends in Working Hours, 1968–2001," Working Paper, Survey Research Center, University of California, Berkeley, June 2002, cited with permission of authors; AFL-CIO Working Women's Department, http://www.aflcio.org/women; Family Caregiver Alliance, http://www.caregiver.org.

3.13 Urban Institute, "Fast Facts on Welfare Policy" and "Nearly 3 Out of 4 Young Children with Employed Mothers are Regularly in Child Care," http://www.urban.org; Linda Giannarelli et al., "Getting Help with Child Care Expenses," Urban Institute Occasional Paper No. 62.

3.14 Janet Gornick and Marcia Meyers, *Families That Work: Policies for Reconciling Parenthood and Employment* (New York: Russell Sage Foundation, 2003).

3.15 Alan Guttmacher Institute, "Top 10 Ways Sexual and Reproductive Health Suffered in 2004," News Release, Dec. 20, 2004, http://www.guttmacher.org/media/nr/2004/12/20/index.html; Nicholas D. Kristof, "Bush's Sex Scandal," NYT, Feb. 6, 2005, p. A21; Lawrence Finer and Stanley Henshaw, "Abortion Incidence and Services in the United States in 2000," Tables 3 and 4, *Perspectives on Sexual and Reproductive Health*, Vol. 35, No. 1 (Jan./Feb. 2003), http://www.gutt macher.org/pubs/journals/3500603.html.

3.16 Center for American Women and Politics, "Women in Elective Office 2005," http://www.cawp.rutgers.edu/Facts.html.

CHAPTER 4: PEOPLE OF COLOR

4.1 SA 2004/5, Table 16; J. Passel, "Projections of the U.S. Population and Labor Force by Generation and Educational Attainment: 2000–2050," Urban Institute, 2003.

4.2 Census, "The Hispanic Population: 2000," Census 2000 Brief, May 2001, p. 1, and "The Asian Population: 2000," Census 2000 Brief, Feb. 2002, p. 9, Table 4.

4.3 SA 2004/5, Table 5; Sheldon Danziger and Peter Gottschalk, "Diverging Fortunes: Trends in Poverty and Inequality," Population Reference Bureau, http://www.prb.org; George J. Borjas, "Increasing the Supply of Labor Through Immigration," Center for Immigration Studies, May 2004, http://www.cis.org.

4.4 Jeffrey S. Passel, "Estimates of the Size and Characteristics of the Undocumented Population," Pew Hispanic Center Report, Mar. 21, 2005, http://pewhispanic.org. Note: The category of "legal permanent residents" covers green-card holders including amnesty recipients under the Immigration Reform and Control Act of 1986. "Legal temporary residents" includes students, professors, high-tech workers, and those in a number of other temporary visa categories.

4.5   ERP 2004, p. 260, Table B-42.

4.6   EE, Jan. 2005, p. 204, Table 7; "Hispanics and the Bottom Rung," Hispanic American Center for Economic Research, http://www.hacer.org/current/US084.php; "Labor Market Outcomes of Hispanics by Generation: ERIC Digest," http://www.ericdigests.org/2004-2/labor.html.

4.7   SA 2004/5, Table 212.

4.8   EE, Jan. 2005, pp. 216–17, Tables 12 and 13; SA 2004/5, Table 669.

4.9   EE, Jan. 2005, p. 190, Table D-19.

4.10   Carmen DeNavas-Walt et al., *Income, Poverty, and Health Insurance Coverage in the United States: 2003* (CPR P60-226), pp. 40–45, Table B-1, http://www.census.gov/prod/2004pubs/p60-226.pdf.

4.11   Sourcebook of Criminal Justice Statistics, Table 6.33, http://www.albany.edu/sourcebook/pdf/t633.pdf; Federal Bureau of Prisons, "Quick Facts," Aug. 27, 2005, posting, http://www.bop.gov/news/quick.jsp. Note: As a result of changes in the presentation of data by the source, this series differs from that published in the previous edition of the *Field Guide,* showing sentenced prisoners rather than number of adults held. See also Betty Pettit and Bruce Western, "Mass Imprisonment and the Life Course: Race and Class Inequality in U.S. Incarceration," *American Sociological Review,* Vol. 69, No. 2 (2004).

4.12   Nell Bernstein, "Left Behind," *Mother Jones,* July 10, 2001; Kiaran Honderich, "The Real Cost of Prisons for Women and Their Children," Real Cost of Prisons Project, http://www.realcostofprisons.org/papers.html#background; Center for Children of Incarcerated Parents, http://www.e-ccip.org/publication.html; "Learning Behind Bars," American School Board Journal, http://www.asbj.com/current/research.html.

4.13   SA 2004/5, Table 59.

4.14   SA 2004/5, Table 60; Nancy Folbre, "Our Children, Ourselves: Social Reproduction in the U.S.," manuscript, Department of Economics, University of Massachusetts.

4.15   Roland Fryer and Glenn Loury, "Affirmative Action and Its Mythology," *Journal of Economic Perspectives,* (Summer 2005).

4.16   Marianne Bertrand and Sendhil Mullainathan, "Are Emily and Greg More Employable than Lakisha and Jamal? A Field Experiment on Labor Market Discrimination," National Bureau of Economic Research, Working Paper No. 9873, July 2003;

Devah Pager and Bruce Western, "Discrimination in Low-Wage Labor Markets: Evidence from an Experimental Audit Study in New York City," Department of Sociology, Princeton University, paper presented at the meetings of the Population Association of America, April 2005; National Community Reinvestment Coalition, "Fair Lending Disparities by Race, Income, and Gender in All Metropolitan Areas in America," March 2005, http://www.ncrc.org/pressandpubs/press_releases/documents/HMDA_Pricing_Report.htm; Caroline E. Mayer, "Car-Loan Rates Marked Up More for Blacks," WP, Oct. 1, 2003, p. E01.

CHAPTER 5: GOVERNMENT

5.1   BUSG FY2006, Historical Tables, Tables 15.2; BLS, Employment Situation Release, Table A-1, http://www.bls.gov/webapps/legacy/cpsatab1.htm, and Table B-1, http://www.bls.gov/webapps/legacy/cesbtab1.htm. See the note in 5.2 below.

5.2   OECD, *Economic Outlook,* No. 77, Statistical Annex Table 25, June 2005, http://www.oecd.org/document/61/0,2340,en_2649_201185_2483901_1_1_1_1,00.html; OECD, "Health Care Data 2005," Table 7, http://www.oecd.org/document/16/0,2340,en_2825_495642_2085200_1_1_1_1,00.html;

information from SIPRI, "SIPRI Military Expenditure Database"; Census, "Health Insurance Coverage: 2004," Table 7, http://www.census.gov/hhes/www/hlthins/hlthin04/hi04t7.pdf. Note: Charts 5.1 and 5.2 make it appear as though government spending as a share of GDP in the U.S. increased by 5% between 2004 and 2005. However, this is actually the result of different methods of calculation used by our sources for the two charts. According to the OECD's calculations, there was almost no change in government spending as a percentage of GDP in those two years.

5.3   BUSG, FY2006, Historical Tables, Tables 3.1, 3.2, 7.1, 8.5, and 8.7, and Analytical Perspectives, Table 8.5; Andrew Hacker, "After Welfare," *New Republic,* Oct. 11, 2004, http://www.jasondeparle.com/TNR_110704.html. Note: TANF is Temporary Assistance for Needy Families; SCHIP is State Children's Health Insurance Program.

5.4   BUSG, FY2006, Historical Tables, Table 3.2. On affordable housing: NPP, "NPP Database." On hunger: Mark Nord et al., "Household Food Security in the United States, 2003," USDA, Economic Research Service, Research Brief, Oct. 2004, Section 1, p. 3, http://www.ers.usda.gov/publications/fanrr42/; ibid., "Household Food Security in the United States 2002," USDA, Section 1, p. 4, http://www.ers.usda.gov/publications/fanrr35/. Note:

"The FMR [fair market rent] is devised by HUD and is the amount of money needed to pay gross rent (shelter plus utilities) for privately-provided, safe, sanitary, rental housing of a modest nature, in a given area. Affordable rent is defined as rent consuming no more than 30% of one's income. Therefore, a renter who cannot afford FMR, is a renter who would need to pay more than 30% of his/her income in order to pay for the FMR of a 2-bedroom unit." Definition from NPP.

5.5 NPP, "Better Security for Less Money in the United States," June 2005; Center for Defense Information and Foreign Policy in Focus, *The Report of the Task force on A Unified Security Budget for the United States, 2006,* http://www.cdi.org/pdfs/Unified-Security-Budget-2006.pdf.

5.6 NPP, "New National Security," Aug. 15, 2005; information from SIPRI, "SIPRI Military Expenditure Database"; U.S. Department of Defense, "Active Duty Military Personnel Strengths by Regional Area and by Country," June 30, 2005, http://web1.whs .osd.mil/mmid/military/history/hst0605.pdf; White House, "President Bush Announces Major Combat Operations in Iraq Have Ended," May 1, 2003, http://www.whitehouse.gov/news/releases/2003/ 05/iraq/20030501-15.html; Michael O'Hanlon and Nina Kamp, *Iraq Index*, Brookings Institution, Sept. 29, 2005, pp. 5, 7, and 10, http://www.brookings .edu/fp/saban/iraq/index.htm; Peter Grier, "The Rising Economic Cost of the Iraq War," *Christian Science Monitor,* May 19, 2005, http://www .csmonitor.com/2005/0519/p01s03-usmi.htm. Note: North Atlantic Treaty Organization (NATO) members are Belgium, Bulgaria, Canada, Czech Republic, Denmark, Estonia, France, Germany, Greece, Hungary, Iceland, Italy, Latvia, Lithuania, Luxembourg, Netherlands, Norway, Poland, Portugal, Romania, Slovakia, Slovenia, Spain, Turkey, United Kingdom, and U.S.A. The chart slice labeled "Other close allies" covers Australia, Israel, Japan, and South Korea.

5.7 BUSG, FY2006, Historical Tables, Table 1.1.

5.8 BUSG, FY2006, Historical Tables, Table 7.1; Bureau of the Public Debt, "Historical Monthly Statements," Table 1, Aug. 31, 2005, http://www.publicdebt .treas.gov/opd/opds082005.htm.

5.9 BUSG, FY2006, Historical Tables, Table 2.1; ITEP, "Federal Taxation of Earnings versus Investment Income in 2004," May 2004.

5.10 CTJ, "The Bush Tax Cuts: The Most Recent CTJ Data," July 18, 2005.

5.11 ITEP, *Who Pays? A Distributional Analysis of the Tax Systems in All 50 States,* 2nd edition, Jan. 2003. Note: Values in the table do not add up perfectly due to independent rounding.

5.12 Robert McIntyre and T.D. Nguyen, "State Corporate Income Taxes 2001–2003," CTJ/ITEP, Feb. 2005;

McIntyre and Nguyen, "Corporate Income Taxes in the Bush Years," CTJ/ITEP, Sept. 2004.

5.13   CRP, "Tracking the Payback," http://opensecrets.org/payback/index.asp.

5.14   Census, "Voting and Registration in the Election of November 2004," Tables 4a, 5, 7, and 9, http://www.census.gov/population/www/socdemo/voting/cps2004.html; International Institute for Democracy and Electoral Assistance, "Turnout in the World—Country by Country Performance," http://www.idea.int/vt/survey/voter_turnout_pop2.cfm.

5.15   Census, Historical Poverty Tables—People, Table 3, http://www.census.gov/hhes/www/poverty/histpov/hstpov3.html.

5.16   The 2005 OASDI Trustees Report, Table VI.F7, http://www.ssa.gov/OACT/TR/TR05/VI_OASDHI_dollars.html#wp140103; Chris Chaplain and Alice Wade, "Memorandum: Estimated OASDI Long-Range Financial Effects of Several Provisions Requested by the Social Security Advisory Board," Office of the Chief Actuary, Social Security Administration, Table 15, Feb. 7, 2005, http://www.ssab.gov/financing/2004_update.pdf.

CHAPTER 6: WELFARE AND EDUCATION

6.1   Census, Historical Income Tables—Families, Table F-7, http://www.census.gov/hhes/income/histinc/f07.html.

6.2   Census, Historical Income Tables—Families, Table F-2, http://www.census.gov/hhes/income/histinc/f02.html.

6.3   Carmen DeNavas-Walt et al., *Income, Poverty, and Health Insurance Coverage in the United States: 2003* (CPR P60-226), pp. 4 and 39, http://www.census.gov/prod/2004pubs/p60-226.pdf.

6.4   Ibid., p. 10, Table 3; U.S. Internal Revenue Service, "EITC Assistant," http://www.irs.gov/individuals/article/0,,id=130102,00.html; Census, "Poverty Thresholds 2004," http://www.census.gov/hhes/www/poverty/threshld/thresh04.html.

6.5   Census, Historical Poverty Tables, Table 3, http://www.census.gov/hhes/poverty/histpov/hstpov3.html; Luxembourg Income Study, http://www.lisproject.org/keyfigures.htm.

6.6   Census, Small Area Income and Poverty Estimates, http://www.census.gov/hhes/www/saipe/county.html; Elizabeth Gershoff, "Low Income and the Development of America's Kindergartners," National Center for Children in Poverty, Living at the Edge research brief No. 4, Nov. 2003; Child Trends Data Bank, "Asthma," http://www.childtrendsdatabank

.org/pdf/43_PDF.pdf, and "Foster Care," http://www
.childtrendsdatabank.org/indicators/12FosterCare.cf
m; U.S. Department of Health and Human Services,
Administration for Children, National Center on
Abuse and Neglect, *Third National Incidence Study of
Abuse and Neglect* (Washington, DC, 1996).

6.7 Testimony of Mark Greenberg, Center for Law and
Social Policy, to the Committee on Education and
the Workforce, U.S. House of Representatives,
Mar. 15, 2005, http://www.clasp.org/publications/
greenberg_testimony_031505.pdf.

6.8 Jennifer Mezey, "Threatened Progress: U.S. in
Danger of Losing Ground on Child Care for Low-
Income Working Families," Center for Law and
Social Policy, Brief 2, June 2003, http://www.clasp
.org/publications/CC_brief2.pdf; IWPR, *In Our
Own Backyards: Local and State Strategies to Improve
the Quality of Family Child Care,* 2005, p. 1,
http://www.iwpr.org/pdf/G717.pdf.

6.9 UNICEF, *Child Poverty in Rich Countries 2005,
Report Card No. 6,* p. 15 (Florence: UNICEF
Innocenti Research Centre, 2005), http://www.un-
ngls.org/UNICEF-child-poverty-in-rich-countries-
2005.pdf; David Pichaud and Holly Sutherland,
"How Effective Is the British Government's Attempt
to Reduce Child Poverty," Innocenti Working Paper
No. 77 (Florence: UNICEF Innocenti Research
Centre, 2000), http://www.unicef-icdc.org/
publications/pdf/iwp77.pdf; Isabel Sawhill, ed., *One
Percent for the Kids: New Policies, Brighter Futures for
America's Children* (Washington, DC: Brookings
Institution, 2003). Note: The U.K., like other
European countries but unlike the U.S., defines
poverty in terms of relative income rather than in
terms of an absolute standard. Households
with incomes below 60% of the median income for
households of a similar composition are deemed
poor. ("Median" is explained in Toolkit T.3.)

6.10 Cato Handbook for Congress, 2003, http://www
.cato.org/pubs/handbook/hb108/hb108-33.pdf;
Doug Bandow, "Surprise! Stadiums Don't Pay, After
All," WP, Oct. 19, 2003, p. B01; Philip Mattera and
Anna Purinton, "Shopping for Subsidies: How Wal-
Mart Uses Taxpayer Money to Finance Its Never-
Ending Growth," Good Jobs First, May 2004,
http://www.goodjobsfirst.org/pdf/wmtstudy.pdf.

6.11 Mark Nord et al., "Household Food Security in the
United States, 2003," USDA, Economic Research
Service, Research Brief, Oct. 2004, http://www.ers
.usda.gov/Publications/fanrr42/; The United States
Conference of Mayors, *Hunger and Homelessness
Survey, 2004,* p. 3, http://www.usmayors.org/uscm/
hungersurvey/2004/onlinereport/HungerAndHome
lessnessReport2004.pdf.

6.12 Joint Center for Housing Studies of Harvard
University, *The State of the Nation's Housing 2005,*

http://www.jchs.harvard.edu/publications/markets/son2004.pdf.

6.13 U.S. Conference of Mayors, *Hunger and Homelessness Survey, 2004*; National Low Income Housing Coalition, *Out of Reach 2004,* http://www.nlihc.org/oor2004/.

6.14 National Education Association, *Rankings & Estimates: Rankings of the States 2004 and Estimates of School Statistics 2005,* Summary Table J, June 2005, p. 95, http://www.nea.org/edstats/images/05rankings.pdf; Stan Karp, "Money, Schools, and Justice," *Rethinking Schools,* Vol. 18, No. 1 (Fall 2003), http://www.rethinkingschools.org/archive/18_01/just181.shtml.

6.15 NCES, *Digest of Education Statistics 2003,* Table 315, http://nces.ed.gov/programs/digest/d03/tables/dt315.asp; Gordon C. Winston, "The Awkward Economics of Higher Education," *Journal of Economic Perspectives,* Vol. 13, No. 1 (Winter 1999), pp. 13–36; Congressional Budget Office, *Private and Public Contributions to Financing College Education* (Washington, DC: Congressional Budget Office, 2004).

6.16 The Pell Institute, *Indicators of Opportunity in Higher Education,* Fall 2004, p. 7, http://www.pellinstitute.org/statusreport/5b_Indicators_CvrsTxt.pdf; Congressional Budget Office, *Private and Public Contributions to Financing College Education*

(Washington, DC: Congressional Budget Office, 2004); Investment Company Institute, *Profile of Households Saving for College,* Fall 2003, p. 19, http://www.ici.org/statements/res/1rpt_03_college_saving.pdf.

CHAPTER 7: HEALTH

7.1 HUS 2004, Tables 115, 116, and 131.

7.2 HUS 2004, Tables 25, 26, and 115; Richard Wilkinson, *The Impact of Inequality* (New York: The New Press, 2005), Chapter 3.

7.3 OECD, "OECD Health Data 2005," Table 7, http://www.oecd.org/dataoecd/44/15/35044328.xls, and Table 10, http://www.oecd.org/dataoecd/43/56/35044601.xls; CMS, "Facts About the Centers for Medicare & Medicaid Services"; SA 2004/05, Table 3. Note: The dollar values shown in the text and graph are calculated in "purchasing power parity" (PPP). This is a way of comparing money value between countries that adjusts the official exchange rate to account for different purchasing power within each country.

7.4 Annual averages calculated from BLS, Consumer Price Index, Detailed Statistics, Seasonally Adjusted, http://data.bls.gov/cgi-bin/dsrv?cu.

7.5 NCHS, "Summary Health Statistics for the U.S.

Population: National Health Survey, 2003," pp. 11–12, Table 2, http://www.cdc.gov/nchs/data/series/sr_10/sr10_224.pdf; Urban Institute, "National Survey of America's Families: 2002," Online Statistical Analysis, http://anfdata.urban.org/sdaweb/analysis.cfm.

7.6   HUS 2004, Tables 131 and 153; CPS, *2004 Annual Social and Economic Supplement*, Table HI03, http://pubdb3.census.gov/macro/032004/health/h03_001.html; Kaiser Commission on Medicaid and the Uninsured, "Enrolling Uninsured Low-Income Children in Medicaid and SCHIP," March 2005, http://www.kff.org/medicaid/2177-04.cfml; Carmen DeNavas-Walt et al., *Income, Poverty, and Health Insurance Coverage in the United States: 2003* (CPR P60-226), http://www.census.gov/prod/2004pubs/p60-226.pdf.

7.7   Carmen DeNavas-Walt et al., Tables 5 and 6; CPS, *2004 Annual Social and Economic Supplement*, Table HI03; HUS 2004, Table 27; CDC, *National Vital Statistics Reports*, Vol. 53, No. 17 (Mar. 7, 2005), Table E, http://www.cdc.gov/nchs/data/dvs/nvsr53_17 tableE2002.pdf.

7.8   HUS 2004, Tables 6 and 19; HUS 2000, Table 20; HUS 1999, Table 19; HUS 1998, Tables 6 and 20; HUS 1996–97, Table 20; HUS 1993, Table 18; HUS 1989, Table 6; HUS 1985, Table 12; HUS 1982, Table 11; HUS 1981, Table 10; HUS 1980, Table 10; HUS 1976–77, Table 22. Note: For an explanation of a "ratio" scale, see Toolkit T.2.

7.9   BLS, Consumer Expenditure Survey 2003, Table 1, http://www.bls.gov/cex/2003/Standard/quintile.pdf.

7.10   Lawrence Finer et al., "Reasons U.S. Women Have Abortions: Quantitative and Qualitative Perspectives," Table 5, *Perspectives on Sexual and Reproductive Health,* Vol. 37, No. 2 (Sept. 2005), http://www.guttmacher.org/pubs/journals/3711005.pdf; Rachel Jones et al., "Patterns in the Socioeconomic Characteristics of Women Obtaining Abortions in 2000–2001," Table 1, *Perspectives on Sexual and Reproductive Health,* Vol. 34, No. 5 (Sept./Oct. 2002), http://www.guttmacher.org/pubs/journals/3422602.html; Lawrence Finer and Stanley Henshaw, "Abortion Incidence and Services in the United States in 2000," text and Tables 1 and 3, *Perspectives on Sexual and Reproductive Health*, Vol. 35, No. 1 (Jan./Feb. 2003), http://www.guttmacher.org/pubs/journals/3500603.html; Lawrence Finer and Stanley Henshaw, "Estimates of U.S. Abortion Incidence in 2001 and 2002," Alan Guttmacher Institute, http://www.guttmacher.org/pubs/2005/05/18/ab_incidence.pdf.

7.11   NCHS, "Early Release of Selected Estimates Based on Data From the 2004 National Health Interview Survey," Figures 13.1, 13.2, and 13.3, http://www.cdc.gov/nchs/about/major/nhis/

released200506.htm; NCHS, "Mental Health Disorders," FASTATS, http://www.cdc.gov/nchs/fastats/men tal.htm; Substance Abuse and Mental Health Services Administration, "Homelessness," http://www.mentalhealth.samhsa.gov/cmhs/Homeless ness; CDC, "Deaths: Preliminary Data for 2003," National Vital Statistics Reports, Vol. 53, No. 15 (Feb. 28, 2005), Table B, http://www.cdc.gov/nchs/deaths.htm; Carole Gresenz et al., "Income and Mental Health: Unraveling Community and Individual Level Relationships," *Journal of Mental Health Policy and Economics,* Vol. 4 (2001), pp. 197–203.

7.12   David Himmelstein et al., "MarketWatch: Illness and Injury as Contributors to Bankruptcy," *Health Affairs,* Feb. 2, 2005, http://www.healthaffairs.org. Note: Data on Native American infant mortality rates were not available for the years earlier than 1983 and for 1992, 1993, and 1994.

7.13   Harvard Center for Cancer Prevention, "Chronic Disease: Impact and Prevention Fact Sheet," http://www.yourdiseaserisk.harvard.edu/hccpquiz.pl?lang=english&func=show&page=generalfactsheet; HUS 2004, Tables 30 and 31 and text p. 33; A.H. Mokdad et al., "Actual Causes of Death in the United States, 2000," *Journal of the American Medical Association,* (Mar. 10, 2005); J. Michael Harris et al., *The U.S. Food Marketing System, 2002,* Appendix Table 30, USDA Agricultural Economic Report No. 811, June 2002, http://www.ers.usda.gov/publications/aer811.

7.14   Dee Mahan, "Profiting from Pain: Where Prescription Drug Dollars Go," Families USA, http://www.familiesusa.org/assets/pdfs/PPreport89a5.pdf; Kaiser Family Foundation, "Trends and Indicators in the Changing Healthcare Marketplace," Exhibit 1.21, http://www.kff.org/insurance/7031/ti2004-1-21.cfm; Marc Kaufman, "Merck CEO Resigns as Drug Probe Continues," WP, May 6, 2005, p. A01; Marcia Angell, "The Truth About the Drug Companies," *New York Review of Books,* Vol. 51, No. 12, Jul. 15, 2004, http://www.nybooks.com/articles/17244; Gardiner Harris and Eric Koli, "Lucrative Drug, Danger Signals and the F.D.A.," NYT, June 10, 2005, p. A1.

7.15   UNAIDS, *AIDS Epidemic Update 2004,* "Introduction," December 2004, p. 3; UNAIDS, "Factsheet: Africa," Apr. 3, 2005; UNAIDS, *2004 Report on the Global HIV/AIDS Epidemic: 4th Global Report,* "The Impact of AIDS on People and Societies" and "Table of Country-Specific HIV/AIDS Estimates and Data, as of End 2003," http://www.unaids.org/bangkok2004/GAR2004_html/GAR2004_00_en.htm; WHO, *Progress on Global Access to HIV Antiretroviral Therapy: An Update on "3 by 5,"* p. 13, Table 1, http://www.who.int/3by5/fullreport

June2005.pdf; HUS 2004, Table 29. Note: HIV is the human immunodeficiency virus. It causes acquired immunodeficiency syndrome (AIDS). HIV attacks a person's immune system, leaving the individual susceptible to other diseases. A person can have HIV and show no symptoms; when the person becomes sick enough, he or she is said to have developed AIDS. It is usually transmitted from one person to another through unprotected sex (sex without proper use of a condom) or the sharing of needles used for injecting drugs.

7.16 HDR 2004, "Human Development Indicators," Tables 6, 7, and 9, http://hdr.undp.org/reports/global//2004; WHO, *World Health Report 2005*, "Statistical Annex," Table 3, http://www.who.int/whr/2005/en/index.html; Richard Adams, "International Migration, Remittances and the Brain Drain: A Study of 24 Labor-Exporting Countries," World Bank Policy Research Working Paper 3069, June 2003, http://econ.worldbank.org/external/default/main?pagePK=64165259&theSitePK=469372&piPK=64165421&menuPK=64166093&entityID=000094946_03062104301450; Ashnie Padarath et al., "Health Personnel in Southern Africa: Confronting Maldistribution and Brain Drain," EQUINET Discussion Paper No. 3, 2003, p. 23, http://www.equinetafrica.org/bibl/docs/DIS3hres.pdf; World Bank, *World Development Indicators 2005*,

Tables 2.14 and 2.15, http://devdata.worldbank.org/wdi2005/section2.htm.

CHAPTER 8: ENVIRONMENT

8.1 WRI, *Millennium Ecosystem Assessment: Ecosystems and Human Well-being, Biodiversity Synthesis*, (Washington, DC: WRI, 2005), Box 2.2, p. 39; http://www.millenniumassessment.org/en/Products.Synthesis.aspx. Note: As in the WRI source, the smallest values were used to compare net benefits when a range of estimates were reported. "Net present value" is defined in the Glossary.

8.2 SA 2004/5, Table 372; SA 1998, Table 408; James Boyce and Manuel Pastor, *Building Natural Assets: New Strategies for Poverty Reduction and Environmental Protection* (Amherst, MA: PERI, 2001), p. 10, http://www.umass.edu/peri/pdfs/RR3.pdf; WRI, *World Resources 2005*, (Washington, DC: WRI, 2005) p. 10, Table 1.1.

8.3 "The Toxic 100: Top Corporate Air Polluters in the United States," PERI, http://www.umass.edu/peri/resources/Toxics100table.htm. Note: The toxic release score is calculated as follows: the number of pounds of toxic substances released into the environment by facilities owed by the company *multiplied by* the level of toxicity of each substance released *multi-*

plied by the number of people exposed. For more information, see PERI, "Toxics 100: Technical Notes," http://www.umass.edu/peri/resources/Toxics100-technotes.htm.

8.4   Janet Currie and Matthew Neidell, "Air Pollution and Infant Health: What Can We Learn from California's Recent Experience," *Quarterly Journal of Economics*, Vol. 120, No. 3 (Aug. 2005), pp. 1003–30; Jane Houlihan et al., "Body Burden: The Pollution in Newborns," Environmental Working Group, June 2005, p. 33, http://www.ewg.org/reports/body burden2/contentindex.php. Note: Some chemicals affect multiple body systems and are counted in each category. Also, "chemicals listed as linked to cancer are those classified by the National Toxicology Program as 'known' human carcinogens, or 'reasonably anticipated' to be human carcinogens; or those classified by the Environmental Protection Agency as 'known' or 'probable' human carcinogens" (Houlihan et al.).

8.5   Manuel Pastor et al., "The Air Is Always Cleaner on the Other Side: Race, Space, and Ambient Air Toxics Exposures in California," *Journal of Urban Affairs*, Vol. 27, No. 2 (2005), p. 137, Figure 2; Manuel Pastor et al., "Which Came First? Toxic Facilities, Minority Move-in, and Environmental Justice," *Journal of Urban Affairs*, Vol. 23, No. 1 (2001); Michael Ash and T. Robert Fetter, "Who Lives on the Wrong Side of the Environmental Tracks?" PERI, Working Paper 50, Dec. 2002, http://wwwx.oit.umass.edu/~peri/html/3/73.html. Note: The Census collects and presents information at many levels of geographic detail. From broadest to narrowest, they are: United States; Region; Division; State; County; County subdivision; Place (or part); Census tract (or part); Block group (or part); and Census block. "Census tract" is defined above in the Glossary. Additional information on Census geographic terms and concepts is at, http://www.census.gov/geo/www/tiger/glossry2.pdf.

8.6   James Boyce et al., "Power Distribution, the Environment, and Public Health: A State-Level Analysis," *Ecological Economics*, Vol. 29 (1999), pp. 127–40; James Boyce, "Inequality and Environmental Protection," PERI, Working Paper 52, Jan. 2003, http://wwwx.oit.umass.edu/~peri/html/9/79.html. Note: The "power distribution index" is a composite measure consisting of voter participation, tax fairness, Medicaid accessibility, and educational attainment. The "environmental stress index" is a composite measure consisting of state-level environmental policies, population density, and the degree of manufacturing and urbanization. Data to construct the indices are from various years. (See Boyce et al., pp. 129 and 131.)

8.7   SA 2004/05, Table 464 (2004 values estimated); SA

1995, Table 522; Danny Hakim, "E.P.A. Holds Back Report on Car Fuel Efficiency," NYT, July 28, 2005; Rebecca Clarren, "Fields of Poison," *The Nation,* Dec. 29, 2003.

8.8   Peter Barnes and Marc Breslow, "The Sky Trust: The Battle for Atmospheric Scarcity Rent," in *Natural Assets,* pp. 135–49, edited by James Boyce and Barry Shelley (Washington, DC: Island Press, 2003); EPA, Clean Air Markets, "Acid Rain Program 2003 Progress Report," http://www.epa.gov/airmarkets/cmprpt/arp03/summary.html; Ray Hilborn et al., "State of the World's Fisheries," *Annual Review of Energy and the Environment,* Vol. 28, No. 1 (2003), pp. 384–87. Note: In the graph, the benefits and costs are estimated for the year 2010 (and reported in 2004 dollars), based on an assumption that the U.S. would have targeted CO_2 emissions to be in compliance with the Kyoto Protocol.

8.9   WRI, "EarthTrends: Forests, Grasslands and Drylands," Searchable Database Tables, http://earthtrends.wri.org/searchable_db/index.cfm?theme=9; Helmut Geist and Eric Lambin, "Proximate Causes and Underlying Driving Forces of Tropical Deforestation," *BioScience,* Vol. 52, No. 2, (2002), pp. 143–50; Philip Fearnside, "Amazonia: Deforestation," National Institute for Research in the Amazon, http://philip.inpa.gov.br/publ_livres/Preprints/2002/ENCYCLOP.pdf; Joan Martinez-

Alier, *The Environmentalism of the Poor,* chapter 5 (Northampton: Edward Elgar, 2002).

8.10   World Conservation Union, "IUCN Red List of Threatened Species: Summary Statistics," Table 1, http://www.redlist.org/info/tables/table1; Juliet Eilperin, "Wave of Marine Species Extinctions Feared," WP, Aug. 24, 2005, p. A01; Rainforest Action Network, "Species Extinction," http://www.ran.org/info_center/factsheets/03b.html. Note: The term "threatened" is used by the World Conservation Union to refer to species that have been evaluated as "critically endangered" (i.e., "facing an extremely high risk of extinction in the wild"), "endangered" (i.e., "facing a very high risk of extinction in the wild"), or "vulnerable" (i.e., "facing a high risk of extinction in the wild").

8.11   USDA, National Agricultural Statistics Service, "Quick Stats: Agricultural Statistics Data Base: US & State—Farm Numbers," http://www.nass.usda.gov/QuickStats; BEA, "U.S. International Trade in Goods and Services: Annual Revision for 2004," Exhibit 14, http://www.bea.doc.gov/bea/newsrelarchive/2005/trad1305.pdf; Jeffrey Hopkins and Robert Johansson, "Beyond Environmental Compliance: Stewardship as Good Business," *Amber Waves*, USDA, Economic Research Service, Apr. 2004, http://www.ers.usda.gov/Amberwaves/April04/Features/BeyondEnvironmental.htm; Craig Osteen, "Agricultural

Resources and Environmental Indicators: Pest Management Practices," USDA, Economic Research Service, Table 4.3.1, Sept. 2000, http://www.ers.usda.gov/publications/arei/ah722/arei4_3/DBGen.htm; USDA, Economic Research Service, "Food Marketing and Price Spreads: USDA Marketing Bill," Table 1, http://www.ers.usda.gov/Briefing/Food PriceSpreads/bill/table1.htm; Public Citizen, Global Trade Watch, "Down on the Farm: NAFTA's Seven-Years War on Farmers and Ranchers in the U.S., Canada and Mexico," pp. 23–25, http://www.citizen.org/documents/ACFF2.PDF.

8.12   Census, "Journey to Work and Place of Work," http://www.census.gov/population/www/socdemo/journey.html; American Farmland Trust, "Farming on the Edge: Sprawling Development Threatens America's Best Farmland," http://www.farmland.org/farmingontheedge/index.htm; SA 2004/05, Table 1069; Federal Highway Administration, *Highway Statistics 2003*, Table HM-10, http://www.fhwa.dot.gov/policy/ohim/hs03/htm/hm10.htm; Federal Highway Administration, *Highway Statistics* (various years), Table VM-2M, http://www.fhwa.dot.gov/policy/ohpi/hss/hsspubs.htm; Howard Frumkin, "Urban Sprawl and Public Health," *Public Health Reports,* Vol. 117 (May-June 2002), pp. 201–17, http://www.med.harvard.edu/chge/course/driving/urban/FrumkinUrbanSprawl.pdf.

8.13   AER, Tables 3.5, 5.1, 5.3, 5.4, 11.5, and 11.7; James Fearon, "Primary Commodities Exports and Civil War," *Journal of Conflict Resolution,* forthcoming, http://www.stanford.edu/~jfearon/papers/sxpfinal.pdf; Elise Ackerman, "Chevron Paid Agents Who Destroyed Villages," *Mercury News*, Aug. 2, 2005, http://www.mercurynews.com/mld/mercury news/12285441.htm; Joan Martinez-Alier, *The Environmentalism of the Poor* (Northampton: Edward Elgar, 2002), pp. 102–107; Jim VandeHei and Justin Blum, "Bush Signs Energy Bill, Cheers Steps Towards Self-Sufficiency," WP, Aug. 9, 2005, p. A03; Gwich'in Steering Committee, http://www.gwichin steeringcommittee.org.

8.14   AER, Tables 2.1b, 2.1c, 2.1d, 2.1e, and 2.1f; IEA, Tables E.1, E.2, E.3, E.4, C.6 and 7.2; SA 2004/05, Table 2; Census, "Total Midyear Population for the World: 1950–2050," http://www.census.gov/ipc/www/worldpop.html; Census, "International Data Base," http://www.census.gov/ipc/www/idb new.html; Federal Statistical Office Germany, "Time-Series: Population by Area," http://www.destatis.de/indicators/e/lrbev03ae.htm; Lawrence Livermore National Laboratory, "U.S. Energy Flow—2002," http://eed.llnl.gov/flow/02flow.php; Rocky Mountain Institute, "Electric Efficiency," http://www.rmi.org/sitepages/pid321.php; U.S. Department of Transportation, "Summary of Fuel Economy

Performance: March 2004," http://www.nhtsa
.dot.gov/cars/rules/cafe/docs/Summary-Fuel-
Economy-Pref-2004.pdf.

8.15   WRI, "Climate and Atmosphere Overview 2005,"
        Earthtrends: Climate and Atmosphere: Data Tables,
        http://earthtrends.wri.org/datatables/index.cfm?
        theme=3; Intergovernmental Panel on Climate
        Change, "Climate Change 2001: Synthesis Report:
        Summary for Policymakers," http://www.ipcc.ch/
        pub/reports. htm; AER 2004, Table 12.1; United
        Nations Framework Convention on Climate Change,
        "Kyoto Protocol: Status of Ratification,"Aug. 2,
        2005, http://unfccc.int/essential_background/
        kyoto_protocol/status_of_ratification/items/2613.ph
        p. Note: In the text, greenhouse gas emissions are
        reported in carbon dioxide equivalent. That is, non-
        CO_2 gases are reported as an equivalent amount of
        CO_2 based on the relative strength of their effect on
        the climate. For example, one pound of methane is
        23 times more powerful as a greenhouse gas than one
        pound of CO_2. In the graph, we relied on a different
        source than for the previous edition. Our new source,
        World Resources Institute, includes CO_2 emissions
        that result from changes in land use, such as defor-
        estation and certain agricultural methods. While not
        normally considered in public discussion of global
        warming, land use is a major contributor to the con-
        centration of greenhouse gasses in the atmosphere.

For example, because large areas of farmland in the
U.S. were allowed to revert to forest, U.S. land use
between 1950 and 2000 actually resulted in negative
net CO_2 emissions of 26 billion metric tons. On the
other hand, deforestation and agricultural methods in
Latin America between 1950 and 2000 have produced positive net CO_2 emissions equal to 76% of
the region's total emissions. Considering only emissions resulting from fossil fuel use and cement production, the U.S.'s cumulative emissions between
1950 and 2000 are significantly greater than those of
Asia and Oceania. See WRI, "Climate and
Atmosphere Overview 2005," Earthtrends: Climate
and Atmosphere: Data Tables. For a quick primer on
the basics of global warming, see http://www.pewcli-
mate.org/global-warming-basics/facts_and_figures/
greenhouse.cfm.

8.16   DOE, Office of Civilian Radioactive Waste
        Management, "How Much Nuclear Waste Is in the
        United States?" http://www.ocrwm.doe.gov/ymp/
        about/howmuch.shtml; EIA, "U.S. Nuclear
        Reactors," http://www.eia.doe.gov/cneaf/nuclear/
        page/nuc_reactors/reactsum.html; U.S. Government
        Accountability Office, "NRC Needs to Do More to
        Ensure that Power Plants Are Effectively Controlling
        Spent Nuclear Fuel," GAO-05-339, Apr. 2005, p. 1,
        http://www.gao.gov/new.items/d05339.pdf; Nuclear
        Energy Institute, "Common Objections to the Yucca

Mountain Project, and What the Science Really Says," http://www.nei.org/index.asp?catnum=2&catid=197; Matthew Wald, "Interest in Reactors Builds, but Industry Is Still Cautious," NYT, May 2, 2005, p. A19; Peter Eisler, "Special Report: Fuel for Nuclear Weapons Is More Widely Available than the Public Has Been Told," *USA Today,* Feb. 27, 2003, p. 1A; Giles Tremlett, "Al-Qaida Leaders Say Nuclear Power Stations Were Original Targets," *Guardian* (U.K.), Sept. 9, 2002, http://www.guardian.co.uk/international/story/0,,788331,00.html; Robert Alvarez et al., "Reducing the Hazards from Stored Spent Power-Reactor Fuel in the United States," *Science and Global Security,* Vol. 11 (2003), p. 10, http://www.princeton.edu/~globsec/publications/pdf/11_1Alvarez.pdf.

CHAPTER 9: MACROECONOMICS

9.1   BEA, NIPA Table 1.1.1. Note: In this edition of the *Field Guide,* we're including NBER recessions where the growth rate did not become negative. The previous edition of the *Field Guide* did not include these episodes in its chart.

9.2   Jason Venetoulis and Cliff Cobb, "The Genuine Progress Indicator 1950–2002 (2004 Update)," March 2004, http://www.redefiningprogress.org/newpubs/2004/gpi_march2004update.pdf.

9.3   BEA, NIPA, Table 1.1.1. Note: In the chart, the period covered by each full business cycle begins with the first quarter of recovery (after a trough) and ends on the quarter of the next trough, as identified by the NBER.

9.4   BEA, NIPA, Table 5.1.

9.5   BLS, Major Sector Productivity and Costs Index statistics series PRS85006092 and PRS85006152, http://data.bls.gov/cgi-bin/surveymost?pr. Note: See 9.3 above for definition of "business cycle."

9.6   BEA, *Fixed Assets and Consumer Durable Goods in the United States, 1925–97* (Washington, DC: BEA, 2003), Table 4.1; BEA, "All Fixed Asset Tables," Table 4.1, http://www.bea.gov/bea/dn/FA2004/SelectTable.asp; BEA, NIPA, Table 6.19D.

9.7   BLS, Consumer Price Index, ftp://ftp.bls.gov/pub/special.requests/cpi/cpiai.txt.

9.9   ERP 2005, pp. 296–97, Table B-73; BEA, NIPA, Table 1.1.4.

9.10 ERP 2005, pp. 296–97, Table B-73.

9.11 FDIC, Historical Statistics on Banking, Table CB01, http://www2.fdic.gov/hsob/SelectRpt.asp?EntryTyp=10. Note: Only FDIC-insured commercial banks are included in the chart.

9.12 Federal Reserve Board of Governors, Flow of Funds Accounts, 1945–2004, Flow Table F-100 and Level Table L-100, http://www.federalreserve.gov/

releases/z1/current/default.htm. Note: The full name of the bankruptcy reform bill of 2005 is the Bankruptcy Abuse Prevention and Consumer Protection Act.

9.13   U.S. Department of Housing and Urban Development, Office of Federal Housing Enterprise Oversight, House Price Index, http://www. ofheo.gov/download.asp; BLS, Consumer Price Index; Michael Powell, "A Bane Amid the Housing Boom: Rising Foreclosures," WP, May 30, 2005, p. A01; Daniela Deane, "Middle Class Drives Soaring Purchases of Second Homes," WP, Mar. 2, 2005, p. E01.

9.14   ERP 2005, pp. 320–21, Table B-96.

9.15   BEA, U.S. International Transactions Accounts, Tables 1 and 11, http://www.bea.gov/bea/inter national/bp_web/list.cfm?anon=624&registered=0.

9.16   Federal Reserve Board of Governors, "Price-Adjusted Broad Dollar Index," http://www.federalreserve.gov/ releases/H10/Summary/indexbc_m.txt.

Chapter 10: The Global Economy

10.1   WDI 2005 (CD-ROM).

10.2   WDI 2005 (CD-ROM); HDR 2004, pp. 139–42, Table 1, http://hdr.undp.org/reports/global/ 2004/?CFID=11959576&CFTOKEN=65100468.

10.3   WDI 2005 (CD-ROM); WDI, "Reducing Poverty and Hunger," http://www.worldbank.org/data/ wdi2005/wditext/Section1_1_1.htm.

10.4   Authors' calculations based on data from WDI 2005 (CD-ROM). Note: The values in the chart do not add to 100% due to independent rounding. Household consumption expenditures and per capita income were adjusted to reflect differences in pur- chasing power as estimated by the World Bank.

10.5   United Nations, Department of Economic and Social Affairs, *World Economic and Social Survey 2004,* pp. vii, 24 (Table II.1), 51 (Table II.15), and 107 (Table IV.3), http://www.un.org/esa/policy/wess.

10.6   Ibid., pp. 97–101; WDI 2005 (CD-ROM).

10.7   International Labour Organization (ILO), *Global Employment Trends* 2004, p. 1, Table 1, http://www .ilo.org/public/english/employment/strat/global04. htm; ILO, *World Employment Report 2004/5*, p. 24, http://www.ilo.org/public/english/employment/strat/ wer2004.htm.

10.8   BLS, Foreign Labor Statistics, "International Comparisons of Hourly Compensation Costs for Production Workers in Manufacturing, 2003," Table 2, Nov. 18, 2004, http://www.bls.gov/news.release/ ichcc.toc.htm; Judith Banister, "Manufacturing Employment and Compensation in China," BLS, Foreign Labor Statistics, Dec. 2004, http://www .bls.gov/fls/chinareport.pdf.

10.9   United Nations Conference on Trade and

Development (UNCTAD), "Globstat: Development and Globalization: Facts and Figures," http://globstat.unctad.org/html/index.html.

10.10 Kate Bronfenbrenner and Stephanie Luce, "The Changing Nature of Corporate Global Restructuring: The Impact of Production Shifts on Jobs in the U.S., China, and Around the Globe," report submitted to the U.S.-China Economic and Security Review Commission, 2004, p. 55, Table 10, http://www.uscc .gov/researchpapers/2004/cornell_u_mass_report.pdf.

10.11 World Intellectual Property Organization (WIPO), "PCT Statistical Indicators Report 1978–2004" Apr. 2005, http://www.wipo.int/ipstats/en/statistics/patents/pdf/yearly_report_2004.pdf.

10.12 Martin Khor, "WTO Wrangle Over the 'Singapore Issues,'" Third World Network, Dec. 2003, http://www.twnside.org.sg/title2/gtrends0309.htm;

Oxfam, "Cultivating Poverty: The Impact of U.S. Cotton Subsidies on Africa," http://www.oxfam.org .uk/what_we_do/issues/trade/downloads/bp30_cotton.pdf.

10.13 BEA, NIPA, Tables 6.17b-d.

10.14 UNCTAD, *World Investment Report 2004,* pp. 367–71, Table B1, http://www.unctad.org/Templates/WebFlyer.asp?intItemID=3235&lang=1. Note: In the chart, "Developed countries" includes North America, Western Europe, Japan, New Zealand, and Australia.

10.15 WDI 2005 (CD-ROM).

10.16 Ilene Grabel, "Averting Crisis? Assessing Measures to Manage Integration in Emerging Economies," *Cambridge Journal of Economics*, Vol. 27 (2003), pp. 317–36.

10.17 WDI 2005 (CD-ROM).

10.18 HDR 2004, p. 196.

ALSO AVAILABLE FROM THE NEW PRESS

Doug Henwood
AFTER THE NEW ECONOMY
The Binge . . . And the Hangover That Won't Go Away
(PB, 1-56584-983-3, 304 pages with 30 charts and graphs)
Economist Doug Henwood scrutinizes the 1990s and brilliantly dissects the so-called new economy.

Beth Shulman
THE BETRAYAL OF WORK
How Low-Wage Jobs Fail 30 Million Americans
(PB, 1-56584-733-4, 272 pages)
How the United States turns its back on the working poor.

Meizhu Lui, Barbara Robles, Betsy Leondar-Wright, Rose Brewer, and Rebecca Adamson
THE COLOR OF WEALTH
The Story Behind the U.S. Racial Wealth Divide
(PB, 1-59558-004-2, 320 pages)
Written by five leading experts on the racial wealth divide, this is a uniquely comprehensive multicultural history of American wealth.

Susan Linn
CONSUMING KIDS
The Hostile Takeover of Childhood
(HC, 1-56584-783-0, 304 pages)
A shocking expose of the $15 billion marketing maelstrom aimed at our children and how we can stop it.

Edited by Juliet B. Schor and Douglas B. Holt
THE CONSUMER SOCIETY READER
(PB, 1-56584-598-6, 528 pages)
The definitive reader on the nature and evolution of consumer society.

Chuck Collins and Felice Yeskel
with United for a Fair Economy and Class Action
ECONOMIC APARTHEID IN AMERICA
(PB, 1-59558-015-8, 272 pages with illustrations, charts, and tables throughout)
An engaging activist guide to closing the gap between the rich and everyone else in America.

Sarah Anderson and John Cavanagh, with Thea Lee
FIELD GUIDE TO THE GLOBAL ECONOMY
Revised and Updated
(PB, 1-56584-956-6, 160 pages with illustrations, charts, and tables throughout)
An eye-opening guide to the myths and realities of the international economy.

Priscilla Murolo and A.B. Chitty
FROM THE FOLKS WHO BROUGHT YOU THE WEEKEND
A Short, Illustrated History of Labor in the United States
(PB, 1-56584-776-8, 384 pages with 30 black-and-white illustrations)
An engrossing history of American labor that captures the full sweep of working people's struggles.

Medard Gabel and Henry Bruner
GLOBAL INC.
An Atlas of the Multinational Corporation
(PB, 1-56584-727-X, 176 pages with 200 full-color maps, charts, and graphs throughout)
A unique and startling visual representation of the rise of the global corporation.

Saskia Sassen, foreword by K. Anthony Appiah
GLOBALIZATION AND ITS DISCONTENTS
Essays on the New Mobility of People and Money
(PB, 1-56584-518-8, 288 pages with 7 black-and-white charts)
Groundbreaking essays on the new global economy from one of the leading experts on globalization.

Richard G. Wilkinson
IMPACT OF INEQUALITY
How to Make Sick Societies Healthier
(HC, 1-56584-925-6, 368 pages)
How inequality—more than destroying health and social status—affects the very way people view their lives.

R. Emmett Murray
LEXICON OF LABOR
More Than 500 Key Terms, Biographical Sketches, and Historical Insights Concerning Labor in America
(PB, 1-56584-456-4, 208 pages)
An innovative and informative mini-encyclopedia of work and workers in America.

Robert Pollin and Stephanie Luce
THE LIVING WAGE
Building a Fair Economy
(PB, 1-56584-588-9, 272 pages)
A comprehensive examination of the economic concept that has yielded dramatic results across the nation.

Andrew Ross
LOW PAY, HIGH PROFILE
(PB, 1-56584-893-4, 272 pages with 31 black-and-white photographs)
Anti-sweatshop activist and commentator Andrew Ross presents case studies from around the world to showcase the success and strength of the fair labor movement.

George Monbiot
MANIFESTO FOR A NEW WORLD ORDER
(HC, 1-56584-908-6, 288 pages)
A global perspective on the current state of democracy, from the most realistic utopian of our time.

Howard Zinn
PEOPLE'S HISTORY OF THE UNITED STATES
Abridged Teaching Edition, Revised and Updated
(PB, 1-56584-826-8, 640 pages)
Zinn's original text available specifically for classroom use, including exercises and teaching materials to accompany each chapter.

Stephen J. Rose
SOCIAL STRATIFICATION IN THE UNITED STATES 2000
The New American Profile Poster: A Book-and-Poster Set
(PB, 1-56584-550-1, 48 pages with one full-sized poster)
A book and poster set on American comparative wealth, based on the most
recent census data.

Edward Wolff
TOP HEAVY
*The Increasing Inequality of Wealth in America and What Can Be Done
About It*
(PB, 1-56584-665-6, 128 pages)
Compelling evidence on the growing gap between America's rich and poor.

William K. Tabb
UNEQUAL PARTNERS
(PB, 1-56584-722-9, 288 pages)
An eye-opening primer on some of the less explored aspects of
globalization.

**Randy Albelda, Nancy Folbre, and the Center for Popular
Economics**
WAR ON THE POOR
A Defense Manual
(PB, 1-56584-262-6, 144 pages)
An incisive look at self-perpetuating poverty in America.

Lori Wallach and Patrick Woodall, Public Citizen
WHOSE TRADE ORGANIZATION?
The Comprehensive Guide to the WTO
(PB, 1-56584-841-1, 416 pages)
A meticulous chronicle of how the WTO has eroded democracy around
the world.

Studs Terkel
WORKING
*People Talk about What They Do All Day and How They Feel about What
They Do*
(PB, 1-56584-342-8, 640 pages)
A timeless snapshot of people's feelings about their working lives, consisting
of over 100 interviews.

To order, call 1-800-233-4830

To learn more about The New Press and receive updates on new titles, visit www.thenewpress.com.